The Music of the Spheres in the Western Imagination

The Music of the Spheres in the Western Imagination

David J. Kendall

LEXINGTON BOOKS
Lanham • Boulder • New York • London

Published by Lexington Books
An imprint of The Rowman & Littlefield Publishing Group, Inc.
4501 Forbes Boulevard, Suite 200, Lanham, Maryland 20706
www.rowman.com

86-90 Paul Street, London EC2A 4NE

Copyright © 2022 by The Rowman & Littlefield Publishing Group, Inc.

All rights reserved. No part of this book may be reproduced in any form or by any electronic or mechanical means, including information storage and retrieval systems, without written permission from the publisher, except by a reviewer who may quote passages in a review.

British Library Cataloguing in Publication Information Available

Library of Congress Cataloging-in-Publication Data

Names: Kendall, David J., 1980- author.
Title: The music of the spheres in the Western imagination / David J. Kendall.
Description: Lanham : Lexington Books, 2022. | Includes bibliographical references and index.
Identifiers: LCCN 2022037026 (print) | LCCN 2022037027 (ebook) |
  ISBN 9781793650351 (cloth) | ISBN 9781793650375 (paperback) |
  ISBN 9781793650368 (ebook)
Subjects: LCSH: Music and literature. | Music in literature. |
  Science fiction--History and criticism. | Fantasy fiction--History and criticism. |
  Church music. | Music--Philosophy and aesthetics. | Harmony of the spheres.
Classification: LCC ML3849 .K47 2022 (print) | LCC ML3849 (ebook) |
  DDC 780/.08--dc23/eng/20220803
LC record available at https://lccn.loc.gov/2022037026
LC ebook record available at https://lccn.loc.gov/2022037027

∞™ The paper used in this publication meets the minimum requirements of American National Standard for Information Sciences—Permanence of Paper for Printed Library Materials, ANSI/NISO Z39.48-1992.

To Dad
Miles Elwyn Topham (1947–2006)

To my sister
Melinda Ann Landis Whedon (1978–2009)

To a wonderful student and friend
Leqi Lily Yan (1985–2022)

****

To Sheng, Mina, and Ela

Matibay ang walis
Palibhasa'y magkabigkis

To Angel and Yuki

Pangur, white Pangur,
How happy we are
Alone together, Scholar and cat.

****

[M]a già volgeva il mio disio e 'l velle,
sì come rota ch' igualmente è mossa,
l'amor che move il sole e l'altre stelle.

Figure 0.1 *Musica Mundana.* *Source*: Nancy Chiu. All rights reserved. Used with permission.

Contents

Acknowledgments	ix
Introduction	1
1 "The Heavens Make a Harmony": *Musica Mundana, Musica Humana,* and *Musica Instrumentalis* in the Ancient and Early Christian World	7
2 "Thy Hearing is Mortal Even as Thy Sight": Human Perception in the Heavenly Journey of Dante's *Paradiso*	35
2.5 "I Noticed That the Grass Did Not Bend Under Their Feet": Solid People, Ghosts, and the Sense of Touch in a Heavenly Journey of C. S. Lewis	59
3 "Behold Your Music!": Music as a Force of Creation, Destruction, and Re-Creation in the Worlds of J. R. R. Tolkien and C. S. Lewis	67
3.5 Powerful Music: Horns, Trumpets, Voices, and Other Magical Instruments in Tolkien and Lewis	99
4 When the Celestial Laws Change	113
5 To Conserve, Exploit, or Embrace?: The Human and the Non-Human in Christian Hymnody	131
5.5 "Still, It May Be Useful": The Ring of Sauron and the Value Axis	157

6	***Bent* Roads and *Bent* People**	165
6.5	***Musica Humana* and the Limits of Musical Genius**	199
7	**The Music of the Spheres and the Modern Worship Wars**	207

Conclusion: *Da Capo*   227

Bibliography   231

Index   241

About the Author   249

Acknowledgments

I have many people to thank for their part in seeing this book through to publication, though many may be unaware of the roles they played. Going *way* back, my parents had homes filled with books, where reading and learning was encouraged. Many were the afternoons I spent hiding in an empty room, with a copy of *The Hobbit* for company. I was oddly well-prepared in junior high school by Ken Bursey, who hammered graduate-level vocabulary into me, thus opening up a whole world of literature I would have otherwise had to wait years for. In high school, Norman and Allyson Ault continued to expand my horizons in English literature. During my undergraduate years at La Sierra University, I was fortunate enough to have a mentor in Dr. René Ramos, who showed me that musicology could become a true vocation, and others like Dr. Barbara Favorito, Dr. William Chunestudy, Dr. Elvin Rodríguez, Dr. Don Thurber, Dr. Kimo Smith, Prof. Ty Rust, and Dr. Richard Hoffmann, who helped me learn about professionalism and keeping an open mind. Graduate studies at the University of California, Riverside, were made especially meaningful by mentors like Dr. Fred Gable, Dr. Walter Clark, Dr. Renée Coulombe, Dr. Barbara Bennett, Dr. Paulo Chagas, Dr. Rogério Budasz, Dr. Leonora Saavedra, Dr. René Lysloff, and Dr. Jonathan Ritter. Those years at UCR exponentially expanded my outlook, my knowledge base, and the endless vistas of possibility in research and learning.

I have had the kind help of many colleagues in the various fields I dabble with in this book. Voluminous thanks belong to Dr. John Jones, Dr. Wonil Kim, and Dr. John Webster, in the fields of religious and theological studies; and to Dr. Sam McBride and Dr. Debbie Higgens, in C.S. Lewis and J.R.R. Tolkien studies. But the brightest star in this constellation is Dr. Ihor Kokhan who, for well over a year, met with me for several hours a week in our writing group, and has read multiple versions of every last passage in this book.

If the ideas and thoughts laid down in this volume make any sense at all, it is largely due to his patient advice and wise suggestions. Thanks also to Diane, Alexander, and Leonardo, for sharing Ihor with me. May God shower many blessings on your potatoes!

I would also like to thank Lexington Books for believing in this project, and for following up with me over the course of several years while I vacillated. Thanks to Courtney Morales and Emma Ebert for shepherding me through the process. Special thanks also to my illustrator Nancy Chiu, who seemed to know what I had in mind even before I asked. Finally, I must honor my wife, Shiela, and my daughters, Carmina and Mikaëla, who demonstrated divine levels of patience with my countless hours of reading, writing, and editing. Between my children and my cats, I was never alone while writing this book!

Introduction

> This is my Father's world.
> E'en yet to my listening ears
> All nature sings, and around me rings
> The music of the spheres.[1]

These are the opening words to a hymn popular when I was growing up in the 1980s. Most of the words were easily understandable to me and the other children in my church and school, and they went on to glorify the created world, made up of "rocks and trees" and "skies and seas." However, as children often do, I repeated the words "the music of the spheres" with no real understanding of what I was singing—I probably did not even know what a sphere was at that early age. Even after acquiring that bit of knowledge in the geometry curriculum, I certainly had no concept of the *meaning* of that portion of text, neither did I think about it, or even to *think* to think about it. The first time I recall reflecting on the notion was my freshman year at college in the late 1990s when, during a school event, one of my undergraduate professors jokingly and playfully ridiculed the concept. "Who can hear the music of the spheres? They don't even make sound!" he laughed, and we laughed with him. But a seed was planted, though dormant for many years, and I later begin to consider the idea, wondering what the music of the spheres was, and how it had become a part, however trivial, of our collective cultural consciousness. Little did I realize how important a concept it is, and how fundamental a part of our consciousness it continues to be, though buried beneath layers of definition, usage, and commentary that are nearly geological in depth and complexity.

I learned a little more about the music of the spheres in my undergraduate music history courses, but dismissed the theory of an all-encompassing celestial music as an ancient and outmoded philosophical concept—nothing more than required reading before moving on to the "real" music that, as a practicing performer, most interested me. However, as is often the case with realities we attempt to ignore, the music of the spheres continued to waylay me, this time in graduate musicology coursework, especially in a particularly good seminar on the history of music theory.[2] Later dissertation research made it necessary to read and translate a large number of theoretical treatises on music, all of which simply took the concept of the music of the spheres for granted, being the foundation upon which each was written. Finally, and after much foolish avoidance on my part, I began to consider the idea of celestial music to be worth a fair and thoughtful look. In the years that have elapsed since, I have come to the conclusion that the notion of divine music serves not only as the foundation for *musical* thought and practice in the Western world, but also the foundation of the *entire* cosmic system—the universe as we know and conceive of it, with all its component parts. This notion is neither novel nor has it been entirely forgotten and assigned to the dustbin of history. A better metaphor is that the concept has *sunk* below the level of everyday discourse but, in the manner of things that sink, has become the bedrock for everything subsequently built upon it. Indeed, it is rather shocking to see the extent to which the music of the spheres continues to surreptitiously dominate our collective understanding of theology, religious worship, philosophy, metaphysics, sociology, psychology, literature, and musical performance. These various disciplines may have largely stripped away their overtly musical terminologies but, like music itself, continue to resonate and echo in the discourses of each of these fields.

Despite my assertions as to its universal nature, this book is not intended to be, nor could it be, an encyclopedic compendium of all Western thought built on musical concepts. Rather, it attempts to identify important and thought-provoking instances of the celestial-musical model that illustrates its ubiquity, depth, and application over millennia. This is an attempt to examine a fair range of Western thought through the lens of music, or to be more accurate, *musica*. The philosophical system of cosmic music includes three component parts: *musica mundana, musica humana*, and *musica instrumentalis*. Though not given these particular labels until at least the sixth-century CE, they were understood as such centuries prior, to at least the era of the great classical Greek philosophers. Each chapter in this book will explore some aspect of Western thought, practice, or cultural output in terms of one or more of these three kinds of *musica*.

OUTLINE

I have designed this book to correspond roughly to a medieval astronomical equilibrium. At the beginning and end are short chapters that serve to prepare and to debrief the reader. The symmetrically placed chapters 1, 4, and 7 focus on different eras in Western history that provide historical and theoretical contexts to the idea of *musica*, while following its evolving meanings and usages. Chapters 2, 3, 5, and 6 are deeper analyses of particular examples or applications of *musica*. Each of these is followed by a shorter chapter-vignette, in which the specific context or conclusion treated in the paired chapter is tangentially applied to a different aspect of Western cultural thought or production.

In chapter 1, we explore the works of Boethius and several centuries of his followers and commentators, while closely defining the categories of *musica mundana*, *musica humana*, and *musica instrumentalis*. This will also take us into numerology and its applications in practical music, as well as pre-Christian and Christian notions of systems of perfection, systems of imperfection, and systems of greater perfection.

Chapter 2 applies these concepts to the *Paradiso*, the third part of Dante's *Divine Comedy*. Here, the celebrated Florentine takes the reader on a heavenly journey experienced through the senses of sight, sound, and understanding, where we will see the *Paradiso* functioning as a speculative essay on the nature of human sensory perception among the celestial spheres. In the subsequent chapter-vignette, we travel with C. S. Lewis on a similar heavenly expedition, observing the nature of human perception from a different, twentieth-century perspective.

Chapter 3 is an analysis of the works of C. S. Lewis and J. R. R. Tolkien, and their use of music as an initiating creative force for their fictional worlds. This chapter focuses particularly on the idea of consonance and dissonance in these created universes, as well as within and among the characters populating them. We also discuss a number of concepts analogous to music, such as water, light, and darkness, while considering the role of music in healing and *re*-creation. The following chapter-vignette explores the use of musical instruments, including trumpets, horns, and voices in the works of Tolkien and Lewis, specifically their powers as weapons of offense or defense.

Chapter 4 continues the work of chapter 1, with a focus on the evolution of the celestial laws of music in theoretical works. This evolution causes friction between speculative music theorists, who argue for the retention of traditional musical forms and materials, and practical musicians, who desire to expand upon these materials for purposes of expression. The chapter explores the importance of the human ear in determining what is allowable in practical performance, as well as major changes in the theoretical acceptance of musical dissonance around the turn of the twentieth century.

In chapter 5, we examine a range of hymn texts from Western Christianity, seeing what they tell us about the connection between the human and non-human created worlds. Two of the categories of *musica*, namely *musica mundana* and *musica humana*, come into potential conflict, making an analysis of their relationship important. The examined hymn texts demonstrate how mankind views creation along an axis of value, from the mere acknowledgment of its existence, to the display of an attitude of subjugation, to the adoption of creation as a part of the human family. The chapter-vignette explores the same value axis, but as a method of analyzing the perceived value of Sauron's Ring in Tolkien's *The Lord of the Rings*.

Chapter 6 is an expanded analysis of *bentness* as defined and explored by C. S. Lewis in *The Space Trilogy*. The idea of *bentness* closely aligns with the musical concepts of consonance and dissonance, and are read in much the same way. We explore *bentness* in terms of shapes and other physical phenomena, but primarily as it manifests itself in characters from a cross-section of Western literature of the nineteenth and twentieth centuries. The subsequent chapter-vignette serves as a case study in how the critical reception of Western composers of music can evolve, especially as attitudes toward their character and morals shift over time.

Chapter 7 completes the historical survey, through an examination of music for Christian worship, from the Protestant Reformation through the "worship wars" of the second half of the twentieth century. We explore the musical attitudes of such sixteenth-century figures as Martin Luther and Jean Calvin, various church dicta regarding music and worship, reactions among Christians to the rise of modernity, and the problematic concept of the "African" in discourses about music.

The final chapter traces the concept of *musica* even further back in time than in chapter 1, re-establishing and strengthening the foundational aspects of musical thought in Western culture.

A NOTE ON SOURCES

The focus of this book is the influence of *musica* on the Western imagination. Though I am relatively selective of the fields I am treating, they do represent a broad cross-section of scholarship, and there are distinct limits to such a treatment. Whether the subject is medieval music theory, the works of Dante, nineteenth-century literature, Tolkien studies, hymnody, the history of sociology, music history, or the symbolism of C. S. Lewis, my use of sources is far from exhaustive, and in no way represents the most up-to-date or current state of the fields represented. There are many potentially excellent books and articles I have not consulted, and thus many valuable perspectives that will not be included. However, I believe that enough has been included to make the argument that *musica* is a valid and compelling epistemological lens through which to view many aspects of Western culture. I am not attempting to do any more—or any less—than that. This may not satisfy all readers, who will note the ubiquitous inclusion of points of view that have been overwhelmingly dominant in the West, namely those of heterosexual, cisgender, (largely) Christian, white males. Unfortunately, the fact remains that much of what survives as representative of Western culture is the result of dynamics in which the powerful and privileged have their stories told, to the exclusion of others. Ultimately, my purpose is to identify a cosmology based on music and musical principles, how theorists and practitioners attempted to live within this universal system, and some of the ways the Western imagination uses this cosmic model to create its own worlds. That these theories and created worlds come from the imaginations of the dominant members of the societies of which they are a part, is fully conceded.

To continue my confession of potential weaknesses, my sources for literary works and musical treatises are those I have been able to get my hands on, and I am aware that more reliable translations of some of them may exist.[3] For instance, I use a particular translation of Dante's *Paradiso* because it is a reading and commentary that I happen to enjoy more than others. My copies of Lewis' and Tolkien's works are either mass-market paperbacks or well-worn and dog-eared copies from childhood. The examples I use from the world of English-language literature reveal my own literary preferences and biases. My strong distaste for certain kinds of racial discourse may assert itself in chapter 7, and my lifelong love of the created worlds of Lewis and Tolkien will affirm itself throughout. Finally, I will attempt to let the sources speak for themselves and refrain from adding special emphasis in quoted passages, trusting in the reader to appreciate their significance in the context of the discussion. Any remaining emphasis exists in the original source.

It may be successfully argued that, as a musician, I see music wherever I look. While this may be true, I believe that there is *indeed* music everywhere we look, and this book is an attempt to illustrate that fundamental truth.

NOTES

1. Maltbie Davenport Babcock, *Thoughts for Every-Day Living* (New York: Charles Scribner's Sons, 1901), 180.

2. This course was taught in early 2006 by Dr. Renée Coulombe at the University of California, Riverside.

3. Given that this book was written entirely during the recent global pandemic, accessing certain sources and alternative translations was challenging, and in many cases, impossible.

Chapter 1

"The Heavens Make a Harmony"

Musica Mundana, Musica Humana, *and* Musica Instrumentalis *in the Ancient and Early Christian World*

For even the universe itself is said to have been put together with a certain harmony of sounds, and the very heavens revolve under the guidance of harmony.[1]

Thou tun'dst this world below, the spheres above,
Which in the heavenly round to their own music move.[2]

The Western world owes much to a well-educated Roman patrician, philosopher, and politician named Anicius Manlius Severinus Boethius. Born around the time the last Western Roman Emperor was deposed, later serving as an official in the court of the Ostrogothic king Theodoric the Great, Boethius translated several important classical Greek works, and authored many "handbooks," or compilations, of ancient scholarship on various subjects. In these latter capacities Boethius is largely credited for the transmission of what was known of classical Greek thought to the Western Christian world for most of the next thousand years, before European rediscoveries of original sources.[3]

In the introductory chapter, I mentioned the concept that underpins this book, namely a threefold categorization of music—*musica mundana, musica humana,* and *musica instrumentalis*—as coined and described by Boethius. In addition to defining these concepts, we will explore mathematical and numerological principles common in discussions of music theory and practice, as well as competing cosmological models, such as systems of perfection and of imperfection. Much of this originates in ancient musical and mathematical treatises collected and transmitted by Boethius, and later commented and expanded upon by his disciples and followers.

THE LONG SHADOW OF BOETHIUS

Boethius' *De Institutione Musica*, a handbook written in the first decades of the sixth century, is primarily a mathematical and theoretical treatise, and has little to say about the practical performance of music. Among other things, it considers the mathematical foundations of harmony, and their applications to aspects of observable reality, from the actual sounds produced and detected by the sense of hearing, to the balance of elements within the human body and among members of human societies, to the changes of the seasons, the interactions of the material elements, and movements of bodies within the visible universe. All these orderly and regular aspects of reality are *musical* in nature. Boethius describes a cosmos in which everything has its origin and being in musical concepts, and where the component parts exist in reciprocal and symbiotic relationships. Boethius' treatise is not the only example of this type from his era, but it is by far the most significant and consequential in the later history of the Western world. Though many of the conceptual models are no longer widely known by the particular terms Boethius provided, they are still foundational in Western musical, theoretical, and theological thought, including his tripartite definition of *musica*. Each of these is treated in detail below

MUSICA MUNDANA

Though the very notion may be met with skepticism or derision by the modern mind, as I shared in the previous chapter, this is the "Music of the Spheres." While *musica mundana* was not always a particular object of scorn, it has nonetheless caused a certain amount of confusion among scholars, theorists, and practical musicians over the centuries. Perhaps the chief cause of bewilderment is the simple fact that something called "music" can be entirely *inaudible* to the human sense of hearing. The sixteenth-century theorist Gioseffo Zarlino acknowledged this difficulty, while providing potential solutions to such a paradox:

> Moreover, philosophers affirm that the revolving heavens make a harmony, which we do not hear because they revolve too fast, or are too far away from us, or for some other unknown reason.[4]

Taking a slightly different position, Michael Ward notes that in the medieval context, "the planets were silent and sounding at the same time: their music was not heard on earth because it was always heard."[5] I am inclined to blend these two statements, noting that the heavenly music is indeed silent to the human sense of hearing, but always "heard" in the manifestation of its actual effects. More on this below.

It is essential to understand the contexts in which the term *musica mundana* is used, and how it has been read and applied over time. The Latin word *mundana* commonly translates as "mundane," referring to things that are "of the world" or earthly—as opposed to heavenly—and often those that are ordinary, uninteresting, or dull. While *mundana* does have connotations of the worldly, we must recognize that the understanding of what constitutes "the world" has evolved over time. Rapid advances in the science of astronomy, especially since the eighteenth century, have created a perception of the world—specifically, the Earth—as a small, decentralized, and increasingly unimportant object in a universe of startlingly vast dimensions. Our ability to image celestial objects in ever-increasing detail, together with the advent of satellites, probes, and human spaceflight, provides a perspective that allows us to categorize objects as either terrestrial or *extra*-terrestrial, of the world or *not* of the world. However, ancient models did not consider any part the observable universe as separable from the human realm, and all the celestial bodies were considered an integral part of the world. This conceptual inseparability is strengthened by the fact that *musica mundana* includes the Earth itself, the balance and proportion of its elements, and the orderly procession of its seasons—the Earth being the locus and center around which all else revolves. For ancient theorists, the universe was a unified macrocosm, a single entity in which all parts were related, and where all parts influenced one another. For these philosophers and theorists, there was no difference between the "world" and the "universe," rather they were one in the same, and all embraced by *mundana*.

The other half of the phrase, *musica*, is a term whose meaning and usage has similarly evolved, expanded, and contracted. Music, as an academic or theoretical discipline in the ancient world, was primarily concerned with proportions, typically of objects set into motion. As such, music was not conceptualized as one of the arts or humanities, but rather one of the sciences, being largely based on observation and measurement. In the early educational curriculum, *musica* was a part of the *quadrivium*, together with arithmetic, geometry, and astronomy.[6] Indeed, arithmetic was a prerequisite for the study of music, with music an important cognate for the study of astronomy. For the classical or medieval scholar, music was the study of proportions in the observable universe, thus all things possessing balance and proportion were *musical*.

The perceived mathematical—and musical—perfection of the cosmos was based on the observed proportions and symmetries among its various elements. This was both implicitly and explicitly stated by Boethius and his contemporaries, and generations of subsequent music theorists. Cassiodorus, a disciple of Boethius, says, "Whatever design there is in the heavens and on earth which accords with the governance of the Creator Himself occurs only through [music]."[7] Writing in the ninth century, Aurelian of Réôme notes, "truly, the construction of this world and its natural order somehow contain an harmonious balance."[8] In a seventh-century work, Isidore of Seville ends his discussion of arithmetical relationships in music thus: "this ratio of the circling of the spheres exists in the heavens."[9] Johannes Lippius links music and the cosmos in the following elegant passage from his early seventeenth-century treatise: "[God] is the wisest and sweetest Architect Who designed the universe according to weight, number, measure, and harmony, namely, Jehova, the eternal Geometrician and Musician."[10] Remembering that the universe conceived by these theorists includes the Earth, balances and proportions existing in the heavenly bodies apply also to those nearer at hand, including observed phenomena on the Earth itself. Aurelian includes the following in his discussion of *musica mundana*:

> And if a certain harmony did not join the diversities of the four seasons—of winter, spring, summer and autumn—how could it happen that they come together into a single body and substance? But each season is such that it either brings forth its own fruit or helps the other to bring forth theirs.
>
> For what winter binds, spring releases; what summer warms, autumn ripens . . .[11]

Divine harmony, which manifests itself in the ordered motions of the celestial bodies, as well as the regular changes of earthly seasons and elements, is not sequestered within those particular domains, but flows from the heavens and the Earth, as it were, *into* the human frame, as described in another exposition by Lippius:

> The most beautiful harmony, I say, dwells in our triune God, Archetype and Source of all things. It abides in the choir of good angels; it resides in the physical macrocosm, in the heavens, in elements, mixtures, meteors, metals, stones, plants, and beasts; it dwells in man, the microcosm.[12]

It is to this we now turn—the music that exists within mankind.

MUSICA HUMANA

In many theoretical texts, as in Lippius, mankind is described as a microcosm that reflects or imitates the perfection and balance of the macrocosm.[13] The idea of mankind as microcosm did not originate with Boethius, but was theorized much further back, as Johannes de Grocheo reminds us in his fourteenth-century treatise:

> We also agree with the opinion . . . that man, as Plato and Aristotle say, is like a cosmos, hence he is called by them a microcosmos, that is, a small world. Hence, his laws and operations ought to imitate divine law as completely as possible.[14]

According to Grocheo, the best and most effective human state of being is one that aligns—*attunes* itself—to divine principles. The alignment of the human microcosm with the universal macrocosm is achieved "through the best mixture of elements in it,"[15] that is, within the human frame. However, this notion of an alignment between the *musica mundana* and the *musica humana* presents an essential problem. Music theorists universally describe the music of the celestial bodies—and often the earthly seasons and elements—as fundamentally *perfect*, while the same theorists, all well-educated Catholics,[16] and many of them priests and trained theologians, would have known from their St. Augustine and the doctrine of original sin, that mankind is inured to a state of sin and *imperfection*.

Theorists were aware of this central contradiction, and helpfully described it in musical terms. Cassiodorus states: "in short, music is the art of being well-tuned."[17] Isidore clarifies this by noting that mankind can, and does, fail to reflect the perfect balances and mathematical ratios observed in the heavens, so that "if man lacks this perfect ratio, he is not in tune."[18] While such statements contrast divine perfection with the human failure to reflect that perfection, the question remains, how may one *become* "well-tuned"? What are the means and methods by which such a change might be accomplished? Cassiodorus provides some guidance in the following passage:

> The study of music therefore permeates all that we do in life, especially if we keep the commandments of the Creator and obey with pure hearts the laws which He has laid down. For whatever we say and whatever we feel deep within, as evidenced by the beating of our hearts, shows by the musical flow whether it is in accord with the Virtues.
>
> [. . .]
>
> If we habitually live in agreement with the good, we always show that we are allied with music. But when we engage in evil, we do not have music within us.[19]

Cassiodorus makes the case that the capacity for mankind to be well-tuned is dependent upon its alignment with the requirements set down in divine laws and precepts—by being in agreement with good and avoiding evil. To be good is to be musical, or conversely, to be musical is to be *good*. Lippius provides a slightly different perspective on the juxtaposition between being tuned well and tuned ill:

> All things stand by virtue of harmony. Through disharmony all things crumble. Nothing is raised, replenished, or restored, unless it is first brought back and reconciled to harmony. Thus the devil in his disharmony lies fallen once and for all. Man, whom he deceived, can rise again only through the grace of God. In this way peace and justice are reinstated, and the harmonic image of God, previously lost through defiance, is restored to the human race.[20]

While this passage focuses in part on how disharmony came into the universe and was manifested within humankind, it also tells us by what means harmony may be regained. Lippius admits that the process of regaining harmony with the divine is continually ongoing, involving an active struggle between the competing influences of harmony and disharmony. Though the process of salvation has "freed [us] from everlasting, horrid, and infernal dissonance," nonetheless, our nature, still tainted by the stain of original sin, exists in a state of "harmony [. . .] still exist[ing] somehow mixed with its opposing discord," compelling us to "still aspire for that ineffable heavenly concord."[21] According to Lippius, victory over disharmony, personified in the devil as "that agitator of all noise, that raging screech owl, that roaring lion," is achieved through the agency of "the Arch-Musician and God-Man, Our Lord Jesus Christ."[22] On the one hand, Cassiodorus stresses obedience to divine laws and commandments as the method by which one becomes well-tuned, while on the other hand, Lippius focuses on an aspirational, gradual approach, attainable only through divine grace.

Having good and well-tuned *musica humana* is not only a spiritual exercise but also applies to the physical and mental health of humankind. Isidore notes that "music stirs the emotions; it rouses and transforms our feelings," "music soothes the soul," and "music . . . calms the passions."[23] Illustrating the medicinal power of music, Cassiodorus relates the biblical story of King Saul who, when oppressed by an evil spirit over which doctors and their medicines had no power, was restored to sanity by hearing the soothing music of David and his harp. Cassiodorus also tells the story of the physician Asclepiades who restored a madman through the use of music, and adds other extraordinary accounts, saying, "many miracles of healing have been performed through this art."[24]

Musica humana is not limited to the spiritual, physical, and mental health of individuals, but also signifies harmonious interactions between humans in their personal relationships, and within their larger societal structures. In short, wherever individual humans are "in tune" with divine principles—ensuring the proper balance of elements within themselves—human societies will likewise enjoy harmony. In the *Timaeus*, Plato notes that God gave humans the sense of sight so they could see the movements of the celestial bodies, and "apply them to the courses of our own intelligence which are akin to them," in order to identify "the irregular and graceless ways which prevail among mankind . . . and to help us against them."[25] In short, well-tuned *persons* make a well-tuned *people*.

MUSIC HUMANA AND VOCAL MUSIC

As a brief aside, a number of early theorists, including Boethius and some of his successors, categorize singing, or vocal music, as part of *musica humana*. However, it is fairly clear that these theorists are separating the *science* of singing, which belongs to *musica humana*, from the *practice* of singing, which belongs to the third and final category of *musica instrumentalis*, discussed in the next section. Aurelian illustrates this when he draws on Boethius and Nicomachus, a first-century Neopythagorean scholar, to define *musica humana* in three component parts: harmonics, rhythmics, and metrics. *Harmonics* is the ability to distinguish between low and high sounds, *rhythmics* the relationship of words to one another, and *metrics* the placing of words into different meters. None of these directly treat practical, audible, performed vocal music, but rather indicate the skills necessary for a listener to suitably judge a musical-poetic composition.[26] Aurelian says as much when he identifies a musician—one with well-tuned *musica humana*—as "one who has the faculty of judging without error with regard to reasoning, purposeful reflection, and musical convention, concerning quantities and rhythms, the kind and relationships of melodies, and the songs of the poets."[27] Later he says, "a musician is one who has with well-weighed intellect attained the science of singing not by the servitude of labor, but by the rule of contemplation."[28] Thus, a musician is not one who creates sounds as the result of mere physical labor, but is one who understands the silent *science* of music. Lippius agrees and expands on this when he states that a musician first "understands, notates, and composes a . . . piece according to the prescribed rules governing the science," after which "he finally actuates it on some instrument."[29] Among the many instruments on which a composition may be realized is the human voice, as well as other kinds of instruments like pipes and strings.

Aurelian describes the human body's capacity for creating audible music in instrumental terms: "even man himself . . . will not doubt the great harmony with which he is equipped for this discipline: for in this throat he has a pipe for singing; in his chest, a kind of harp, adorned with strings, as it were, the fibers of his lungs."[30] This was still understood as such in the early fourteenth century, when Grocheo notes that *musica instrumentalis* is "music which is caused by sounds of instruments, natural or artificial."[31] It is clear that the voice is such a natural instrument, and can be understood to belong to *musica instrumentalis*, to which we now turn our attention.

MUSICA INSTRUMENTALIS

In Western musical scholarship beginning with Boethius in the sixth century, we can detect a shift in focus from the theoretical to the practical. The earliest theorists had little to say about practical music or methods of performance. Their treatises usually contained passages describing the eight melodic modes, and their applications in different musical settings, but most often these were vehicles for the authors to demonstrate their skill in categorizing the many possible mutations and arrangements of the modes, with the characteristic delight in classification common to the Scholastics. Many earlier theorists did not think highly of practical music or, for that matter, of practical *musicians*. Such individuals were often considered little more than tradesmen, identified simply by the instruments they played (vocalist from voice, cithara player from cithara, harpist from harp, etc.), in much the same way a hammerer is named because of his use of the hammer.[32] Boethius identifies three classes of people who are "concerned with the art of music." First are instrumentalists and singers, who "are cut off from the understanding of musical science, since they are servants [. . .] who do not make any use of reason, and are altogether lacking in thought." Second are poets, who are "attracted to song not so much by speculation and reason as by a certain natural instinct," and who are likewise "separated from music." Thirdly and finally are those who have "the skill of judging," who can "[weigh] rhythms and melodies and the whole of song" and are considered properly musical because they rely "entirely upon reason and speculation."[33] Only members of this third category may be given the title of *musician*.

Early treatises listed musical instruments in categories, such as wind instruments, string instruments, and percussion instruments, but included little commentary and description of their uses and effects, and the amount of space given to them is small when compared with the lengthy passages devoted to *musica mundana* and *musica humana*. From this, it is clear that *musica instrumentalis* occupies the lowest position among the three types of music. These relative positions are illustrated in an illuminated page from a ca. 1300 edition of Beothius' *De institutione musica* (see figure 1.1). There, we see three scenes with three enthroned personifications of *musica*. First is *musica mundana*, where *musica* points with her rod at a depiction of the heavenly bodies, including the sun, moon, and stars, and the various earthly

Figure 1.1 MS Pluteo 29.I. *Source:* Held in the Biblioteca Medicea Laurenziana, Florence.

elements—earth, water, wind, and fire. Second is *musica humana*, where *musica* points to a group of men whose harmonious nature, both individual and collective, is shown by their mild postures and joining of hands. Finally there is *musica instrumentalis*, in which *musica* pulls back her rod, and waves a warning finger at the string player and his group of instruments. This further demonstrates the lowly position held by practical, audible music, as well as its potential dangers if not properly controlled and moderated. An important corollary to this illustrated warning is Raphael's *St. Cecilia Altarpiece*, also known as *The Ecstasy of St. Cecilia*, painted in the early sixteenth century, shown in figure 1.2. According to legend, Cecilia was a second- or third-century martyr who was betrothed to a pagan nobleman, though she had already taken a vow of perpetual virginity as part of a spiritual "marriage" to Christ. As musicians played during her wedding feast, St. Cecilia ignored the music, instead singing in her heart to God. In time, St. Cecilia would become the patron saint of musicians, and it is in this capacity that Rafael depicts her

Figure 1.2 Ecstasy of St. Cecilia. *Source*: Oil painting by Raphael, c. 1514–1517. Held in the Pinacoteca Nazionale Bologna.

in the *Ecstasy*. The early seventeenth-century composer and theorist Adriano Banchieri says the following about the painting:

> Guided by his marvelous imagination, [Rafael] portrayed her holding an organ which was broken and upside down, with other broken instruments at her feet. She turned to the harmony of heaven with a compassionate look, carried away by holy zeal, in a manner that seems to say, "Go away, go away, sounds, songs, and all you worldly pleasures; return to your ancient mother. I yearn only to be placed in that most holy musical chapel among those chosen, virtuous musicians and organists who play continually before my most sweet spouse Jesus, Holy, Holy, Holy."[34]

With such divine messages and warnings in mind, how can *musica instrumentalis* be suitably and safely performed? The means is the correct application of the "higher" forms of music: *musica mundana* and *musica humana*. As a "lower" form of music, *musica instrumentalis* improves the quality of mankind's own internal harmony if, and only if, it aligns with proper divine principles. This is elaborated upon by Lippius:

> There dwells something divine in music when it is taught properly. As it penetrates the human structure, it often succeeds in awakening, establishing, and eliciting man's internal harmony.
> [. . .]
> In the wave of human events man's inner and intellectual harmony [is] aroused, established, maintained, and enriched by audible external harmony.[35]

In the dedicatory passage to his 1549 treatise, Nicolaus Listenius also notes the potential power of properly taught music in the education of young noblemen:

> Many great and serious reasons are established by learned and intelligent men, for all men of genius . . . must be versed in music and habituated to it. It influences souls to humanity, suavity, even-temper; it restrains all immoderate affections, grief, wrath; it represses violence and obscene desires, for it calms them; as in sounds and songs, so in all the actions of life we may conserve harmony.
> [. . .]
> With all peoples at all periods of music, it has been used in sacred observances, not as a useless voluptuousness, to play some kind of game, but in song, as souls are made more tranquil and are aroused to understand the harmony of divine guidance and are attuned to the correct movement of heavenly teaching; hence its doctrines will more efficiently move souls when song arises.[36]

As just alluded to by Listenius, appropriate practical music is suitable for education *because* of the imprint of divinity that exists and is retained there. For example, Grocheo argues that the ability of mankind to perceive three—and only three—perfect consonant sounds, reflects the "image of the Trinity," and that "the human soul, directly created from the beginning, retains the type or image of its Creator." It is because of "this natural awareness [that] the human soul perceives a triple perfection in sounds."[37] Thus, some measure of awareness of divine musical principles is instilled in the very nature of mankind, and without the need for formal musical training. It is integral to the *musica humana* of a created human being, or as Gaspar Stoquerus says, "those rules are known by nature and seem to be evident even to the untaught."[38] However, this innate capacity can be improved through the agency and application of human reason, so that musicians who are "talented and skilled in their art, because they are outstandingly gifted with reason," create music that "in [its] correct correspondence with reason [. . .] closely approach[es] the truth."[39] This clearly illustrates the essential interconnectedness of the three kinds of *musica*: a human gifted with good reason (*musica humana* via *musica mundana*) creates good music (*musica instrumentalis*), that in turn reflects eternal truths (*musica mundana*).

PYTHAGORAS AND THE DISCOVERY OF NUMBERS IN MUSIC

Being at its conceptual core an art based on observation, music has much to do with numbers. Regarding music's relationship to numbers and mathematics, Pietro Aaron says, "The power of number has precedence over music,"[40] and Aurelian adds, "Music has the greatest correspondence to mathematics."[41] These statements neatly summarize the attitudes of music theorists on the power of mathematics and numbers—specifically numerical ratios—and their ability to bequeath power to music. This ability derives from the nature and structure of the universe itself, as Lippius noted at the head of this chapter, that God "designed the universe according to weight, number, measure, and harmony."[42] Just *which* numbers and measures have ability to bestow power on music belongs to the realm of numerology, the study and application of the spiritual and magical properties of numbers and proportions.

The most common story describing the discovery of numerical relationships in music is that of Pythagoras and the Hammers (see figure 1.3). While there are differing versions of the story, the general outlines remain fairly consistent. One day, while reflecting on mathematical principles, Pythagoras takes a stroll through town, and "as by divine inspiration"[43] his feet lead him toward a blacksmith's forge, where he hears the ringing of hammers striking the anvil. Occasionally, two hammers strike the anvil at the same time, and Pythagoras hears the simultaneous pitches that are produced as a result. Sometimes the interval between two striking hammers is pleasing to the ear, while with other combinations of hammers, the sound is unpleasant. Pythagoras takes the hammers,[44] weighs them, and learns that the numerical ratios of the weights of the hammers determine whether or not they sound pleasing when struck together. For instance, when a hammer weighing 12 pounds and one weighing 6 pounds are sounded, the 2:1 ratio between their weights creates a pleasing sound. In the same way, the striking of a 12-pound and an 8-pound hammer (making a 3:2 ratio), and a 12-pound and a 9-pound hammer (4:3 ratio), are likewise agreeable. However, when a 9-pound and an 8-pound hammer are struck together (9:8 ratio), the sound fails to delight the ear. In this way, Pythagoras discovers the three pleasing, or consonant, sounds produced by means of these ratios, known collectively as the *perfect consonances:* the perfect octave, the perfect fifth, and the perfect fourth.

According to Aurelian, "it was . . . not without divine approval that . . . Pythagoras was able to discover how different proportions are related to

"The Heavens Make a Harmony" 19

Figure 1.3   From Franchino Gafurio's *Theorica Musice* (1492). Clockwise from top left: Pythagoras (in this panel Renamed IVBAL [Jubal]) and the blacksmith's hammers; Pythagoras experimenting with ratios on bells and glasses of water; Pythagoras and his disciple Philolaus creating intervals with pipes; Pythagoras experimenting with ratios using string tension created by different weights. *Source*: From Franchino Gafurio's *Theorica Musice* (1492).

consonant sounds."[45] Pythagoras followed up on this divine inspiration, conducting further inquiries and tests with his disciple Philolaus (see figure 1.3), discovering that the same proportions and ratios observed with the hammers applied to other means of creating sound. Whether by striking bells of different weights, playing musical glasses filled with different amounts of water, plucking strings under differing tensions, or blowing through tubes of various lengths, these numerical principles were confirmed.[46] The numerological significance of this discovery was important in the expression of Greek and Judeo-Christian religious traditions, as the component numbers of the ratios of the three perfectly consonant intervals are 1, 2, 3, and 4. These are the first four simple and radical numbers, known as the Pythagorean quaternary,[47] they also represent the *tetragrammaton*, the four Hebrew letters making up the name of God, and when conceived of as a collection of points in a triangular figure they create the *tetractys*, an important mystical symbol in Pythagorean religious worship. Added together, the numbers make ten, the *dekad*, the point at which numbers are "reborn" and begin again, and represent the number of the ten commandments. With such mystical and spiritual implications, it is clear that musical intervals comprised of these numbers have potency, as Lippius notes: "divine music gives special powers to these proportions."[48]

That the perfect consonances also conform to the number of persons in the Trinity was not lost on music theorists in the Christian world. Grocheo already connects these consonances with the Godhead in a passage above, and goes on to support the use of numerological principles when stating that mankind's "laws and operations ought to imitate divine law as completely as possible."[49]

Though our guiding principle has been, and will continue to be, Boethius' threefold categorization of music into *musica mundana*, *musica humana*, and *musica instrumentalis*, there are many other musical principles and categories conveniently (and at times, arbitrarily) encountered in sets of three. Aurelian divides *musica humana* into three parts: harmonics, rhythmics, and metrics.[50] Listenius categorizes music into theoretical, practical, and poetic foci;[51] he divides the rhythmic tactus, or "beat," into total/integral, general/common, and special types;[52] and he provides for three elements of rhythmic modality in *modus, tempus,* and *prolatio*.[53] According to Grocheo and many other theorists, rhythms using patterns of three constitute a *perfectio*, a perfection, "just as perfection is expected in bodies made up of a triple constitution, so in sounds they have called a perfection something made from three."[54] The fundamentally perfect nature of "three-ness" is confirmed by Tinctoris when he says, "every ternary number [. . .] according to musicians is perfect,"[55] and again by Marcin Kromer: "Musicians [. . .] call anything perfect that is complete in threes."[56]

The power of the number three derives directly from the Trinity, through its imprint on the nature of humanity, where it reveals itself in humanity's musical compositions. Lippius, speaking of the musical triad, which becomes the theoretical basis for musical harmony from the seventeenth century onward, describes the triad in terms that are as theological as they are musical:

> The harmonic, simple, and direct triad is the true and unitrisonic root of all the most perfect and most complete harmonies that can exist in the world. It is the root of even thousands and millions of sounds [. . .]. The triad is the image of that great mystery, the divine and solely adorable Unitrinity (I cannot think of a semblance more lucid).[57]

There are uncounted further examples illustrating the importance and power of the number three, but let the above suffice, as there are still other essential and efficacious numbers found in music.

The number four derives much of its power by being the number of the observed earthly elements of earth, water, air, and fire. According to the anonymous compiler of the Berkeley manuscript, "since the harmony of the world is composed of four elements, the ecclesiastical harmony disposes its finals in four letters."[58] Likewise for Lippius, the four voices of the choir, discant (soprano), alto, tenor, and bass, "are analogous to the four elements of earth."[59] The number seven is powerful, and tied to Greek and Christian cosmology. The Berkeley author claims that the seventh-century BCE musician Terpander of Lesbos added a seventh string to the lyre to "establish a musical likeness to the seven planets."[60] Grocheo notes, "seven are the gifts of the spirit and there are seven planets in heaven and seven days in the week," and "similarly [. . .] there are seven concords in sound."[61] Lippius identifies the particularly miraculous nature of the number seven, saying that it is "the first virginal and sacred number" because, though "it stands apart and begets no consonances [. . .] it amazingly spells out the total number of [. . .] consonances."[62] In other words, though the number seven does not appear in any of the numerical ratios of the consonances, it nonetheless encompasses within itself the entirety of their quantity. The number eight also possesses a measure of efficacy. Echoing Grocheo's statement that human operations should imitate divine law, Aurelian explains that there are eight musical modes that "seem to imitate celestial motions," which include "seven of the planets and one of that which is called the Zodiac, which all say make the sweetest harmony of song."[63] Grocheo says that these eight modes may be compared to "the manner of the eight Beatitudes [. . .] or perhaps considering it more from an arithmetical standpoint, by looking at the logic and propriety of eight, which is the first of the cubes."[64] The anonymous author of the ninth-century *Musica Enchiriadis* explains that the Greek term for the interval of the octave, *diapason*, means "from all things," because "of old no more than eight strings were used" on a stringed instrument, and that through the octave "the voice is once more renewed."[65]

It is clear that numerical and mathematical concepts were highly valued in music. They represented the imprint of the *musica mundana*—observed in the numbers and attitudes of celestial and natural phenomena, and the number and types of spiritual principles—on the practical and audible nature of *musica instrumentalis*. As the theorists and commentators have asserted above, this imprint fully or partially imbues the music with *perfection*. With this in mind, we will now examine a range of musical systems that partake of, or aspire to, perfection.

TOWARDS SYSTEMS OF PERFECTION

Having observed many of the ways perfection was theorized in early musical treatises, it is important to see how—or if—these principles are put into practice. In practical, performed music, perfection can be maintained, at least conceptually, by remaining within certain patterns. For example, early polyphony—music in which more than one pitch sounds at a time—was permitted in religious and liturgical music if the intervals used were among the three perfect consonances: perfect octave, perfect fifth, or perfect fourth. It follows that polyphonic music using these prescribed consonances will thus be perfect, and this is *mostly* true. However, *complete* perfection is not possible when using the consonance of the perfect fourth. The author of the *Musica Enchiriadis* provides instructions and procedures for creating polyphonic music using perfect consonances, but must also describe methods to avoid problems, or *imperfections*, that unavoidably arise. In most cases, creating this early style of polyphony is as simple as taking an original line of melody, adding a second melody above or below at a distance of one of the perfect consonances, and then moving in strict, parallel motion. However, at the interval of the perfect fourth, due to the nature of the musical scale itself, the sound produced in some cases will not be the consonance of the perfect fourth at the 4:3 ratio, but rather the *tritone*, with the decidedly *imperfect* ratio of 729:512. This interval was considered so imperfect and dissonant that it was given the name *diabolus in musica* ("the devil in music"), and was to be avoided at all costs.[66] The author of the *Enchiriadis* notes that "somehow they [i.e., these sounds] accord so sweetly in [their] mingling, [but] other sounds are indeed more unpleasantly out of harmony, refusing to be mixed together,"[67] and provides instructions on how to elude the troublesome interval by using other intervals in its place. These substituted intervals are not perfect, but not *as* imperfect as the tritone. So in the case of the perfect fourth, it is only through the use of a *lesser* imperfection that a *greater* imperfection is avoided. The inability of musicians to achieve musical perfection even with perfect consonances is, according to the *Enchiriadis*, "a more profoundly marvelous principle, even among the most important of nature's most secret secrets," through which "God permitted us in this matter to attain [only] partial results."[68] It is thus clear that perfection exists, but God, by holding back some of the "most secret secrets" of nature, does not permit humanity to fully attain perfection, leaving it with imperfection. However, because such a system of perfection is *conceivably* possible, if mankind were to discover these "most secret secrets," we are still left with a true system of perfection, but which on Earth attains only "partial results."

Other examples illustrate the possibility of perfection, but not necessarily the *desire* to achieve it. Many treatises treat the subject of rhythm, and the various ways in which rhythms at different levels can be combined effectively. A *perfectio* in rhythm occurs when metrical and rhythmic devices are organized into sets of three. However, early theorists and composers of music, perhaps chafing under the relative limitations imposed by perfect rhythm, became interested in rhythms *not* composed in sets of three. This was accomplished in two ways. One, a more conservative approach, shied away from abandoning established numerological principles, and posited *spiritual* arguments for the use of rhythms in proportions other than three. Tinctoris explains his support of rhythmic division by two, by addressing the idea of the union of humanity and divinity: "After a fullness of time had passed, in which that greatest musician, Jesus Christ, our peace, made both one in duple proportion."[69] The second method of justifying duple rhythms did not bother addressing the spiritual aspects of rhythmic proportion at all, and instead simply illustrated the ways in which rhythmic imperfection could be used most effectively in practice,[70] or how perfect and imperfect rhythms could be combined and used in tandem.[71] While the strictly spiritual aspects of perfect and imperfect rhythms were largely ignored by later theorists, the continued use of the word *perfection* indicates that a greater value was still attached to it, even if the results left much to be desired by more modern ears.

As with rhythm, movement beyond the three previously accepted intervals in harmony was inevitable, as composers explored musical possibilities outside the limitations of the perfect consonances. Their reasoning was often strictly sensory in nature, in that non-perfect intervals were acceptable simply because they pleased the ear, and not because they were mathematically or theoretically suitable.[72] In his thirteenth-century treatise, Johannes de Garlandia ranks the intervals by the degree to which their sound is pleasing (concordant) or displeasing (discordant) to the ear. In Garlandia's classifications, concords and discords each contain three subcategories indicating the extent to which the different sounds are perceived by the ear as compatible or incompatible. These include the following: (1) perfect concords, which include the perfect unison[73] and the perfect octave; (2) intermediate concords, including the perfect fifth and perfect fourth;[74] (3) imperfect concords, comprised of the major third and minor third; (4) imperfect discords, containing the major sixth and minor seventh; (5) intermediate discords, including the major second and the minor sixth; and (6) perfect discords, consisting of the major seventh, the minor second, and the tritone.[75] A curious addition to the overall theoretical dialogue is Garlandia's identification of sets of *contrasting perfections*, which include the perfect concords (1) versus the perfect discords (6). With the latter, he identifies a set of intervals that are *perfectly imperfect*, or cannot contain more imperfection.[76] Though Garlandia's continuum of intervals includes those that are imperfect, it nonetheless maintains the *theoretical* possibility of perfection, even where there is no desire to attain it, and thus, like rhythm, exists within a larger system of perfection.

Lippius makes another provision for potential perfection in his discussion of melodic scales. He compares the tuning of the diatonal diatonic scale, whose invention was attributed to Pythagoras, with that of the newer syntonal diatonic scale, developed by Gioseffo Zarlino in the sixteenth century. Lippius characterizes the Pythagorean scale as "strange and awkward," one that "because of its imperfection [. . .] has become antiquated, and with good reason."[77] While advocating for the use of the newer scale, he notes: "Although this [scale] is not totally perfect, nevertheless it has a greater perfection, naturalness, simplicity, agreeableness, sobriety, variety, suitability to harmonic composition, admirableness, and divinity."[78] Lippius' use of "a greater perfection" again assumes a place for perfection in the system, especially as he points toward the concept by ascribing a measure of "divinity" to the scale.

SYSTEMS OF IMPERFECTION

As we have seen, the notion of musical perfection by spiritual and numerological means underlies the theory and practice of many centuries of musical development. Even when imperfections were deliberately used, the *idea* that perfection existed, and was potentially accessible, was an important notion for many theorists and composers. However, for speculative music theorists, as well as for astronomers—both intimately concerned with *musica mundana*—technical advances proved that classical systems of cosmological perfection did not, and could not, exist. The following discussion treats this as part of systems of *imperfection*.

The notion of proper tuning was of particular concern to theorists and practical performers alike, as we saw above with Lippius and the tuning of diatonic scales. The proper performance of harmonic intervals according to simple numerical ratios—particularly the perfect intervals—was critical, because such intervals were considered spiritually and theoretically correct, and because they sounded "sweet" to the human ear. It follows, even today, that when an instrument, such as a guitar or a piano, is tuned, intervals should conform to these ratios. Obvious though it may seem, it is nevertheless mathematically impossible. This is clearly illustrated when attempting to tune the two purest perfect intervals—the perfect octave and the perfect fifth—on a keyboard instrument, such as the piano. The tuner can tune a cycle of pitches at perfect octaves (2:1 ratio), as shown on the left side of figure 1.4. Beginning at the lowest note (called "C"), the octaves can be tuned perfectly, with each subsequent "C" sounding at twice the frequency of the one below it, all the way to the highest "C" on the keyboard. Similarly, the perfect fifth is tuned from the same place, with each fifth tuned higher than the one below it at a perfect 3:2 ratio, until the highest "C" is reached,[79] as seen on the right side of figure 1.4. The total ratio between the lowest and highest perfect octaves will come out to 128:1 (or $2^7:1^7$), dividing to an even 128. However, the cycle of perfect fifths comes to 531,441:4,096 (or $3^{12}:2^{12}$), which divides out to an *uneven* 129.5. Thus, the instrument cannot accommodate both perfect octaves

Figure 1.4 Cycle of Perfect Octaves (Left) and Cycle of Perfect Fifths (Right). *Source*: Author.

and perfect fifths; one or the other (or both) must be tuned imperfectly. The space taken up by the cycle of perfect fifths is larger than that of the perfect octaves by about 1%, a difference very noticeable to the human ear. This difference is known as the "Pythagorean comma," and the question of what to do with the comma—how to distribute its difference among other pitches and intervals so that the result is tolerable to the ear—has been the concern of practical musicians for centuries.[80]

While Boethius and subsequent theorists acknowledged the comma, its existence was sometimes couched in terms of imperfection caused by sin and a fallen world. David Tame describes the potential consequences of the comma's existence:

> The comma produces huge cosmological, as well as practical, implications and results. Since this system . . . does not perfectly complete the octave, the . . . pitches it produces are imperfect for use together in harmony.
>
> [. . .]
>
> If the system resulted, as it did, in the harmony of mortal music being imperfect, then this had to be borne as a manifest symbol of man's fall from grace, and of the inherent imperfection of the non-heavenly realm of time and space.[81]

What makes the issue of tuning different from the other practical considerations we have explored in this chapter, is that there is no parallel system of perfection for tuning. For polyphonic music we may simply avoid the tritone, or admit that there is a secret method not yet revealed to mankind, and with rhythm we can stay within the restrictions of the *perfectio*, even if it does bore us. But tuning does not allow for any such prevarication—it is a *complete* system of imperfection. It is here that we observe some of the Greco-Roman foundations over which much of Christian music theory, theology, and metaphysics is built. In systems of perfection, theorists and practitioners may allow for the imperfect and the sensual, but they are not comfortable without the *potential* for perfection, even if achieving it is difficult or not desired. Pythagoras stands in both places: the Pythagorean comma proves the impossibility of perfection in tuning, while the story of Pythagoras and the hammers establishes the three perfect consonances. Though total perfection is occluded in some cases, as with the perfect fourth, at least *some* perfection is possible. Tame suggests as much when he notes that these imperfections are part of a world in its fallen state—a state that that will someday be remedied and perfected. However, there do exist musical accounts from the ancient, pre-Christian world that have no trouble whatsoever with systems of imperfection as a natural part of the created world.

Describing these pre-Christian foundations, Hans Jonas famously depicts them in their epic, herculean proportions, ones that are familiar—disconcertingly familiar—to Christian readers:

> Out of the mist of the beginning of our era there looms a pageant of mythical figures whose vast, superhuman contours might people the walls and ceiling of another Sistine Chapel. Their countenances and gestures, the roles in which they are cast, the drama which they enact, would yield images different from the biblical ones on which the imagination of the beholder was reared, yet strangely familiar to him and disturbingly moving. The stage would be the same, the theme as transcending: the creation of the world, the destiny of man, fall and redemption, the first and the last things. But how much more numerous would be the cast, how much more bizarre the symbolism, how much more extravagant the emotions! Almost all the action would be in the heights, in the divine or angelic or daimonic realm, a drama of pre-cosmic persons in the supranatural world, of which the drama of man in the natural world is but a distant echo.[82]

These myths and epics and the characters that inhabit them are set in cosmic, extra-human environments, but the divinities are themselves *very* human, and the universe likewise blemished and imperfect. This is not the world of John Milton in which paradise and perfection are shown to exist precisely *because* they can be lost and regained. It is rather a world where perfection has never existed, nor is it expected to exist at any future time. The flaws of the characters populating this universe, deities though they may be, are ridiculously outsized—their pride, rashness, avarice, pettiness, greed, recklessness, lust, and wrath not just of human, but of superhuman, proportions. Humans themselves are not at the center of this story, neither is there any hint of redemption or return to a pre-fall state of perfection.[83]

With such a foundational concept of the imperfection of the universe in mind, let us examine two Greek stories that describe the origins of music. These accounts exist in many versions, but their general outlines are similar. The first story features one of the Greek gods, usually Apollo,[84] walking along the banks of the Nile River. The river has receded from its annual flood stage and the body of a tortoise, having died after being stranded on high ground, is lying on a bank. The tortoise has decayed to the point that all that remains is its shell and a number of sinews that have dried, and are now stretched taut across the hollow section. Apollo picks this up, plucks one of the dried sinews, hears the resulting musical tone, and thereby discovers music as well as the primitive form of the lyre.[85] The second story treats Hermes[86] and the miraculous events of his first day of life. On the day of his birth to the nymph Maia and the god Zeus, Hermes leaves his cradle, intent on precocious mischief. Determined to steal the cattle of his elder half-brother Apollo, he leaves his mother's cave, and on the way out meets a tortoise passing near the threshold. He quickly kills her, creates a lyre from her shell, and composes a hymn, thus simultaneously inventing musical instruments and singing. Hermes eventually steals Apollo's cattle, and when he is forced to return them, he also gives Apollo the newly created lyre as a gift, passing to him the status as divine patron of music.[87]

These musical origin stories illustrate a fundamental difference between Christian and ancient Greco-Roman cosmologies. Whereas the theorists following Boethius posit patterns of perfection in the *musica mundana*, toward which the practical, performed music of *musica instrumentalis* should strive, the Greco-Roman system ties the very creation of music to death and decay. Theorists in the Christian West "baptized" the mathematical and musical foundations ascribed to Pythagoras, going so far as to rechristen him as Jubal or King David.[88] Despite attempts to graft perfection onto them, these adapted systems are, ultimately, systems of *imperfection*.

MAIOR PERFECTUM: GREATER PERFECTION

An extension of systems of perfection is the *maior perfectum*: a system of greater perfection. The fifteenth-century theorist Bonaventura da Brescia hints at this in a discussion of the three different mutations used when singing with solfége syllables: "Note that we have three types of mutation, that is, a most perfect mutation, a perfect mutation and an imperfect mutation."[89] The author of the *Musica Enchiriadis* identifies the three consonant intervals, but sets apart the octave because "in it there is a more perfect consonance than in the others,"[90] and later that it "resound[s] . . . with the greatest possible perfection."[91] Aurelian identifies the double octave as "that greatest consonance," more perfect than the other perfect intervals.[92] There are other examples, identified as "most perfect" or "greater than perfect" throughout the theoretical literature, and they create a logical conundrum. Namely, how can a thing be *more* perfect than perfect? A biblical passage from the book of Hebrews hints at such a possibility, at least in the heavenly realm: "But Christ came as High Priest of the good things to come, with the greater and more perfect tabernacle not made with hands, that is, not of this creation."[93] This passage assumes the existence of a perfect tabernacle, with which a "more perfect" one contrasts. Another analogue for *maior perfectum* comes out of Christian theology, which generally includes the doctrine of humanity created in a state of perfection, followed by a fall into sin and imperfection, and an eventual return to perfection. This return is often presented in terms of a return to the original state of perfection, with the further expansion or enlargement of that state. An illustration of this principle is found in the third verse and refrain of the late nineteenth-century hymn "Holy, Holy, Is What the Angels Sing," written by Johnson Oatman, Jr. Here, the author illustrates that, in heaven, humanity will have something they have *never* had before, which will be expressed musically:

Then the angels stand and listen, for they cannot join that song,
Like the sound of many waters, by that happy, blood-washed throng;
For they sing about great trials, battles fought and vict'ries won,
And they praise their great Redeemer who hath said to them, "well done."
Holy, holy, is what the angels sing,
And I expect to help them make the courts of heaven ring;
But when I sing redemption's story, they will fold their wings,
For angels never felt the joys that our salvation brings.[94]

In Oatman's understanding, humanity, after having attained salvation and renewed perfection, possess something not known to the other created classes, even the unfallen angelic orders. In the afterlife, the *musica humana* of redeemed mankind even achieves the ability to enhance the *musica mundana* of the heavenly realms. This is accomplished through humanity's fall into sin, and its subsequent salvation, the reality of which is conceived of as an essential *improvement* on mankind's pre-fall state. The idea is explored in a theological concept known as *Felix peccatum Adae*, the "blessed sin of Adam," or *Felix culpa*, the "blessed fault." This concept contends that the fall is ultimately a net benefit to humanity, because the experience of salvation that comes as a result could not have occurred without sin. Thus, humankind's eventual condition is one that is better—more perfect—than if no fall had taken place. St. Augustine explores this in an early fifth-century work, saying that God "foresaw that man would make a bad use of his free-will, that is, would sin, [and] arranged His own designs rather with a view to do good to man even in his sinfulness." Rather than having a will that has power to choose either right or wrong, as in its originally created state, redeemed mankind "shall be much freer when it shall be wholly impossible for him to be the slave of sin."[95]

According to Augustine, humanity's eventual position in the future paradise is greater than what was possible on the pre-fall earth, and he notes that mankind will take up positions in the heavenly hierarchy formerly held by fallen angels. This points to a *maior perfectum* that is not simply a greater *degree* of perfection, but a greater *capacity* for perfection. Another perspective is that of the second-century bishop and author Irenaeus, who argued that humanity was not initially created in complete perfection. Comparing primordial, pre-fall mankind to an infant that is fed first on milk before moving on to richer, solid foods, Irenaeus says that God *could* have granted total perfection, but because man "was only recently created, he could not possibly have received it, or even if he had received it, could he have contained it, or containing it, could he have retained it."[96] The remedy for this initial lack of capacity is time and growth. The end point of this growth is a perfection analogous to godhood, for "we have not been made gods from the beginning, but at first merely men, then at length gods."[97] The process of receiving this greater perfection is described as follows:

> Now it was necessary that man should in the first instance be created; and having been created, should receive growth; and having received growth, should be strengthened; and having been strengthened, should abound; and having abounded, should recover [from the disease of sin]; and having recovered, should be glorified; and being glorified, should see his Lord.[98]

The end point of this process is open-ended, and Irenaeus describes mankind as moving closer and closer to the potential and capacity for perfection equal to God himself. This would be a course of growth, a *maior perfectum*, of infinite capacity, taking place over an infinite amount of time.

Ultimately, these systems of imperfection, perfection, and greater perfection illustrate different methods for visualizing the workings of the universe—the *musica mundana*. In one case, the imperfections we perceive are an integral part of the original design; in another, they are the result of negative forces which break up the original perfection, to which we may still be restored; in yet another, the negative forces are not only remedied, but are reversed "with compound interest," resulting in an infinitely expanding perfection. Since these cases are concerned with the eventual fate of humanity, and the intricacies of its own inner workings, its subject is also *musica humana*. Finally, mankind's practical music, the *musica instrumentalis*, reflects all of this: our perception of the universe, and our own place within it. In the next chapter, we explore these notions of imperfection, perfection, and greater perfection in the imagination of Dante as he takes a journey into heaven, experiencing the expressions and limitations of all three kinds of *musica*.

NOTES

1. Ernest Brehaut, *An Encyclopedist of the Dark Ages: Isidore of Seville* (New York: Longmans, Green & Co., 1912), 137.
2. J. Nichols, *A Select Collection of Poems*, vol. 5 (London: J. Nichols, 1782), 305.
3. Boethius' works are largely Aristotelian and Neoplatonic in flavor, and later rediscoveries of works of other ancient schools of thought created tensions in Catholic philosophy and theology. However, in terms of music, Boethius reigned supreme, and authors of music treatises respectfully deferred to his musical-theoretical authority well into the nineteenth century.
4. Leo Treitler, general ed., *Source Readings in Music History – Vol. 3: The Renaissance*, Gary Tomlinson, ed. (New York and London: W.W. Norton and Co., 1998), 18.
5. Michael Ward, *Planet Narnia: The Seven Heavens in the Imagination of C.S. Lewis* (New York and Oxford: Oxford University Press, 2008), 21–2.
6. Boethius specifically mentions these four subjects as an integral part of education, echoing earlier scholars from the fifth-century CE theorist Martianus Capella back to Pythagoras and Plato.
7. Helen Dill Goode and Gertrude C. Drake, trs. *Cassiodorus - Institutiones: Book II, Ch. V; Isidore of Seville - Etymologies: Book III*, Ch. 15 - 23 (Colorado Springs: Colorado College Music Press, 1980), 9.
8. Joseph Ponte, tr. *Aurelian of Réôme – The Discipline of Music (Musica Disciplina)* (Colorado Springs: Colorado College Music Press, 1968), 6.
9. Goode and Drake, *Cassiodorus and Isidore of Seville*, 20.
10. Benito V. Rivera, tr., *Johannes Lippius – Synopsis of New Music (Synopsis Musicae Novae)* (Colorado Springs: Colorado College Music Press, 1977), 14.
11. Ponte, *Aurelian of Réôme*, 10. The last part of this passage is a direct quote from Boethius.
12. Rivera, *Johannes Lippius*, 1.
13. Mankind is not considered to be *outside* the larger created macrocosm in any of the theoretical texts, but for purposes of categorization, as well as the understandably anthropocentric viewpoints of the authors, humanity is always treated separately.

14. Albert Seay, tr., *Johannes de Grocheo – Concerning Music (De Musica)*, 2nd ed. (Colorado Springs: Colorado College Music Press, 1973), 7–8.
15. Ibid., 10.
16. Some later theorists, beginning in the sixteenth century, were Protestants.
17. Goode and Drake, *Cassiodorus and Isidore of Seville*, 3.
18. Ibid., 20.
19. Ibid., 3–4.
20. Rivera, *Johannes Lippius*, 1–2.
21. Ibid., 2.
22. Ibid., 4.
23. Goode and Drake, *Cassiodorus and Isidore of Seville*, 14.
24. Ibid., 9.
25. Piero Weiss and Richard Taruskin, *Music in the Western World: A History in Documents* (New York and London: Schirmer Books, 1984), 10.
26. It should be made clear that in ancient music theory, music and poetry were not separable categories—they existed as a single entity known as *melos*. This was the case for Plato in his fourth-century BCE treatise the *Republic*, as well as for the fourth-century CE neo-Platonist Aristides Quintilianus, both of whom were known to Boethius and his followers. Leo Treitler, general ed., *Source Readings in Music History – Vol. 1: Greek Views of Music*, Thomas J. Mathiesen, ed. (New York and London: W.W. Norton and Co., 1998), 10, ff. 2.
27. Ponte, *Aurelian of Réôme*, 12.
28. Ibid., 20.
29. Rivera, *Johannes Lippius*, 14.
30. Ponte, *Aurelian of Réôme*, 6.
31. Seay, *Johannes de Grocheo*, 10.
32. Ponte, *Aurelian of Réôme*, 20.
33. Leo Treitler, general ed., *Source Readings in Music History – Vol. 2: The Early Christian Period and the Latin Middle Ages*, James McKinnon, ed. (New York and London: W.W. Norton and Co., 1998), 32.
34. Lee R. Garrett, tr., *Adriano Banchieri – Conclusions for Playing the Organ (1609)* (Colorado Springs: Colorado College Music Press, 1982), 3.
35. Rivera, *Johannes Lippius*, 3.
36. Albert Seay, tr., *Nicolaus Listenius – Music (Musica)* (Colorado Springs: Colorado College Music Press, 1975), 1.
37. Seay, *Johannes de Grocheo*, 6–7. Grocheo notes that this imprint is not detectable by the other created orders, such as animals, though such "brutes" may be delighted by musical sounds in general. The ability of mankind to recognize the perfect consonances—the imprint of the Trinity—illustrates its favored position in the hierarchy of creation. Much more will be said about this hierarchy in chapter 5.
38. Albert C. Rotola, SJ, tr. and comm., *Gaspar Stoquerus – Two Books on Verbal Music (De Musica Verbali)* (Lincoln and London: University of Nebraska Press, 1988), 193.
39. Ibid.

40. Peter Berquist, tr., *Pietro Aaron – Toscanello in Music, Book II, Chapters I – XXXVI* (Colorado Springs: Colorado College Music Press, 1970), 43.
41. Ponte, *Aurelian of Réôme*, 14.
42. Rivera, *Johannes Lippius*, 14.
43. Seay, *Johannes de Grocheo*, 3.
44. With permission, it is hoped.
45. Ponte, *Aurelian of Réôme*, 9.
46. I should note that most of these experiments do *not* produce the results described in the account. It does, however, make for a very good story.
47. Rivera, *Johannes Lippius*, 36.
48. Ibid., 17.
49. Seay, *Johannes de Grocheo*, 8.
50. Ponte, *Aurelian of Réôme*, 11.
51. Seay, *Nicolaus Listenius*, 3.
52. Ibid., 39.
53. Ibid., 30.
54. Seay, *Johannes de Grocheo*, 22.
55. Seay, *Johannes Tinctoris*, 46.
56. Albert Seay, ed. and tr., *Marcin Kromer – De Musica Figurata [1534]* (Colorado Springs: Colorado College Music Presss, 1980), 13.
57. Rivera, *Johannes Lippius*, 41.
58. Oliver B. Ellsworth, tr. and comm., *The Berkeley Manuscript* (Lincoln and London: University of Nebraska Press, 1984), 191.
59. Rivera, *Johannes Lippius*, 45.
60. Ellsworth, *The Berkeley Manuscript*, 201.
61. Seay, *Johannes de Grocheo*, 7.
62. Rivera, *Johannes Lippius*, 36.
63. Ponte, *Aurelian of Réôme*, 21–2.
64. Seay, *Johannes de Grocheo*, 33.
65. Léonie Rosenstiel, tr., *Anonymous – Music Handbook (Musica Enchiriadis)* (Colorado Springs: Colorado College Music Press, 1976), 14.
66. The special case of the fourth will be treated further in chapter 4.
67. Rosenstiel, *Musica Enchiriadis*, 31.
68. Ibid.
69. Seay, *Johannes Tinctoris*, 1–2.
70. Seay, *Nicolaus Listenius*, 37–8.
71. Berquist, *Pietro Aaron*, 47–9.
72. Sarah Fuller, "Theoretical Foundations of Early Organum Theory," *Acta Musicologica* 53 (1981): 67. Some theorists and authors cited the importance of the ear in determining what is perfect or pleasing, though the ear was, in turn, expected to confirm the numerological and theological principles. Theorists admitted that the ear could be "tricked" into enjoying sounds that are not theoretically acceptable. This will be treated further in chapter 4.
73. This interval was not discussed in the above description of perfect consonances, because it was not agreed upon whether the unison is an interval to begin

with. It has a 1:1 ratio, and so can be characterized as two voices singing the same pitch. Bonaventura da Brescia considered it a perfect consonance "because it has no difference at all." Albert Seay, tr., *Bonaventura da Brescia – Rules of Plain Music (Breviloquium Musicale)* (Colorado Springs: Colorado College Music Press, 1979), 10.

74. Surprisingly, the perfect fifth and perfect fourth are two of the three perfect consonances as defined by the author of the *Musica Enchiriadis*, but Johannes de Garlandia considers them "neither perfect nor imperfect [in consonance], but seem to be partially perfect and partially imperfect," likely because the ear can begin to distinguish the difference between the sounds that comprise the intervals. Stanley H. Birnbaum, tr., *Johannes de Garlandia – Concerning Measured Music (De Mensurabili Musica)* (Colorado Springs: Colorado College Music Press, 1978), 16.

75. Birnbaum, *Johannes de Garlandia*, 15–17.

76. We will explore the concept of the "perfectly imperfect" later in the book.

77. Rivera, *Johannes Lippius*, 20.

78. Ibid., 20–1.

79. Technically, the highest note reached in the figure is "B#," which can be considered the same as "C" through the practice of enharmonic spelling.

80. There are many historical tuning schemes that place the Pythagorean comma within certain intervals, or between particular pitches. The most common modern tuning system is *equal temperament*, in which the comma is divided and spread equally among the twelve pitches of the octave. Modern ears generally tolerate this compromise.

81. David Tame, *The Secret Power of Music* (Rochester, VT: Destiny Books, 1984), 249. It is telling that Tame specifies that this system of imperfection exists in the *non-heavenly* realm, which assumes a reality that is heavenly, and outside of time and space. This sounds very much like Dante's concept the Empyrean heaven as described in the *Paradiso*, which we will discuss in the next chapter.

82. Hans Jonas, *The Gnostic Religion*, 2nd rev. ed. (Boston: Beacon Press, 1972), xiii.

83. The human and animal world is also underpinned by essential conflict. In the *Metamorphoses*, Ovid notes that life on earth is driven by the opposition of fire and water, in the form of "moist heat," and "this discordant harmony is suited to creation." Mary M. Innes, tr., *The Metamorphoses of Ovid* (New York: Viking Penguin, 1955), 40.

84. Sometimes other characters are identified instead of Apollo, such as his son Linus of Thebes. Ellsworth, *The Berkeley Manuscript*, 197.

85. Early Greek lyres used tortoise shells as resonators.

86. In the Roman pantheon, he is named Mercury.

87. Susan C. Shelmerdine, "Hermes and the Tortoise: A Prelude to Cult," *Greek, Roman, and Byzantine Studies* 25/3 (September, 1984): 201–8.

88. According to Genesis 4:21 (KJV), Jubal "was the father of all such as handle the harp and organ." King David was famous for his skill at singing and playing the harp, and many of the biblical psalms are attributed to him. Scripture quotations marked (KJV) are from The Authorized (King James) Version. Rights in the

Authorized Version in the United Kingdom are vested in the Crown. Reproduced by permission of the Crown's patentee, Cambridge University Press.

89. Seay, *Bonaventura da Brescia*, 8.
90. Rosenstiel, *Musica Enchiriadis*, 16.
91. Ibid., 26.
92. Ponte, *Aurelian of Réôme*, 16.
93. Hebrews 9:11. Scripture taken from the New King James Version®. Copyright © 1982 by Thomas Nelson. Used by permission. All rights reserved.
94. John R. Sweney, H. L. Gilmour, and J. H. Entwisle, eds., *Songs of Love and Praise No. 4* (Philadelphia and Chicago: John J. Hood, 1897), 42–3.
95. Henry Paolucci, ed., *St. Augustine – The Enchiridion on Faith, Hope and Love* (Chicago: Henry Regnery Co., 1961), 122–3.
96. Rev. Alexander Roberts and James Donaldson, eds., *Ante-Nicene Christian Library: Translations of the Writings of the Fathers*, vol. IX (Edinburgh: T. & T. Clark, 1869), 43.
97. Ibid., 44–5.
98. Ibid., 44.

Chapter 2

"Thy Hearing is Mortal Even as Thy Sight"

Human Perception in the Heavenly Journey of Dante's **Paradiso**

> So did I see the glorious wheel move, and render voice to voice in concord and in sweetness which cannot be known save there where joy is everlasting.[1]

The descriptions of *musica mundana* in the previous chapter were, for the theorists and musicians depicting them, essentially *real* from a theoretical, scientific, and theological point of view. There were also many for whom the nature of the cosmos was a source of speculation, and inspiration for imaginative fiction. Perhaps foremost among these was the exiled Florentine poet Dante Alighieri who, in the fourteenth century, wrote a poetic and speculative account of a journey through the hereafter that is widely considered among the finest works of literature in Western history. Nevertheless, for many casual readers of Dante's three-part *Comedia*, the treatment of the afterlife can feel somewhat uneven. The *Inferno* and the *Purgatorio* are full of graphically creative imagery, including humans being immersed in rivers of excrement, frozen in blocks of ice, or having their eyes sown shut with pieces of wire—gripping reading indeed, though not anything most readers would wish to experience personally. When the extended climb down through the levels of Hell and back up the terraces of Purgatory are finally accomplished and the *Paradiso* opens, it may strike readers as an overly-long denouement to what had been a thrilling journey through vivid scenes of torture and penance. The *Paradiso* may appear an almost stereotypical account of heaven, full of angels strumming harps while seated on puffy clouds. At the very least, I will admit this as my *own* reaction the first time(s) I attempted the journey through this part of Dante's work. For years, my *Inferno* and *Purgatorio* volumes were well thumbed-through, while my copy of the *Paradiso*, apart from a few abortive attempts to get through the first few cantos, remained on the shelf in pristine condition. At length girding my loins, I finally undertook the heavenly voyage with Dante, to my own great profit.

As a brief summary, Dante begins his *Comedia* with a first-person account of awaking, lost in a dark and pathless forest, and pursued by wild beasts. He is rescued by the first-century BCE Roman poet Virgil, who offers to take him on a tour of the afterlife. The two of them pass through the gates and vestibule of Hell, and down through its nine levels, where different varieties of impenitent souls are punished for eternity. The midpoint of the lowest level is occupied by Satan who, in his position at the very center of the Earth, and thus at the furthest point possible from God in the geocentric cosmos, is frozen in ice. Dante and Virgil then make their way to the other side of the Earth, to the mountain of Purgatory, where those who will eventually enter paradise are having their sins purged, in order to be made fit for heaven. At the top of the mountain is the Garden of Eden, where the souls of those whose sins have been expunged achieve pre-fall human perfection, and prepare for their ascent upward into the celestial realms. Here, Virgil is replaced as Dante's guide by Beatrice,[2] who leads him through the heavenly spheres, including the Moon, Mercury, Venus, the Sun, Mars, Jupiter, Saturn, the region of the Fixed Stars, and the Primum Mobile (or Crystalline sphere). The final destination is the Empyrean, or Heaven, which is not a physical sphere but the abode of God himself, which exists outside time and space. In each successive sphere Dante encounters the souls of the redeemed, and often has lengthy conversations with them about current political matters, as well as theological and metaphysical concepts.

My own initial reticence notwithstanding, this heavenly journey is fascinating, not only due to the interesting paths Dante and Beatrice take through the heavenly spheres, or the many souls of historical figures they encounter along the way, but because of the manner in which Dante experiences the journey through the lens of his human senses. The method of presenting the journey is, as one would expect, chronological, and his ascent through the spheres is accompanied by increasingly greater wonders, all of which he attempts to perceive and describe to the reader. As Rachel Jacoff notes, "Dante's approach to the final vision is staged sequentially, with the pilgrim gradually becoming a more adequate observer."[3] In this chapter, we will follow this journey, discussing the specific aspects of Dante's "sequential adequacy" as an observer. Dante experiences this celestial excursion through three distinct modes of perception. First, his mental faculties: Dante's ability to understand and integrate the various aspects of theology, philosophy, and metaphysics that are revealed to him by his guide, and by the personages he meets in the different spheres. Second, his sense of sight: what he is able to observe of the heavenly realities through his physical eyes. Third, his sense of hearing: specifically his ability to hear and understand *music* in the heavens.

In the *Paradiso*, these three senses are not treated in the same manner, and I argue that this is a deliberate decision on the part of the author. As a result, the *Paradiso* becomes a speculative discourse by Dante on the nature and capacity of human sensory perception. The first two senses, those of sight and understanding, gradually improve as he ascends, the first in response to the increasing quality and intensity of light, and the second as the theological concepts propounded by his celestial respondents become ever more obscure and esoteric. However, this is *not* the case with Dante's sense of hearing. Dante's ears are progressively less able to perceive and understand music as he rises through the spheres, until he is ultimately confronted by silence. Only after this occurs are his ears "leveled up," so that his aural capacity matches that of his understanding and sight.[4] It is important to remember that at the beginning of the *Paradiso*, Dante stands at the summit of the mountain of Purgatory, and within the Garden of Eden. At this point he has attained *human* perfection, and enjoys the full measure of spiritual, mental, and physical faculties intended for humanity in its original, unfallen state. He now has a perfectly tuned *musica humana*. Why then does Dante require divine aid in order to fully perceive the heavenly realities he is about to experience?

Dante is operating within a cosmological model in which the universe revolves around the Earth and the human realm. While the heavenly bodies do indeed exist within "the world" as Dante would have conceived of it, there is nothing to indicate that humanity would be "at home" among them—they were not made for mortal occupancy. The fact that the celestial spheres are not amenable to humanity does not suggest any sensory *imperfection*, but rather a limitation in human sensory *capacity*. Humanity's created state, even when perfect, is simply not designed for these heavenly environments, just as the human body is not designed to endure the vacuum of space without the aid of supportive technology. To be fair, a perfect *musica humana* does not even assume the ability to perceive all *earthly* sounds. Though written nearly three centuries after the *Comedia*, the following passage from Johannes Lippius undoubtedly belongs here:

> The limits of good and bad sound are not the same as the limits of hearing. [. . .] For while the depth and height of sound can be almost infinite, the nature of the human ear is not only obviously finite but also of humble mediocrity in the small body of the microcosm. Hence man cannot make a correct judgement regarding sounds that plunge to excessive depths, tear away to excessive heights, or stretch out to both extremities. Rather, he can perceive and be duly moved and delighted by sounds that are attuned to him.[5]

Thus, perfection in hearing is the ability to properly perceive and judge sounds *within* the imposed limits of human design. The anonymous author of the *Musica Enchiriadis* contributes something of a similar sort:

> For along with other things that we can see only in part and allegorically, this art also has a foundation that is never to be completely revealed.[6]

The *Enchiriadis* author also notes that true and complete musical understanding is like Orpheus' lost wife Eurydice, who "vanishes even as we imagine we see her."[7] Thus, even *perfection* in hearing within the human realm comes with its own limits and mysteries.

How then does Dante confront the problem of limited human capacity? It is not merely a figure of speech to say that Dante is a wordsmith—he indeed *makes* words. When the Tuscan dialect he uses in the *Comedia* does not possess the word he needs to describe a concept, he simply creates a new word that does. At the beginning of the *Paradiso*, he coins the world *trasumanar*, meant to describe the transcending of human mental, spiritual, and physical capacities, a transcending that is necessary to make the journey outside the human environment. This enlarging of his capacity for perception allows Dante to see, hear, and understand things he never could under other circumstances. His transcendence is an example of a *maior perfectum*, a system of greater perfection, which allows humanity to expand beyond its original specifications.

A brief note about my choice of text and translation of the *Paradiso*. I am using, almost exclusively, John D. Sinclair's 1939–1946 side-by-side prose translation of Dante's original Tuscan. I find the format very useful for examining musical terms used in the fourteenth-century original, and for contemplating their uses in modern English.[8] Also, allowing the beautiful original Tuscan *terzets* to occupy the page is a bit of a tribute to Dante himself.

Being now properly provisioned for the expedition, we follow Dante as he explores the heavenly spheres, experiencing with him his lesson on the limits of human perception. We begin in the Garden of Eden, where the author and his guide Beatrice are gazing into the heavens:

[E] fissi li occhi al sole oltre nostr' uso, Molto è licito là, che qui non lece alle nostre virtù, mercè del loco fatto per proprio dell'umana spece. Io nol soffersi molto, nè sì poco, ch' io nol vedessi sfavillar dintorno, com ferro che bogliente esce del foco; e di subito parve giorno a giorno essere aggiunto, come quei che puote avesse il ciel d'un altro sole adorno. Beatrice tutta nell'etterne rote fissa con li occhi stava; ed io in lei le luci fissi, di là su remote.	[A]nd beyond our wont I fixed my eyes on the sun. Much is granted there that is not granted here to our powers, by virtue of the place made for possession by the race of men. I had not borne it long, yet not so briefly as not to see it sparkling like iron that comes boiling from the fire; and of a sudden it seemed there was added day to day, as if He that is able had decked the sky with a second sun. Beatrice stood with her eyes fixed only on the eternal wheels, and on her I fixed mine, withdrawn from above.

Nel suo aspetto tal dentro mi fei,	At her aspect I was changed within, as was
qual si fè Glauco nel gustar dell'erba	Glaucus[9] when he tasted of the herb that
che 'l fè consorte in mar delli altri Dei.	made him one among the other gods in the
Trasumanar significar per verba	sea. The passing beyond humanity cannot
non si porìa; però l'essemplo basti	be set forth in words; let the example
a cui esperïenza grazia serba.	suffice, therefore, for him to whom grace reserves the experience.[10]

Dante's common sense wisely counsels him not to stare directly into the sun, but here in Eden—the region of human perfection—he is able to do so, at least for a while.[11] This ability is among the things that are "granted there that is not granted here," not available to those weakened and tainted by sin.[12] The quoted passage is significant because it describes the means by which Dante will transcend (*trasumanar*) his limited capacity, *humanly* perfect though it is here in the Garden of Eden. The means is Beatrice. As Dante turns his attention from the sun, he looks at Beatrice as she stands gazing into the heavens, and the sight of her transforms him, like Glaucus, into a being that can endure immersion in an unnatural environment. Throughout the *Paradiso* the power of Beatrice's eyes, or alternatively her smile, is nearly always the means by which Dante is prepared for his ascent into higher spheres. However, as Jacoff notes above, this is a *sequential* process that must be newly performed at each level.[13]

Because this chapter focuses primarily on the enhancement of Dante's *hearing*, I will simply state that his understanding and sight are indeed improved, chiefly through the agency of Beatrice, at the times when improvements are required. Though I make incidental references to Dante's understanding and sight, these serve the larger project of analyzing his hearing. Also, I will not describe the music that Dante hears in any particular detail, or at least the kind of detail that may be desired by musicologists and performing musicians. Dante's descriptions are not always helpful when describing music in terms that we can understand at a distance of eight centuries, though they were certainly understood by his contemporary audiences.[14] We do know, however, that the afterlife experienced by Dante is full of music. Francesco Ciabattoni argues that the musical environment Dante experiences throughout the *Comedia* is a progression—from an antimusical cacophony in the *Inferno*, full of screams and bellowing, to a limited monophonic music in the *Purgatorio*, and finally to the splendor of grand polyphonic music in the *Paradiso*.[15] This is as good a practical description of the heavenly music as any other, and it may serve readers well who desire such an aural image.

Now, having read Dante's initial description of what he *sees* in the above-quoted passage, let us observe what he *hears* at this point early in the *Paradiso*:

Quando la rota che tu sempiterni desiderato, a sè mi fece atteso con l'armonia che temperi e discerni, parvemi tanto allor del cielo acceso della fiamma del sol, che pioggia o fiume lago non fece mai tanto disteso. La novità del suono e 'l grande lume di lor cagion m'accesero un disio mai non sentito di cotanto acume.	When the wheel which Thou, being desired, makest eternal held me intent on itself by the harmony Thou dost attune and distribute, so much of the sky seemed then to be kindled with the sun's flame that rain or river never made a lake so broad. The newness of the sound and the great light kindled in me such keenness of desire to know their cause as I had never felt before.

This wheel that Dante names is the Primum Mobile, the highest sphere of the physical universe, and the furthest away from the Earth. It spins at an infinite speed due to the desire of all its parts to be in simultaneous contact with the Empyrean heaven, the abode of God and the angels. The velocity of rotation of this outermost sphere gives motive power to the lower spheres, each moving at its own designated speed,[16] and results in the particular "attunement" of the physical universe—the *musica mundana*. Additionally, each sphere exercises its influence on the sphere immediately below it, as well as on various parts of the Earth, including the plants and animals,[17] and also on the human disposition, where it influences the *musica humana*.[18]

At this point in his reverie, Beatrice spirits Dante away from the Garden of Eden, and the travelers arrive in the sphere of the Moon, where they discuss its physical properties. Dante begins to realize that his own earthly knowledge of the physical sciences is of little use here among the heavenly bodies. He also has the opportunity to speak with some of the souls, including Piccarda Donati,[19] who inhabitant this sphere, and who relate experiences from their own time on earth. These conversations end with the following:

Così parlommi, e poi cominciò '*Ave Maria*' cantando, e cantando vanìo come per acqua cupa cosa grave. La vista mia, che tanto la seguìo quanto possibil fu, poi che la perse, volsesi al segno di maggior disio, e a Beatrice tutta si converse;	She [Piccarda] spoke thus to me, then began singing *Ave Maria* and singing vanished, like a weight through deep water. My sight, which followed her as long as it was possible, turned, when it lost her, to the mark of its greater desire and bent itself wholly on Beatrice; but she so flashed on

ma quella folgorò nel mïo sguardo sì che da prima il viso non sofferse; e ciò mi fece a dimandar più tardo.	my gaze that at first my eyes could not bear it, which made me slower to question her.[20]

In this passage, we perceive the influence of Beatrice's eyes, which contain the power to expose Dante's ignorance, making him reticent to continue his questioning. The passage also illustrates the limitations of Dante's sight, as Beatrice temporarily blinds him. Of particular interest is what happens to Dante's hearing—namely nothing at all. Dante hears Piccarda sing the *Ave Maria* as she recedes into the surface of the Moon, and he recognizes the song for what it is, with no need for further commentary.

After more conversation, Dante and Beatrice ascend to the second sphere, that of Mercury. The time spent in this sphere is mostly occupied by a conversation with Justinian, the sixth-century Roman emperor who reconquered much of the former Western Empire, and who is credited with the rewriting and codification of Roman civil law. As in the Moon, Dante's conversation with his respondent ends with a song and subsequent disappearance:

"*Osanna, sanctus Deus sabaoth, superillustrans claritate tua felices ignes horum malacoth!*" Così, volgendosi alla nota sua, fu viso a me cantare essa sustanza, sopra la qual doppio lume s'addua: ed essa e l'altre mossero a sua danza, e quasi velocissime faville, mi si velar di subita distanza.	"Hosanna, holy God of hosts, making more resplendent with Thy brightness the happy fires of these realms!" —thus, wheeling to his own notes,[21] that spirit, on whom a double light is joined, was seen by me to sing, and he and the others moved in the dance and like swiftest sparks were veiled to me by sudden distance.[22]

Again, Dante's hearing is in perfect working order as he hears and understands Justinian's parting song, a gloss on the *Sanctus* of the Mass. The full functioning of Dante's hearing is emphasized by the presence in the passage of the entire text of the song, or at least what can be heard before Justinian's spirit speeds away out of sight and hearing. Again, there is nothing whatsoever to discuss about Dante's aural capacity.

Beatrice next leads Dante into the sphere of Venus. As is common throughout the *Paradiso*, Dante is not aware that he is traveling from one sphere into another—the fabulous velocities required for this almost instantaneous interplanetary travel do not register on him. This may be because Dante is distracted, either by meditating on a conversation he has just finished with some glorious saint of the past, or because he is looking at Beatrice. This latter reason is how Dante becomes aware that he has ascended to Venus, as the following passage illustrates:

Io non m'accorsi del salire in ella;	I was not conscious of rising into it, but
ma d'esservi entro mi fè assai fede	of being within it my Lady gave me full
la donna mia ch' i' vidi far più bella.	assurance when I saw her become more
E come in fiamma favilla si vede,	fair. And as within a flame a spark is seen,
e come in voce voce si discerne,	and within a voice a voice is distinguished
quand'una è ferma e l'altra va e riede,	when one holds the note and the other
vid' io in essa luce altre lucerne	comes and goes, so I saw within that light
muoversi in giro più e men correnti,	other lights in circling movement swifter
al modo, credo, di lor viste eterne.	and slower, in the measure, as I believe,
Di fredda nube non disceser venti,	of their eternal vision. From a cold cloud
o visibili o non, tanto festini,	winds never descended, visible and not, so
che non paressero impediti e lenti	swiftly as not to seem hindered and slow to
a chi avesse quei lumi divini	one that had seen these divine lights come
veduti a noi venir, lasciando il giro	to us, leaving the dance first begun among
pria cominciato in li alti Serafini;	the high Seraphim; and among those that
e dentro a quei che più innanzi appariro	in front sounded a *Hosanna* such that I
sonava 'Osanna' sì, che unque poi	have never since been without the desire
di riudir non fui sanza disiro.	to hear it again.[23]

Dante is aware of having arrived at Venus because Beatrice suddenly becomes more beautiful in his eyes.[24] Interestingly, he describes what he sees using both visual and musical references. The circling movements of the approaching spirits—which include Charles Martel and Rahab—are compared first to sparks within a flame, familiar to anyone who has observed a fire, and then to the movements of voices in a polyphonic musical composition.[25] The foremost members of the group that appear as divine lights sing a transcendently beautiful *Hosanna* that Dante yearns to hear again the rest of his life. Again, as in the preceding spheres, there is nothing to indicate that he has any trouble comprehending the music or the text, since he identifies it as the *Hosanna*, a liturgical passage from the Mass with which he was intimately familiar.

It is in the next sphere, the sphere of the Sun, that something begins to happen to Dante's hearing. In the sun he meets saints known for their wisdom, luminaries—pun intended—of the church like Thomas Aquinas, Albert the Great, Bede the Venerable, King Solomon, and our friends from chapter 1, Boethius and Isidore of Seville. Just as it is certain that these paragons of wisdom will improve Dante's sense of understanding, and that his eyes will be enhanced to endure the brightness of the surface of the sun, we may assume his hearing will likewise be upgraded, or at the very least *retain* the capacity he has demonstrated up to this point. Oddly, his references to music and song are less sure and confident than they were in the previous spheres, as the following passage demonstrates:

Indi, come orologio che ne chiami	Then, like a clock that calls us at the hour
nell'ora che la sposa di Dio surge	when the bride of God rises to sing matins
a mattinar lo sposo perchè l'ami,	to the Bridegroom that he may love her,
che l'una parte l'altra tira e urge,	when one part draws or drives another,
tin tin sonando con sì dolce nota,	sounding the chime with notes so sweet that
che 'l ben disposto spirito d'amor turge;	the well-ordered spirit swells with love,
così vid' io la glorïosa rota	so I saw the glorious wheel move and
muoversi e render voce a voce in tempra	render voice to voice with harmony and
ed in dolcezza ch'esser non pò nota	sweetness that cannot be known but there
se non colà dove gioir s' insempra.	where joy becomes eternal.[26]

Dante uses earthly imagery (of a clock, in this case) to explain a divine reality, and again he uses two pieces of musical imagery: first, of a religious community singing the early morning matins service in praise of God; and second, the sweet sounds of chimes. However, when describing the actual music experienced in this sphere he is not able, as in the previous spheres, to clearly describe the music or the words sung, only that it *cannot* be known except in this celestial environment. In a later passage, still within the sphere of the Sun, Dante makes a similar point from another perspective:

Sì tosto come l'ultima parola	As soon as the blessed flame took up
la benedetta fiamma per dir tolse,	the last word the holy millstone began
a rotar cominciò la santa mola;	to turn, and it had not made a full
e nel suo giro tutta non si volse	circle before another enclosed it round
prima ch'un'altra di cerchio la chiuse,	and matched motion with motion and
e moto a moto e canto a canto colse;	song with song, song which as far
canto che tanto vince nostre muse,	surpassed our Muses and our Sirens
nostre serene in quelle dolci tube,	in those sweet pipes as a first splendor
quanto primo splendor quel ch'e' refuse.	its reflection.[27]

When Dante narrates this scene of the singing of two concentric circles of saints, he describes their song as not only superior to music made by humans, but one that exceeds even the music of the sirens and the muses, just as a primary source of light is superior to its reflection. This is rather telling because, on the Earth, the music of the muses and sirens is *already* superhuman and incomprehensible or overwhelming to human ears—witness the experiences of Odysseus and other sailors of the ancient world. Nevertheless, such music is fundamentally *of* the Earth, while the music heard in the sphere of the Sun is heavenly, surpassing the song of these superhuman, yet still earthly, creatures. But why, when Dante has been able to fully grasp the music of the Moon, Mercury, and Venus, is he now unable to comprehend it in the Sun? It is to this issue we now turn, before resuming our journey into the upper spheres.

In the medieval cosmology in which Dante is operating, the Moon, Mercury, and Venus fully inhabit the heavenly realms, but due to their relative proximity to the Earth, they are subject to some of its influence—they reside "within the shadow" of the Earth. The saints who appear in these first three spheres represent, as do the inhabitants of the other spheres, certain types or classifications of redeemed souls.[28] However, those in the Moon, Mercury, and Venus had suffered during their lifetimes from some spiritual defect, or failed in some spiritual duty.[29] This is why these spheres are sometimes subtitled thus: The Moon—Faithfulness marred by inconstancy; Mercury—Service marred by ambition; Venus—Love marred by wantonness. In contrast, the Sun and the rest of the spheres lie *beyond* the shadow of the Earth, and the spiritual powers personified in the saints at those levels are not marred or overshadowed by anything at all. This reality allows Dante to simultaneously present two speculative scenarios about the human senses, as I argue above. In the first scenario, Dante uses the senses of understanding and sight to illustrate that *any* ascent beyond the earthly realm requires divine aid. In the other scenario, the sense of hearing, Dante receives no divine assistance at all. At first, due to an allowance for earthly influence in the lower three spheres, what he hears there is familiar and understandable. As he continues upward with merely human ears, the familiarity Dante enjoyed in the lower spheres begins to disappear in the sphere of the Sun, where the last traces of earthly influence are left behind. As he ascends, Dante continues to receive aid, sphere by sphere, for his sight and understanding, but he receives no help with his hearing until much later, as we will see.

As a final aside, the question may arise as to the "position" of the souls in the heavenly realms. Do the saints in the earlier spheres rank lower than those higher up? Is there a heavenly hierarchy among the saints, similar to the earthly hierarchies Dante and his readers would have known? Dante has this question in mind when he visits the sphere of the Moon. Beatrice anticipates the question, telling Dante that the spirits seen in each of the spheres do not actually inhabit them as a permanent residence. In fact, they do not *inhabit* them at all—the souls Dante encounters are merely extensions of their own thought, what we might describe as "avatars." The souls of the redeemed truly exist in the Empyrean heaven, seated around the throne of God, where they hold no earthly equivalent ranks, and participate in no hierarchies among themselves. Beatrice explains that they appear to Dante as they do simply to accommodate his own limited capacity of understanding.[30] This equality of the saints before God—their harmony—is an example of perfect *musica humana* as it exists in heaven.

Returning to the journey, we continue up to the "ruddy" sphere of Mars. Dante's visit to the red planet is almost completely taken up by a lengthy and intimate conversation with his great-great-grandfather Cacciaguida. However, just after arriving at Mars, but before meeting his august ancestor, Dante observes the following:

E come giga e harpa, in tempra tesa di molte corde, fa dolce tintinno a tal da cui la nota non è intesa, così da' lumi che lì m'apparinno s'accogliea per la croce una melode che mi rapiva, sanza intender l' inno. Ben m'accors' io ch'elli era d'alte lode, però ch'a me venìa 'Resurgi' e 'Vinci' come a colui che non intende e ode.	And as viol and harp strung with many chords in harmony chime sweetly for one who does not catch the tune, so from the lights that appeared to me there a melody gathered through the cross which held me rapt though I did not follow the hymn. I perceived, indeed, that it was of high praises, for there came to me "Arise" and "Conquer," as one hears without understanding.[31]

Dante's diminishing capacity for perceiving music, hinted at in the Sun as something that "cannot be known," and that "surpasses our Muses and our Sirens," is clearly illustrated here on Mars, where he admits his limitations no fewer than three times in this short passage. While the exact translation of the first part of the passage is not completely clear,[32] it is clear that Dante is suggesting that music can be aesthetically pleasing without being fully comprehended. Most people can relate to such a sentiment, and Dante emphasizes it by saying it twice in different ways: "not follow[ing] the hymn" and "hear[ing] without understanding." He is able, however, to tell that the song is of "high praises" because he catches two of the words, before admitting that he can understand no more.

Dante's hearing continues its steady decline in Jupiter, a sphere inhabited by the most just rulers of history, including the ancient kings David and Hezekiah, and the Roman emperors Constantine and Trajan. These souls create patterns that spell words and form outlines and shapes, the most noteworthy of which is the Eagle of Justice. In one scene, this eagle flies toward Dante in the following manner:

Roteando cantava, e dicea: "Quali son le mie note a te, che non le' ntendi, tal è il giudicio etterno a voi mortali."	Wheeling, it sang, then spoke: "As are my notes to thee who canst not follow them, such is the Eternal Judgment to you mortals."[33]

Here, the eagle reveals its knowledge of Dante's sensory limitations, saying, in essence, "just as you are unable to follow my song, so are you unable to understand God's eternal nature." This is the first indication that the inhabitants of the heavenly spheres are aware of Dante's inability to hear properly, and they tell him so. Other translations of the passage communicate this more effectively. Mandelbaum says "even as are my songs to you—past understanding,"[34] with Ciardi, Hollander, Norton, and Longfellow alike describing the music as beyond understanding or comprehension.[35] This is emphasized in a later passage where the eagle again sings:

[P]erò che tutte quelle vive luci,	For all those living lights, shining
vie più lucendo, cominciaron canti	still more brightly, began songs that
da mia memoria labili e caduci.	slip and fall from my memory.[36]

The nadir of Dante's hearing occurs in Saturn, the furthest and coldest of the planetary spheres. Upon entering this planet, the abode of the contemplative saints, Dante notices two things. First, he sees a ladder reaching up past the limits of his sight with figures ascending and descending on it, one of whom approaches him. Secondly, he notes that, while in the other spheres he has visited there has been music, or at the very least, sound *recognizable* as music, Saturn seems entirely silent. The approaching figure, identified as Peter Damian,[37] addresses himself to Dante and the two begin a conversation. The following is a part—the passage begins with a question posed by Dante, which is then answered by the saint:

"[E] dì perchè si tace in questa rota	"[A]nd say why in this wheel the sweet
la dolce sinfonia di paradiso,	symphony of Paradise is silent which
che giù per l'altre suona sì divota."	through the others below sounds so
"Tu hai l'udir mortal sì como il viso;"	devoutly." "Thy hearing is mortal even as
rispuose a me "onde qui non si canta	thy sight," he answered me "therefore there
per quel che Beatrice non ha riso."	is no singing here for the same reason that
	Beatrice has no smile."[38]

This passage requires some further exploration. Immediately upon entering the sphere of Saturn and just before the above-quoted passage, Dante looks at Beatrice and notices that she is not smiling. We should recall that the smile of Beatrice, and the beauty of her eyes, are most often the means by which Dante's powers of sight and understanding are improved as he ascends through the heavens. Beatrice, always able to anticipate Dante's questions, explains her lack of a smile in the following terms:

Già eran li occhi miei rifissi al volto della mia donna, e l'animo con essi, e da ogni altro intento s'era tolto. E quella non ridea; ma 'S' io ridessi' mi comenciò 'tu ti faresti quale fu Semelè quando di cener fessi; chè la bellezza mia, che per le scale dell'etterno palazzo più s'accende, com' hai veduto, quanto più si sale, se non si temperasse, tanto splende, che 'l tuo mortal podere, al suo folgore, sarebbe fronda che trono scoscende.	Already my eyes were fixed again on the face of my Lady, and with them my mind, which was withdrawn from every other thought; and she did not smile, but "Were I to smile" she began to me 'thou wouldst become like Semele when she was turned to ashes;[39] for my beauty, which thou has seen kindle more the higher we climb by the stairs of the eternal palace, is so shining that if it were not tempered thy mortal powers in its blaze would be as a branch split by a thunderbolt.[40]

As we have seen, Dante is often made aware that he has ascended to a higher sphere because of the increased beauty of Beatrice in his own eyes. She admits as much to him here, while responding to his unspoken question—she is not smiling because, even in the currently "leveled up" state of his senses, he is still inhabiting a mortal body, and any additional display of spiritual power (such as a smile) would destroy him as just Semele was destroyed. Peter Damian confirms this when he explains why there is no singing in Saturn. He is not saying there is *never* singing in Saturn, but only that Dante cannot endure it in his current mortal state. Sinclair's commentary on the passage notes, "if [Beatrice] had smiled or the souls had sung there, the smile or the song would have expressed the truth of God as God is known to these contemplatives, and that is still beyond his capacity."[41] By capacity, he is referring to Dante's *current* capacity, which is limited because he is still largely operating at a human level of comprehension of divine reality, where the limitations of his own *musica humana* are thrown into sharp relief. As Hollander's commentary says, "Dante still thinks as the world thinks and is not yet ready to experience the higher degree of divinity that songs at this level represent."[42] Peter Damian further explains the silence of Saturn, which is especially beautiful in Ciardi's rendering:

"Your sight is mortal. Is not your hearing, too?"
he said. "Our song is still for the same reason
Beatrice holds back her smile—for love of you."[43]

Notwithstanding their love for Dante, the occupants of Saturn at length give him a display of sound—sound so overwhelming as to disprove any idea of the sphere being a realm of silence. Peter Damian completes his conversation with Dante with a denunciation of the current corrupted state of the church, and is joined by the other contemplatives in Saturn with a thunderous cry of righteous indignation:

A questa voce vid' io più fiammelle	At his voice I saw more little flames descend
di grado in grado scendere e girarsi,	from step to step, wheeling, and every turn
e ogni giro le facea più belle.	made them more beautiful. They came
Dintorno a questa vennero e fermarsi,	about him and stopped and raised a cry of
e fero un grido di sì alto suono,	such volume that nothing here could be
che non potrebbe qui assomigliarsi:	likened to it;[44] nor did I understand it, its
nè io lo 'ntesi; sì mi vinse il tuono.	thunder so overcame me.[45]

Immediately upon being stunned by this great sound, Dante turns to Beatrice in fear, just as a child turns to its mother when frightened by a loud noise. Like a mother, she reassures him with these words:

[M]i disse: 'Non sai tu che tu se' in cielo?	[She] said to me: 'Knowest thou not thou
e non sei tu che 'l cielo è tutto santo,	art in heaven? Knowest thou not that
e ciò che ci si fa vien da buon zelo?	heaven is all holy and that whatever is done
Come t'avrebbe trasmutato il canto,	here comes of righteous zeal? How the
e io ridendo, mo pensar lo puoi,	song, and I by smiling, would have
poscia che 'l grido t' ha mosso	confounded thee thou canst now conceive
cotanto;	since this cry has so much moved thee;[46]

Properly reminded of the intense spiritual power of the regions through which he is now traveling, as well as those through which he must yet ascend, Dante is humbled in preparation for the rest of his journey. He is swept up to the next sphere, the sphere of the Fixed Stars, where Beatrice directs him to look down and observe the Earth and all the moving planetary bodies. This vantage point allows Dante, who has traveled through and experienced the regions of the *musica mundana* from below, to see the *musica mundana* from the opposite perspective, from above. Here among the stars, Dante realizes that *all* of his senses are becoming overwhelmed, just as his sense of hearing had been below in Saturn. The spiritual power in Beatrice's eyes and smile now seem insufficient to improve his ability to perceive the mental, visual, and sonic realities of this region. But a greater spiritual power even than that of Beatrice is about to appear to Dante, which will represent the final "leveling up" of his senses, at least within the bounds of the physical universe. None other than Jesus Christ Himself appears in glory for a brief moment and at that sight, Dante is entirely overcome. Beatrice immediately recognizes this and explains:

Oh Beatrice dolce guida e cara!	O Beatrice, sweet guide and dear! She said
Ella mi disse: 'Quel che ti sobranza	to me: "That which overcomes thee is power
è virtù da cui nulla si ripara.	from which there is no defense. Here

Quivi è la sapïenza e la possanza ch'aprì le strade tra 'l cielo e la terra, onde fu già sì lunga disïanza." [. . .] "Apri li occhi e riguarda qual son io: tu hai vedute cose, che possente se' fatto a sostener lo riso mio."	is wisdom and the might that opened the ways between heaven and earth and for which of old there was such long desire." [. . .] "Open thine eyes and look at me as I am; thou has seen such things that thou hast gained strength to bear my smile."[47]

Beatrice is saying that the momentary dazzling of his senses due to the vision of Christ is the means by which Dante will be able to bear what he has been unable to bear since the sphere of Saturn, namely the power of her smile. Sinclair's commentary on this passage puts it succinctly: "it is as if he meant that to see Christ, at all, is to gain a new capacity for all the persuasions of the truth of God."[48] Though it appears that Beatrice is speaking here only of his capacity for sight, this represents the turning point for Dante's capacity for hearing as well. This sense, which had steadily weakened through the spheres of the Sun, Mars, Jupiter, and Saturn, now begins to strengthen, such that Dante can eventually[49] hear and understand the music of the highest heavens as well, if not better, than he did in the bodies within the shadow of the Earth. He soon has the opportunity to test this newly improved ability, as the Virgin Mary now appears to him. The stars encircle her, singing her praises, and remarkably, Dante is able to both hear and understand:

[C]iascun di quei candori in su si stese con la sua fiamma, sì che l'alto affetto ch'elli avïeno a Maria mi fu palese. Indi rimaser lì nel mio cospetto, 'Regina coeli' cantando sì dolce, che mai da me non si partì 'l diletto.	[E]ach of these white radiances reached upward with its flame, so that the deep affection they had for Mary was made plain to me; then they remained there in my sight, singing *Regina coeli* so sweetly that the delight has never left me.[50]

Immediately after this encounter with the Virgin, Dante sees the brightest of the stars that surround her—none other than Peter the Apostle—approach and sing in his presence:

Di quella ch' io notai di più carezza vid' io uscire un foco sì felice, che nullo vi lasciò di più chiarezza; e tre fïate intorno di Beatrice si volse con un canto tanto divo, che la mia fantasia no mi ridice. Però salta la penna e non lo scrivo; chè l'imagine nostra a cotai pieghe, non che 'l parlare, è troppo color vivo.	From the one I noted as the richest I saw come forth a fire so joyful that it left none there of greater brightness, and it wheeled three times round Beatrice with so divine a song that my fancy does not repeat it to me, therefore my pen leaps and I do not write of it; for our imagination, much more our speech, has colours too bright for such folds.[51]

This passage may seem to show that Dante has suddenly lost his newfound ability to hear music. As argued in a previous endnote, I believe that Dante is *gradually* regaining his sense of hearing, as gradually as he earlier lost it. There may be another or parallel reason; however, that is hinted at in the visual reference at the end of the passage. The "folds" that Dante mentions refer to folds of drapery, clothing, and other fabrics that, to be properly rendered in painting, require the artist to have access to extremely subtle shades and pigments. He is likely saying that, just as pigments are not sufficiently subtle to depict the intricacies of folded draperies in painting, so too is human imagination and speech unable to render the complexities of the Apostle Peter's virtuosic chanting. Sinclair notes that "human imagination and language could not deal with the involutions of St. Peter's rendering of plain-song,"[52] and Ciardi says more generally, that "human speech and human imagination are too gross to portray the subtleties of heaven."[53] Of course, the "grossness" of human senses has been all along the cause of Dante's inability to understand music through much of his journey in the *Paradiso*, but whatever the reason for this particular episode, his hearing improves consistently from this point onward. We now move quickly toward the end. During a pause in the conversation between Dante and Peter, the former hears this:

Finito questo, l'alta corte santa	This ended, the high and holy court
risonò per le spere un 'Dio laudamo'	resounded through its circles with a *Te*
nella melode che là su si canta.	*Deum laudamus* in the strains that are sung there above.[54]

Though we can see that he is able to positively identify the *Te Deum*, one of the great songs of praise of the church, Dante notes that it is sung to a heavenly melody, which he is likely unable to fully follow, as was the case during his journey through the middle spheres. Soon afterward, Dante speaks with James the Great, and hears the following as James' brother, John the Apostle, approaches:

E prima, appresso al fin d'este parole,	And first, immediately I had finished
'*Sperent in te*' di sopr' a noi s' udì;	speaking, *Sperent in te* was heard above us,
a che rispuoser tutte le carole.	to which all the choirs responded; then one
Poscia tra esse un lume si schiarì	light among them shone out so that if the
sì che se 'l Cancro avesse un tal cristallo,	Crab held such a gem winter would have
l'inverno avrebbe un mese d'un sol dì.	a month of unbroken day.[55]

Here, Dante makes no mention of the heavenly nature of the melody, its incomprehensibility, or anything else that would make us think that he is not

"Thy Hearing is Mortal Even as Thy Sight" 51

fully enjoying the performance of a well-known sacred antiphon. Next, following his conversation with John the Apostle, Dante is introduced to Adam himself, and as he approaches this greatest of ancestors, all those present sing the opening line of the *Sanctus* from the Mass:

Sì com' io tacqui, un dolcissimo canto	As soon as I was silent, a strain of sweetest
risonò per lo cielo, e la mia donna	song resounded through the heaven, and my
dicea con gli altri: "Santo, santo, santo!"	Lady sang with the rest "Holy, holy holy!"[56]

What is noteworthy here is that Beatrice joins in[57] with the rest of the inhabitants of the starry sphere, something we have not yet seen in the *Paradiso*. After Dante's conversation with Adam, the entire host of stars bursts forth singing the *Gloria Patri*:

"Al Padre, al Figlio, allo Spirito Santo"	"Glory be to the Father, and to the Son, and
cominciò 'gloria!' tutto il paradiso,	to the Holy Ghost!" all Paradise began, so
sì che m' inebriava il dolce canto.	that the sweet song held me rapt;[58] what I
Ciò ch' io vedeva mi sembiava un riso	saw seemed to me a smile of the universe, so
dell'universo; per che mia ebbrezza	that my rapture entered both by hearing and
intrava per l'udire e per lo viso.	by sight.[59]

Again, Dante is well-enough aware of the words and tunes used here that he has no need to excuse himself with the fact that the melodies are heavenly, though undoubtedly they are. Here we see the realization of the increased capacity for sensory perception that Dante received at the earlier sight of Jesus Christ.

Beatrice again smiles at Dante, and this smile transports him to the highest of the spheres that exist within the bounds of space and time, the Primum Mobile. Sinclair notes in his commentary, "by the virtue that comes to him from the eyes of Beatrice—by the further enlargement of his mind—he is snatched away from the Starry Sphere and finds himself in the Crystalline."[60] There, the choirs are heard to sing *Hosanna*—the latter part of the *Sanctus* text from the Mass—to a bright, fixed point in the heavens that marks the location of God. Again, Dante has no trouble at all perceiving the music:

Io sentiva osannar di coro in coro	I heard from choir to choir *Hosanna* sung to
al punto fisso che li tiene alli ubi,	the fixed point, which holds and shall ever
e terrà sempre, ne' quai sempre foro.	hold them in the place where they have ever
	been.[61]

In the Primum Mobile (or Crystalline sphere), Dante learns about the various angelic orders and then, for the last time, the beauty and power of Beatrice's eyes transport him, carrying him out of time and space itself and into the Empyrean heaven, the true abode of God and of the saints.[62] Upon arriving there, Dante becomes aware once again of a deficiency in his senses. Here, outside the physical universe, he is not able to comprehend or understand anything he experiences. At this point, Beatrice cannot help him as she has no power to improve his senses in *this* place. She directs Dante to a river of flowing light, which he drinks in with his eyes. This baptism by light removes the final barriers to his senses—increasing his capacity to the infinite—and he is able to see, hear, and understand everything in the highest courts of heaven. The saints and angels constantly sing *Hosanna* around the throne of God, but the final glorious musical encore of the entire journey of the *Comedia* is Dante's preparation to see the full splendor of Divine Goodness shown in the unveiled face of Christ. To be ready for this experience, Dante must first look into the face of the Virgin Mary so that, by beholding the face that is most like Christ's, Dante may be ready to see Him in His full glory. This is one of the most beautiful scenes in the *Paradiso*, a reenactment of sorts of the Annunciation, in which the archangel Gabriel appears to the Virgin telling her that she will become the mother of the Messiah:

Io vidi sopra lei tanta allegrezza
piover, portata nelle menti sante
create a trasvolar per quella altezza,
che quantunque io avea visto davante
di tanta ammirazion non mi sospese,
nè mi mostrò di Dio tanto sembiante;
e quello amor che primo lì discese,
cantando 'Ave Maria, gratïa plena,'
dinanzi a lei le sue ali distese.
Rispuose alla divina cantilena
da tutte parti la beata corte,
sì ch'ogni vista sen fè più serena.

I saw such gladness rain down upon her,
borne in the holy minds created to fly
through those heights, that all I had
seen before had not held me in such
wonder and suspense nor shown me
such likeness to God, and that loving
spirit which had first descended on her
singing "*Ave Maria, gratia plena*" spread
his wings before her. On all sides the
blessed court sang responses to the
divine canticle, so that every face turned
brighter for it.[63]

The *Ave Maria* acts as a musical bookend for Dante's journey through paradise. It is the very first song he hears in the sphere of the Moon, sung by Piccarda, and it is the last song he hears in the Empyrean, sung by Gabriel to the Virgin herself. It also serves as the song that Dante hears in the two instances when he is in total command of his own sense of hearing: in the first case, having just attained the perfection of his *human* senses in the Garden of Eden, and in the second case, having just achieved the perfection of his *divine* senses—a true *maior perfectum*—by drinking from the Empyrean river of light.[64]

Dante had many inspirations for the writing of his *Comedia*. One was to establish the Tuscan dialect as a legitimate vehicle for serious poetic expression. Another was for Dante to attempt a long-form epic poem in the model of his literary hero Virgil, who "gives" his tacit approval by appearing as a major character in the work. It serves as a panegyric to the love of his life, Beatrice, as well as to his other spiritual mentors among the saints, with special pride of place naturally given to Christ and the Virgin Mary. It is also an acerbic social, religious, and political commentary. Among all these things, it is a fascinating example of applied metaphysics—an attempt at placing the most difficult religious and scientific questions of the time into terms that eyes could see, that ears could hear, and that human intellect could grasp. Here, especially in the *Paradiso*, it is a piece of incredibly imaginative speculative fiction, that imagines how a human traveling through the heavenly realms might perceive and recount the experience. Dante's true innovation is his envisioning of what would happen to human senses when traveling through the celestial spheres, with the application of divine aid on one hand, as is the case with sight and understanding, or with only a limited application on the other, as with the sense of hearing. The *Comedia* stands not only as an important work of theology, metaphysics, and political commentary, it also sets the standard that will be imitated by future authors depicting journeys through the heavens,[65] one of which we will examine in the next chapter.

NOTES

1. Charles Eliot Norton, tr., *The Divine Comedy of Dante Alighieri. III: Paradise*, rev. ed. (Boston and New York: Houghton, Mifflin and Company, 1902), 84.
2. Beatrice was a woman Dante had known since childhood and loved all his life. Though she married someone else and died relatively young, Beatrice forever remained Dante's muse and inspiration.
3. Rachel Jacoff, "Introduction to *Paradiso*," in Rachel Jacoff, ed., *The Cambridge Companion to Dante* (Cambridge: Cambridge University Press, 2007), 118.
4. I should emphasize that this refers specifically to Dante's ability to hear and understand *music*. Dante's hearing is not affected during his conversations with the saints he meets in the heavens, or in any other situation in which his aural sense is needed (detecting rushing winds, hearing flapping wings, etc.).
5. Rivera, *Johannes Lippius*, 39.
6. Rosenstiel, *Musica Enchiriadis*, 31.
7. Ibid.

8. Though no expert on early fourteenth-century Tuscan, I am a musicologist who occasionally translates treatises and other documents. It has been my experience that musical nuances may be lost in translation by scholars who are not deeply familiar with relevant contemporary theoretical and practical music treatises. Sinclair's translation is, in my limited opinion, very good in this respect, which I also value for its elegant prose setting. I am generally wary of translations that attempt to "shoehorn" themselves into English rhythmic and metrical schemes, and that often require questionable word choices in order to make things "fit." I have consulted a number of other translations for purposes of comparison, among them those of Allen Mandelbaum, John Ciardi, John Hollander, Charles Eliot Norton, and Henry Wordsworth Longfellow. At times, I refer to these works for alternative or particularly evocative readings.

9. According to Ovid, Glaucus was a fisherman who, after eating a magical herb, transformed into a fish- or merman-like form and became immortal, joining the other sea gods.

10. Sinclair, *The Divine Comedy: Paradiso*, 20–3.

11. Ciardi renders it thus: "I stared into the Sun so hard that here it would have left me blind," and later, "I had to look away soon." John Ciardi, tr., *The Paradiso* (New York: Signet Classics, 2009), 5. Mendelbaum uses less strong language: "on the sun I set my sight more than we usually do," and, "I did not bear it long." Allen Mandelbaum, tr., *The Divine Comedy* (New York: Everyman's Library, 1995), 380.

12. Sinclair, *The Divine Comedy: Paradiso*, 28–9.

13. This process is not absolute, as Dante remains throughout his journey a human "in the flesh," and not a spirit or disembodied soul. Therefore the "leveling up" of his senses of understanding and sight is at times imperfect, and Dante notes at times that "my memory defeats my skill." However, the premise that he receives divine assistance for these two senses, and not initially for his hearing, still stands. It should also be noted that these incremental improvements to his senses are not provided to Dante until *after* he needs them, meaning that he experiences his limitations *before* receiving relief—an experience not without discomfort or pain. Sinclair quotes a well-known contemporary—one we will meet in the next chapter—whose thoughts belong here: "The suggestion of Mr. C. S. Lewis, made in another connection, is relevant here: 'The joys of heaven are for most of us, in our present condition, an acquired taste.'" Sinclair, *The Divine Comedy: Paradiso*, 442. Sinclair's mention of C. S. Lewis is fortunate, as a portion of another of the author's works is germane to this discussion. In *Perelandra*, the second book of Lewis' *The Space Trilogy*, the protagonist Dr. Elwin Ransom must do a difficult deed while on the planet Venus (this will be explored in some depth in chapters 3 and 6), a deed that when attempted or accomplished will provide no sure guarantee of physical healing, or even of survival. Before attempting the deed, Ransom has the following thought: "And he bowed his head and groaned and repined against his fate—to be still a man and yet to be forced up into the metaphysical world, to enact what philosophy only thinks." C. S. Lewis, *Perelandra* (New York and London: Scribner, 1944), 125.

14. Dante, though very well-read and educated, and knowledgeable in the liturgical and devotional music of his time, was not a professional musician or composer—so

far as we know—and may not have been familiar with all of the musical terminologies current among contemporary musicians. Of course, it is also possible that *we* are not entirely familiar with the musical terminologies common in Dante's time.

15. Francesco Ciabattoni, *Dante's Journey to Polyphony* (Toronto: University of Toronto Press, 2010), 6–7.

16. Ibid., 26.

17. Ibid., 112.

18. Ibid., 45.

19. Piccarda Donati was a thirteenth-century noblewoman from Florence, and likely a personal acquaintance of Dante. At a young age, she left home to enter a convent. Later, she was removed by her brother and forced into a political marriage.

20. Sinclair, *The Divine Comedy: Paradiso*, 54–5.

21. I find this translation of *nota* to be reasonable, as I do Mandelbaum's rendering: "He wheeled to his own music" (Mandelbaum, *The Divine Comedy*, 408). I do not agree with Ciardi's translation, "giving itself to its own harmony" (Ciardi, *The Paradiso*, 63), as this assumes that Justinian is either accompanying himself or is singing with others, neither of which seems supported in this part of the text. Ciardi's translation is organized, however, into tercets that partially approximate Dante's original *terza rima* scheme, and the word "harmony" makes it rhyme.

22. Sinclair, *The Divine Comedy: Paradiso*, 102–3.

23. Ibid., 116–19.

24. Sinclair notes the novel allegorical device, in which Beatrice represents the very truth of God to Dante. As the truth becomes better known to him as he ascends toward its source, it becomes more glorious and beautiful. Ibid., 128.

25. My musicological interests were particularly piqued by this passage, "e come in voce voce si discerne, quand'una è ferma e l'altra va e riede," which Sinclair translates, "and within a voice a voice is distinguished when one holds the note and the other comes and goes." The word *ferma* brings to mind *canto fermo*, or plainchant, a style of singing characterized by a monophonic, unaccompanied melody. Together with the *ferma* ("held") voice, Dante describes another that "comes and goes" ("va e riede"), which sounds suspiciously like a description of *organum*, as developed in the Notre-Dame School of polyphonic composition in the twelfth and thirteenth centuries. In this type of composition, a melody could be sung with slow note values, taken or derived from a passage of plainchant (*ferma*), while a faster and perhaps more rhythmic melody (or multiple melodies) could be sung above or below. The Florentine Dante would certainly have been aware of and familiar with this style of singing, it having been common in Europe for a century or more by his time. Ciardi's translation mostly agrees with such a reading when he writes, "and as two voices may be told apart if one stays firm and one goes lower and higher" (Ciardi, *The Paradiso*, 35). I do not fully agree with Mandelbaum's translation, however, as it reads, "and as, in plainsong, voice in voice is heard—one holds the note, the other comes and goes" (Mandelbaum, *The Divine Comedy*, 413). To be fair, Mandelbaum is aware of early polyphonic music as per his explanatory notes (ibid., 726); however, Dante's description does not seem to refer strictly to plainsong, however broadly defined.

26. Sinclair, *The Divine Comedy: Paradiso*, 152–5.

27. Ibid., 174–5.

28. Just as the levels of the *Inferno* and *Purgatorio* contain different categories of the damned, and of those undergoing purgation.

29. This is not to say that they retained any unrepented or unabsolved sins, as that would place them in Purgatory. We could say that they were, in the end, "good," but that their goodness was not as good as it *could* have been.

30. Sinclair, *The Divine Comedy: Paradiso*, 69.

31. Ibid., 206–7. I am reminded of a passage in *The Silver Chair* from C. S. Lewis' *The Chronicles of Narnia*. When Jill and Eustace open a door to escape from school bullies, they find themselves on a high mountain in another world, and not merely outside the school grounds as they had expected. They have been transported to Aslan's Country, the equivalent of heaven in the world of the *Chronicles*. What they hear (or *how* they hear) echoes Dante's account in Mars:

Instantly there was a quite different sound all about them. It came from those bright things overhead, which now turned out to be birds. They were making a riotous noise, but it was much more like music—rather advanced music which you don't quite take in at the first hearing—than birds' songs ever are in our world.

C. S. Lewis, *The Silver Chair* (New York: HarperCollins Publishers, 1994), 13.

32. Mandelbaum says, "and just as harp and viol . . . produce sweet harmony although each single note is not distinct." Ciardi renders, "and as a viol and a harp . . . make only a sweet tinkle to one who has not studied melody."

33. Sinclair, *The Divine Comedy: Paradiso*, 274–5.

34. Mandelbaum, *The Divine Comedy*, 169–70.

35. In his commentary on this passage, Ciardi notes, "the harmonies and the language of the hymn are beyond Dante's powers of comprehension." Ciardi, *The Paradiso*, 204.

36. Sinclair, *The Divine Comedy: Paradiso*, 286–7. Again, I am reminded of a short scene from *The Chronicles of Narnia*, this time from *The Voyage of the Dawn Treader*. Edmund and Lucy, together with their cousin Eustace, come to the end of the world (the mortal world of Narnia), and for a brief moment see into Aslan's country:

And suddenly there came a breeze from the east. . . . It lasted only a second or so but what it brought them in that second none of those three children will ever forget. It brought both a smell and a sound, a musical sound. Edmund and Eustace would never talk about it afterwards. Lucy could only say, "It would break your heart."

C. S. Lewis, *The Voyage of the Dawn Treader* (New York: HarperCollins Publishers, 1994), 243.

37. Peter Damian was a Benedictine monk and an important church reformer during the eleventh century.

38. Sinclair, *The Divine Comedy: Paradiso*, 304–5.

39. There are several mythical stories about Semele, but one Dante likely knew was that she was a priestess of Zeus and mother of Dionysius. Seduced and impregnated by Zeus (and who wasn't?), she asked him to reveal himself to her in his full divine glory. He did, and she was immediately incinerated.

40. Sinclair, *The Divine Comedy: Paradiso*, 302–3.

41. Ibid., 311.
42. Hollander's translation and commentaries are available online at the Princeton Dante Project. https://dante.princeton.edu/pdp/, Accessed on August 25, 2021.
43. Ciardi, *The Paradiso*, 220.
44. Longfellow translates, "a cry uttered of so loud a sound, it here could find no parallel." Longfellow (Project Gutenburg, https://www.gutenberg.org/files/1004/1004-h/1004-h.htm). Ciardi renders it, "for the peal of that ominous thunder made my senses reel." Ciardi, *The Paradiso*, 222.
45. Sinclair, *The Divine Comedy: Paradiso*, 308–9.
46. Ibid., 316–17. Ciardi's translation is also effective: "Their one cry shakes your senses: you can now see what would have happened to you had they sung, or had I smiled in my new ecstasy." Ciardi, *The Paradiso*, 230.
47. Sinclair, *The Divine Comedy: Paradiso*, 332–3. Norton renders it, "thou art become able to sustain my smile." Norton (Project Gutenberg, https://www.gutenberg.org/files/1997/1997.txt)
48. Ibid., 340. Again, *capacity* is precisely the correct term. Dante is not automatically *given* abilities of sight, hearing, and understanding, but he is now able to receive further leveling-up, which in Saturn he could not receive at the risk of his own destruction. The sight of Christ makes Dante a larger vessel, able to contain more of the heavenly reality.
49. It does not happen instantaneously. Just as Dante experiences an "intermediate" period in the Sun, where limitations in his sense of hearing begin to become apparent, so too does his hearing return gradually during his time in the Fixed Stars.
50. Sinclair, *The Divine Comedy: Paradiso*, 336–7.
51. Ibid., 344–5.
52. Ibid., 354.
53. Ciardi, *The Paradiso*, 258.
54. Sinclair, *The Divine Comedy: Paradiso*, 350–1. Mandelbaum translates, "sung with the melody they use on high." Mandelbaum, *The Divine Comedy*, 495.
55. Sinclair, *The Divine Comedy: Paradiso*, 362–3.
56. Ibid., 376–7.
57. Other translations say that she "joins in" or "speaks" with the rest of them. The verb *dicea* is a form of the word "to speak," but it seems rather odd for Beatrice to speak the words of the *Sanctus* while the others sing it, so I am inclined to agree with Sinclair's rendering.
58. Most translators tiptoe around the word *inebriava*, and the later-used *ebbrezza*. In the Tuscan dialect, the terms are strongly associated with inebriation caused by the consumption of alcohol. Though it is true that some hymns and devotional songs do ask for the believer to be "inebriated" with Christ, it remains a curious concept. I will include Ciardi's much more fearless rendering of the passage for contrast:

"Glory to the Father, the Son, and the Holy Ghost"—
a strain so sweet that I grew drunk with it
rang from the full choir of the heavenly host.
I seemed to see the universe alight
with a single smile; and thus my drunkenness

came on me through my hearing and my sight."
Ciardi, *The Paradiso*, 282.

59. Sinclair, *The Divine Comedy: Paradiso*, 386–7.

60. Ibid., 398.

61. Ibid., 406–7.

62. Ovid describes this region as one of "clear aether that has no weight," and its divine nature established by being "untainted by any earthly particles." Innes, *The Metamorphoses of Ovid*, 31.

63. Sinclair, *The Divine Comedy: Paradiso*, 466–7.

64. This is highly suggestive of mankind's infinite capacity for perfection, as described by Irenaeus near the end of the previous chapter.

65. I would be remiss if I did not mention cosmic visions and journeys previous to Dante's, especially a vision of the twelfth-century abbess, composer, and prophet Hildegard von Bingen. This vision, found in the first book of her work *Scivias*, describes a view of the entire cosmos in the shape of an egg, pulsating with life and motion—a fascinating view of the *musica mundana*. Hildegard supervised the production of illustrations of her visions during her lifetime, and this one is particularly intriguing. A copy of this illustration (with other visions of Hildegard) hangs on my office wall.

Chapter Vignette 2.5

"I Noticed That the Grass Did Not Bend Under Their Feet"

Solid People, Ghosts, and the Sense of Touch in a Heavenly Journey of C. S. Lewis

As with Dante's light-speed flights through celestial space in the *Paradiso*, let us rush forward more than seven centuries in time, and occupy the imagination of the twentieth-century professor, theologian, and author C. S. Lewis. Lewis wrote a number of popular and influential fictional works, some of which I have referenced in endnotes in previous chapters, but the one we will spend time with here is *The Great Divorce*. This short novel contains distinct echoes of Dante's *Comedia* in at least two ways. First, it is a journey from one cosmic location to another, with the journey beginning on Earth—or what is *perceived* as Earth—and moving upward toward a higher, and heavenly, setting. Second, it deals with human senses and their ability to perceive realities that exist in such different places. While these senses include those of sight, hearing, and understanding, as in Dante's work, our examination of Lewis' story will focus on the sense of touch,[1] giving us an additional angle from which to consider the nature of human perception in the heavens.[2] Human sensory perception, we should remember, is an integral part of *musica humana*, and our main interest, as with Dante, is to see what happens to *musica humana* when it comes into direct physical contact with the *musica mundana*.

Originally published as a serial for a religious newspaper in 1944 and 1945, and later released in 1946 as a stand-alone volume, *The Great Divorce* is an account from Lewis' own point of view, as he takes a bus journey from the "grey town" to heaven. Unlike Dante's *Comedia*, this story is less about the journey itself than it is about the destination, namely what happens at and around the heavenly terminus of the bus route. Like Dante, Lewis begins with the narrator finding himself in an unfamiliar place. At the beginning of the *Inferno*, Dante writes, "I came to myself within a dark wood where the straight way was lost,"³ and for Lewis in *The Great Divorce*, "I seemed to be standing in a busy queue by the side of a long, mean street."⁴ For both authors, there are questions as to what realities they are inhabiting: are they asleep, are they experiencing a vision, or are they perhaps dead? Though Lewis' description of his journey is somewhat abbreviated, the short account gives us a number of interesting insights into the nature of the "grey town," as well as the natures of those who inhabit it. While Lewis may suspect this from the beginning, the reader is eventually informed that everyone in the town and on the bus is dead. As the bus leaves the ground and begins flying through the air, Lewis notices that the town stretches as far as his eye can see in every direction. One of his seatmates tells him this is because the inhabitants cannot stand living near one other, so they constantly move out of streets where they have quarreled with their neighbors, to new streets and into new quarrels, and into still new streets, and so on. This is quite easy because, in the gray town, one can simply *think* a house into existence. Not that these homes, or any of the town's buildings, are very substantial. In fact, they are so insubstantial that they appear not to be made of any *substance* at all, since rain falls right through them.⁵ Moreover, all of the buildings, homes, and shops are dingy and run-down, reflecting the minds and attitudes of those who created them—the poor state of their *musica humana*. Another passenger confirms the huge size of the town: since everyone is constantly moving to get away from everyone else, it has grown to be truly astronomical in size. The passenger tells Lewis of two acquaintances who traveled to visit the home of Napoleon, and it took them 15,000 years to make the journey.

We learn more about Lewis and his fellow travelers over the hours of the bus trip, through what *should* be their natural senses. Being quarrelsome, the passengers begin fighting among themselves, stabbing each other with knives and shooting each other with pistols, but Lewis notes, "It all seemed strangely innocuous and when it was over I found myself unharmed."⁶ No one seems to be in any pain and no one is hurt in the fracas, so the passengers' sense of touch appears to be inoperative, at least at this point. Gradually, the bus emerges from the dark and dreary twilight that defines the gray town, and the quality of light changes "from mud-colour to mother of pearl, then to faintest blue, then to a bright blueness that stung the eyes."⁷ This recalls Dante's encounters with light in the *Paradiso*, but in this case the light not only dazzles Lewis and the others, it also reveals their true physical nature. Though the bus windows are closed and covered, the bus is still full of light—a "cruel" light. Lewis looks around at his fellow passengers and is shocked at what he sees:

> I shrank from the faces and forms by which I was surrounded. They were all fixed faces, full not of possibilities but impossibilities, some gaunt, some

bloated, some glaring with idiotic ferocity, some drowned beyond recovery in dreams; but all, in one way or another, distorted and faded. One had a feeling that they might fall to pieces at any moment if the light grew much stronger.[8]

The increasing quality and intensity of light illuminates the true nature of each of the passengers and their lack of physical substance—they are ghosts. This explains why the fight with knives and guns has no real effect, and why something as ephemeral as light is so painful and revealing. As they approach heaven at the end of the bus route, the passengers enter an environment where substance now exists, exposing their own fundamentally insubstantial nature. In the beginning of the *Paradiso*, though Dante achieves a state of human perfection in the Garden of Eden, he is unable to endure the environment of the celestial spheres without superhuman aid. Though it is Dante who inhabits a physical body, while the heavenly souls are spirits, they belong in the heavens while he does not—it is *Dante* who is truly a ghost in that environment.

Lewis and the other passengers are similarly ghostly, and this allows us to explore an aspect of human sensory perception that Dante does not treat in the *Comedia*, that of touch. The first time we are introduced to this sense is when Lewis, responding to the quality of the bright light in the bus, opens the window next to his seat, and "delicious freshness [comes] in."[9] The reactions of other passengers are interesting. His seatmate immediately shuts the window, yelling that they will catch their death in the cold, with similar threatening language from the other passengers.[10] Later, when the bus parks at its destination, Lewis detects a "fresh stillness" in the air. These, however, are more "atmospheric" sensations, and he soon encounters sensations that are much more concrete and direct.

If the faces and forms of the passengers are distorted and faded merely by light leaking in through the closed and covered windows of the bus, the full force of the heavenly environment, when everyone stands outside in the open air, is starkly revealing. At first, Lewis perceives that the other passengers are semi-transparent, "man-shaped stains on the brightness of that air."[11] Then he has a very Dante-esque change of perspective, which bears quoting at length:

> Then some re-adjustment of the mind or some focusing of my eyes took place, and I saw the whole phenomenon the other way round. The men were as they had always been; as all the men I had known had been perhaps. It was the light, the grass, the trees that were different; made of some different substance, so much solider than things in our country that men were ghosts by comparison.[12]

Like Dante, Lewis' senses of understanding and sight are elevated in order to take in this reality, but the sense that truly "feels" the new environment is his sense of touch. The material nature of this place is so different, and the substance of the passengers so weak, that they have almost no ability to physically interact with the environment at all. The grass does not bend when they walk on it, they cannot disturb the dewdrops, and their footsteps do not even make sound. Lewis is unable to pick a daisy or even twist its stalk, and he nearly wears himself out in an effort to move a single leaf on the ground. Walking on the grass and among the plants is sheer torture, as if everything is made of pure diamond and cuts badly into one's feet. Lewis sees and envies a bird he sees running across the path, disturbing the dewdrops in its movement; he realizes that the bird is fully "real" and manifestly *belongs* in this heaven, just as he himself does not. Lewis finds some relief by walking on the surface of a river, though it is very difficult to keep balance with changes in the contour of the water, and where even floating bits of foam bruise his ankles as if they were rocks.

It is entirely valid to wonder about the nature of this place—is it fair to call it heaven when it is a place of exquisite physical discomfort, if not torture?[13] After all, the water cannot be drunk, the food cannot be eaten, and the flowers and plants are solid, sharp, and immovable. The question is answered by the local residents, people who approach and speak to the various passengers exiting the bus. These people are so bright that they can be seen from miles away, and have no difficulty at all interacting with the environment. As with the bird he sees earlier, Lewis knows that these people, the Solid People,[14] intimately *belong* to this place, in the same way Dante sees the spirits as perfectly suited to the heavenly spheres they inhabit.[15] If we also recall the manner through which Dante receives his "leveling up" of mind and sight, he does not receive these sensory upgrades *before* they are needed, but *after*. This forces him always to be confronted with the limitations of his own senses, and in humility to depend on Beatrice and others for divine help.[16] Similarly in *The Great Divorce*, the ghostly passengers receive improvements to their sense of touch, but not until they experience their own natural limitations for a time. The Solid People have come out to meet the bus in an attempt to convince the passengers—their family members and friends—to remain in heaven and come deeper into it, toward the mountains where the true glories of the afterlife await. One of the Solid People tells a ghost, whom he is trying to convince to stay in heaven, "it will hurt at first, until your feet are hardened. Reality is harsh to the feet of shadows."[17] Another of them promises that the ghosts' transparency will wear off too. Lewis notices the range of possibilities in his own brief experience in the heavenly environment: "Once again I realized that something had happened to my senses so that they were now receiving impressions which would normally exceed their capacity."[18] Like Dante, Lewis experiences a tuning of his *musica humana*, and also an expansion of his *capacity* for perfection—a *maior perfectum*.

Here, I would like to share two particularly illustrative and poignant scenes from Lewis' novel. The first is the meeting of one of the passengers, an Episcopal bishop, with a friend of his among the heavenly Solid People. The bishop has, in a way, reasoned himself out of his own faith, largely through pride and an outsized regard for his own intellect. He talks himself out of going further on into heaven, then smiles at his friend and walks away humming the hymn, "City of God, how broad and far."[19] The second is an encounter between the ghost of a man and an angel. The man carries a red lizard on his shoulder, representing lust, and tells the angel he cannot stay in heaven because the lizard will not stay quiet. The angel offers to kill the lizard, but the man hesitates, feeling that this would kill him as well, but he finally relents. When the angel kills the lizard, the ghost of the man falls to the ground and Lewis watches in wonder as he grows into one of the bright, golden, Solid People. The lizard grows into a stallion, representing a healthy sexuality, and man and stallion gallop off toward the heavenly mountains. At this, the very land itself, the earth, the trees, and the waters, sing a song of triumph and victory in a "strange archaic, inorganic noise, that [came] from all directions at once."[20] While Lewis does not elaborate on this music, it is reminiscent of Dante's experience in the heavenly spheres, where he is able to identify the presence of music, but cannot understand it. This is Lewis' own visceral experience of the mysteries of the *musica mundana*.

While Lewis' journey to heaven is not as distinctly "about" the *musica mundana* as it is in Dante's *Paradiso*, it does, like Dante, touch on the effects of the heavenly spheres on the *musica humana*. Though we have focused on Lewis' sense of touch, the novel is largely about people traveling from the gray town up into heaven. These travelers are all decidedly "out of tune"—wrathful, violent, prideful, unbelieving, selfish, close-minded, foolish, and stubborn. These characteristics are what makes them so transparent and insubstantial, and seemingly unable to endure the reality of heaven for long. But the cure for that transparency is, like for Dante, the time spent in that very environment in communion with the Solid People, who have become solid because they have allowed their *musica humana* to become attuned to the *musica mundana* that exists there.

NOTES

1. I should note that sensory analyses are possible in other works of C. S. Lewis, especially *The Chronicles of Narnia* and *The Space Trilogy*. To give only one example from *Perelandra*, the second book of *The Space Trilogy*, the protagonist Dr. Elwin Ransom experiences taste on a higher plane than he does on Earth: "while Ransom was on Perelandra his sense of taste had become something more than it was on Earth: it gave knowledge as well as pleasure, though not a knowledge that can be reduced to words." C. S. Lewis, *Perelandra*, 138. Of course, the connection between eating and

gaining knowledge is part of the biblical story of the fall of mankind, though in that case it had entirely different consequences.

2. Human senses are at times treated through their *absence* in visions and mystical experiences. The sixteenth-century reformer and Doctor of the Church Teresa de Ávila described such experiences in what she called the Prayer of Union, a state of meditation in which all five senses were suspended, and all that remained was pure emotion of joy and delight in the presence of the divine. Such a dulling or elimination of the senses is similar, in some respects, to how Dante initially describes his presence in the Empyrean Heaven, as we saw in the previous chapter.

3. John D. Sinclair, tr. and commentary, *The Divine Comedy of Dante Alighieri: I Inferno* (New York: Oxford University Press, 1961), 23.

4. C.S. Lewis, *The Great Divorce: a Dream* (New York: HarperOne, 2001), 1.

5. One of the travelers on the bus makes the journey for this very reason. He hopes to bring back something from heaven that has true physical substance, something made of matter, so he can create a commodity market for it back in the town. Another passenger comments, "and that passion for 'real' commodities which our friend speaks of is only materialism, you know. It's retrogressive. Earth-bound! A hankering for matter. But we look on this spiritual city—for with all its faults it is spiritual." Lewis, *The Great Divorce*, 16.

6. Ibid., 9.

7. Ibid., 17.

8. Ibid.

9. Ibid.

10. There is no small amount of irony here. How can anyone catch their death of cold if they are already dead? However, I believe this passage illustrates that, just as the ghosts on the bus retain their human personalities, so do they retain their human reactions—nearly all of them violent, self-serving, venal, and dishonest.

11. Lewis, *The Great Divorce*, 20.

12. Ibid., 21. This experience is very similar to one from *The Last Battle*, the final book in the *Chronicles of Narnia*. There, the children who, like Lewis in *The Great Divorce*, have died (though they do not yet know it), find themselves in a beautiful country. They describe it as somehow more *real* than places they had known in England, and subtly different: "Every rock and flower and blade of grass looked as if it meant more." C. S. Lewis, *The Last Battle* (New York: HarperCollins Publishers, 1994), 196.

13. The bus terminal where they disembark is not "exactly" heaven, as one of the inhabitants explains to Lewis, at least not *deep* heaven. Rather, he says that one can think of this place as the "Valley of the Shadow of Life." The true heaven is in the distance, where great mountains loom against the sky with a perpetual promise of sunrise.

14. It is worth noting that C. S. Lewis treats the subject of "solidity," though perhaps "density" may be a better word, in another story about a celestial journey. In *Out of the Silent Planet*, the first book of *The Space Trilogy*, Ransom is taken to Mars, where he discusses the universe with the angelic ruler of that planet. Here, he learns about the ruling angelic spirits whose natural habitat is not a planetary surface, but rather the vacuum of space:

His "light" is a swifter movement which for us is nothing at all; and what we call light is for him a thing like water, a visible thing, a thing he can touch and bathe in—even a dark thing when not illumined by the swifter. And what we call firm things—flesh and earth—seem to him thinner, and harder to see, than our light, and more like clouds, and nearly nothing. To us the [angel] is a thin, half-real body that can go through walls and rocks: to himself he goes through them because he is solid and firm and they are like cloud. And what is true light to him and fills the heaven, so that he will plunge into the rays of the sun to refresh himself from it, is to us the black nothing in the sky at night. These things are not strange . . . though they are beyond our senses.

C. S. Lewis, *Out of the Silent Planet* (New York: Scribner, 2011), 95.

15. Later, Lewis sees these people with what he calls "double vision." On the one hand, they appear as enthroned gods, shining and ageless, and on the other hand, they are recognizable even as they had been known on earth. This is an echo of a biblical passage that Lewis would have known well: "For now we see through a glass, darkly; but then face to face: now I know in part, but then I shall know even as also I am known." 1 Corinthians 13:12 (KJV).

16. Dante's experience is paralleled by that of Lewis, when the guide sent to explain the heavenly world to him helps improve his perception: "Perhaps it was because of his presence that my other senses also appeared to be quickened. I noticed scents in the air which had hitherto escaped me, and the country put on new beauties." Lewis, *The Great Divorce*, 78.

17. Ibid., 39.

18. Ibid., 46.

19. Ibid., 44. The irony doubles with this image of a bishop, ostensibly a man of God, singing a hymn about the kingdom of God, while the very reality of that kingdom sits within his physical line of sight, and he refuses to enter.

20. Ibid., 113.

Chapter 3

"Behold Your Music!"
Music as a Force of Creation, Destruction, and Re-Creation in the Worlds of J. R. R. Tolkien and C. S. Lewis

And God said, Let there be light: and there was light.[1]

Said then th' omnific Word, "your discord end."[2]

Just as centuries of music theorists in the West—and authors like Dante—provided much of the foundational imagery of the universe, so also have C. S. Lewis and J. R. R Tolkien created twentieth-century equivalents that shape modern images of the cosmos in the popular imagination. The worlds created by these authors have heavily influenced much of the literature and media of the past century. Their fictional works have directed readers and scholars back to the theoretical, theological, and philosophical materials that served as primordial ingredients to their created universes. Music plays an essential role in the creation and development of the worlds of Lewis and Tolkien, just as with Dante. These later authors had several centuries of additional material to draw from, such as John Milton's *Paradise Lost* and John Dryden's *A Song for St. Cecilia's Day*, which provide additional imagery for the musical concepts underlying their stories.

As in the *Paradiso*, Tolkien and Lewis explore the nature of music in the celestial realms, but unlike Dante, they expand their scope beyond the current state of the universe as they understand it. For Dante, the trip through Hell, Purgatory, and Paradise happens in the *present* time, the early fourteenth century. In contrast, Tolkien unveils his universe at the instant of its creation, before even the counting of time or the formation of matter. Lewis treats the creation of his universe of Narnia similarly, though Narnia is only one of a large, perhaps an infinite, number of universes that are mutually inaccessible, except to a small number of fortunate children. But both the worlds of Tolkien and Lewis are undisputedly created through music, and by the will and initiative of a single omnipotent creator.

The ability to *create* is not the only power exercised by music in these stories. While the creative act and its immediate effects are a kind of *musica mundana*, music likewise exists within created beings of all kinds, as *musica humana*.[3] Additionally, audible music—*musica instrumentalis*—can have destructive power, as well as power to heal, renew, or recreate.

MUSIC OF CREATION—NARNIA

For Lewis in his world of Narnia, as well as for Tolkien in his Middle-earth legendarium, music is the primary force of material creation. Music initiates the formation of the universe, and acts as the means through which it is sustained and balanced. In *The Magician's Nephew*, the sixth book[4] in the *Chronicles of Narnia*, the children Digory and Polly, Digory's magician uncle Andrew, a London cab driver and his horse, and the witch-queen Jadis, fall into an as-yet uncreated world. Not knowing where they are—though Jadis knows enough to guess—and unsure of their next move, the cab driver suggests they sing a hymn together. Unsure as to what sort of song is appropriate for the situation in which they find themselves, he sings a favorite harvest hymn, with words about gathering wheat into barns, and other solid farming imagery.[5] After finishing the hymn, the group hears a faint voice singing in the distance, which they perceive as beautiful. The sky, which until now was entirely dark and featureless, is suddenly filled with millions of stars, constellations, and planets that immediately join in singing with the first voice. Then, as the horizon slowly brightens, the original voice increases in pitch and volume until, at its highest and most glorious point, the sun rises.[6] The light of the sun allows the group to see that the source of the music is a large lion—Aslan—who sings as he paces slowly toward them. The group soon perceives that the lion's song corresponds to the things being created at any given moment. When Aslan sings "a gentle, rippling music," the bare ground erupts with grasses and plants; when he makes a series of "deep, prolonged notes," a line of fir trees appears on a nearby ridge; and when "burst[ing] into a series of lighter notes," primroses pop up in every direction.[7] At this point, the lion begins to sing animals into existence, and it is not difficult to detect strong echoes of *Paradise Lost* in Lewis' description. In John Milton's seminal work, the archangel Raphael visits Eden to tell Adam the story of creation. Raphael describes the first part of the sixth day of creation in the following exciting and novel narrative:

The sixth, and of creation last, arose
With evening harps and matin; when God said,
Let the Earth bring forth soul living in her kind,

> Cattle, and creeping things, and beast of the Earth,
> Each in their kind. The Earth obeyed, and straight
> Opening her fertile womb teemed at a birth
> Innumerous living creatures, perfect forms,
> Limbed and full grown: Out of the ground up rose,
> As from his lair, the wild beast where he wons
> In forest wild, in thicket, brake, or den;
> Among the trees in pairs they rose, they walked:
> The cattle in the fields and meadows green:
> Those rare and solitary, these in flocks
> Pasturing at once, and in broad herds upsprung.
> The grassy clods now calved; now half appeared
> The tawny lion, pawing to get free
> His hinder parts, then springs as broke from bonds,
> And rampant shakes his brinded mane; the ounce,
> The libbard, and the tiger, as the mole
> Rising, the crumbled earth above them threw
> In hillocks: The swift stag from under ground
> Bore up his branching head: Scarce from his mould
> Behemoth biggest born of earth upheaved
> His vastness . . .[8]

Milton continues with wonderfully vibrant descriptions of the various beasts bursting forth from the earth at God's command. It is worth noting that the sixth day—which would have begun the previous evening, before proceeding through the night and the next day—begins with music, specifically the "evening harps" and the services of *matins*, the part of the liturgical Divine Office that includes the singing of praises to God in the darkness before sunrise. Lewis paints a similarly vivid picture of the creation of the animals of Narnia, as they also break free from the earth:

> Can you imagine a stretch of grassy land bubbling like water in a pot? For that is really the best description of what was happening. In all directions it was swelling into humps. They were of very different sizes, some no bigger than molehills, some as big as wheelbarrows, two the size of cottages. And the humps moved and swelled till they burst, and the crumbled earth poured out of them, and from each hump there came out an animal. The moles came out just as you might see a mole come out in England. The dogs came out, barking the moment their heads were free, and struggling as you've seen them do when they are getting through a narrow hole in a hedge. The stags were the queerest to watch for of course the antlers came up a long time before the rest of them, so at first Digory thought they were trees. The frogs, who all came up near the

river, went straight into it with a plop-plop and a loud croaking. The panthers, leopards and things of that sort, sat down at once to wash the loose earth off their hind quarters and then stood up against the trees to sharpen their front claws.
[. . .]
But the greatest moment of all was when the biggest hump broke like a small earthquake and out came the sloping back, the large, wise head, and the four baggy-trousered legs of an elephant.[9]

The creation of Narnia includes these creatures, all the growing things, and the celestial bodies—everything, in short, that is required for a sustainable, thriving world. Thus, I feel it is no coincidence that Lewis puts a harvest hymn—a song of material sustenance, guaranteed to all—in the mouth of the London cab driver just as creation commences.

Returning to the idea of systems of perfection and imperfection discussed in chapter 1, Narnia is a universe initially created as a system of perfection, similar to the pre-fall world of *Paradise Lost*, and like *Paradise Lost*, evil is imported into Narnia from outside. The witch Jadis,[10] the last ruler and sole survivor of another world, is accidentally brought into Narnia by Digory and Polly, and it is she who introduces evil into this newly created and perfect universe. Aslan speaks to the animals, telling them, "before the new, clean world I gave you is seven hours old, a force of evil has already entered it; waked and brought hither by this son of Adam."[11] Jadis is the means by which the Narnian universe becomes a system of imperfection, with death and decay becoming part of the fabric of its existence. However, just as Adam and Eve in the biblical account are promised that the results of their sin will be mitigated and reversed in the future, Aslan tells the beasts, "as Adam's race has done the harm, Adam's race shall help to heal it."[12] Digory and Polly are then sent to fetch a magic apple that, when planted in Narnia, grows into a tree that prevents Jadis from entering that land for many hundreds of years. Further in the Narnian future, Aslan sacrifices himself to break the power of the witch, just as in the biblical story the promised Messiah is sacrificed to break the power of evil and death.

MUSIC OF CREATION—MIDDLE-EARTH

The creation of Tolkien's world is quite different than that of Lewis' Narnia, but no less musical. Tolkien's universe begins with Eru Ilúvatar,[13] the One, who creates the Ainur,[14] a race of angelic beings, each of which represents a part of Eru's own mind. He teaches the Ainur to sing, then gathers them together, and "declar[ing] unto them a mighty theme,"[15] invites them to adorn the theme with their own musical thoughts and ideas. The resulting music becomes the initiating factor for the creation of the material universe—the music travels out into the uncreated void, and transforms it into matter and substance.[16] However, the mightiest of the Ainur, Melkor, becomes envious of Eru's power and authority, and desires to create things of his own will, apart from the limits of the provided musical theme.[17] Melkor's negative thoughts and desires affect his own parts of the music, immediately causing dissonance in the theme. Some of the Ainur fall silent upon hearing this discord, while others follow Melkor's lead, amplifying his dissonance. Here, Eru stands and smiles, and begins a new and different theme. Melkor again fights against it, causing what Tolkien describes as a "war of sound." Eru stands a second time, with a stern countenance, and initiates yet another musical theme. Melkor continues his assault on the themes by attempting to drown them out through mere repetition of ideas and sheer volume. Nonetheless, Eru takes Melkor's discordant music, and weaves its most brazen dissonances back into Eru's own theme. Finally, Eru stands a third time, and with a face "terrible to behold," ends the music in one great chord.[18]

Tolkien's concept of creative music is different from that of Lewis in a very important way. For Lewis, Aslan's singing creates the universe, its elements, and its creatures *ex nihilo*, in the very instant the words are sung. For Tolkien, the Ainur's music is only a foretaste or foreshadowing of a creation yet to be realized. Eru takes the Ainur into the empty void to show them the results of the music they have just made. He tells them, "Behold your Music!" revealing a vision of the future of the material world, created through the musical contributions and adornments of each of them, according to the grand design of the themes proposed by Eru. Some parts of the music revealed in the vision, including the rise of the races of elves and men (known as the Children of Ilúvatar), were not contributed by the Ainur, and were known only to Eru.[19] Many of the Ainur, upon seeing this vision, desire to go down into this world and inhabit it in anticipation of the coming of the Children. Eru allows those who wish to go into the world to do so, on the condition that their power must remain contained within it, and that they must remain there until its history is complete.[20]

At this point, Eru declares, "*Eä!* Let these things Be!" and immediately the material universe, foreseen in the vision, comes into being. The Ainur who go down into the world immediately perceive, however, that nothing they saw in the vision has yet been created. They realize that they themselves will work to create the things they have sung about and seen in the vision.

DISSONANT CREATION, OR IMPERFECT CREATORS?

Melkor joins the Ainur who come into the world to prepare it for the arrival of the Children. His earlier interference in the music continues, or comes to fruition, as the rest of the Ainur work together to craft the new world. While the others are laboring, Melkor "[meddles] in all that [is] done, turning it if he might to his own desires and purposes."[21] He becomes envious of the others, desiring to dominate and rule over them and their works, becoming a force of destruction rather than creation:

> And they built lands and Melkor destroyed them; valleys they delved and Melkor raised them up; mountains they carved and Melkor threw them down; seas they hollowed and Melkor spilled them; [. . .] for as surely as the [Ainur] began a labour so would Melkor undo it or corrupt it.[22]

Our understanding of the fundamental *dissonance* of Melkor is aided by the fact that the Ainur, after their creation from the mind of Eru, are not initially "developed" musicians. At first they sing "only each alone, or but few together [. . .] for each comprehended only that part of the mind of Ilúvatar from which he came, and in the understanding of their brethren they grew but slowly."[23] As they listen and learn more of each other, they are able to "[come] to deeper understanding, and [increase] in unison and harmony."[24] This is an excellent practical example of *musica humana*, and though the Ainur are not human, they are created beings living in community and relationship with one another. Chiara Bertoglio supports such reading in the following passage: "The more an Ainu hears of another's music, the more their reciprocal knowledge increases; this cannot be done outside a relational framework, since an Ainu's singing is the aural embodiment of his or her deepest being, which is freely given and offered to the others."[25] Not only do the Ainur learn more of each other through their communal music-making, but as each is an embodiment of a part of the mind of Eru, they learn more about him as well, expanding the scope of their *musica mundana*. Melkor, however, is not interested in a harmonious relationship with his peers, rather "he wants to affirm his own singing not only in defiance of Ilúvatar, but also in a hegemonic position with respect to his brethren."[26] In short, Melkor sacrifices the communion of the *musica humana* for the sake of his mere personal *musica instrumentalis*.[27] The resulting lack of harmony among the Ainur is described using the suitable musical terms *disharmony* and *discord*, and Verlyn Flieger notes, "the explicitly musical terms [. . .] are thus metaphorically extended to nonmusical concepts where they become expressive of [. . .] quarrels and contentions."[28] I will only quibble slightly with Flieger to say that, under the different kinds of *musica* we are modeling in this book, such concepts are not only metaphorical, but eminently practical and musical.

The creation of the physical universe in Tolkien's legendarium is novel because, rather than creation as an event initiated and accomplished solely through divine *fiat*, it is rather left to other created beings to realize. These beings, though powerful in themselves, cannot see the complete picture, and moreover, one of them is actively disrupting and sabotaging the collective process of creation. This disruption precedes creation itself, reaching back to the original music, the model for creation. In this way, a system of imperfection is "baked in" to the very fabric of the material universe from before its actual inception. Flieger discusses Tolkien's own thoughts on the subject and, like Lewis, Tolkien notes that Christian mythology includes the entrance of sin and imperfection into creation from an external source.[29] Because of what occurs during the singing of the music, discord and disharmony are destined to become a part of the essence of the universe, coming as it does before, or *outside*, the material creation itself.[30]

The imperfections, or limitations, of the Ainur's creative potential is illustrated in how they perceive the nature of the universe. When they go down into it, they are at first surprised that the world has not yet been created, and that they will have to achieve it through their own initiative and labor. Though they themselves made the music, and saw the vision of the world revealed by Eru, the music was abstract and the vision was as "from afar," and not entirely clear to them. Consequently, when the Ainur enter the world, at many times they see "at unawares [. . .] something new and unforetold."[31] The most important of these new and unexpected elements is the Children of Ilúvatar, whose part in the music originates from the mind of Eru himself. Since the Ainur do not fully understand the themes that bring the Children into the world, they cannot themselves change or add anything to the Children's innate natures, and so they are slow to interfere with the Children, even if for their own good.[32] Furthermore, the Ainur do not know what the end of the world will be, or how it will be brought about. As Flieger notes, "the great design of Eru's initial theme is not carried to its proper conclusion, and so it is never fully achieved."[33] Even when the Ainur are able to fight off the destructive impulses of Melkor, his discord still remains an integral part of the fabric of creation. Thus the Ainur have two great limitations: the residual dissonance of Melkor, and the inability to perceive and realize large parts of the music and the vision.

There are instances, however, when the Ainur *are* given the ability to "replay" the music when important issues arise. The chief and most powerful of the Ainur, after Melkor turns to evil, is Manwë, the master of the sky and winds. Yavanna, in charge of all growing things on the earth, approaches Manwë and asks him to explain why there is no provision for the protection of plants on the earth, while animals have been designed with the ability to flee or defend themselves from those who wish them harm. Here, Manwë experiences the music once again, noticing things he had not before perceived, and Eru also reveals to him a part of the vision, this time clearly and not remote. Manwë sees that when the Children of Ilúvatar awake, divine spirits will enter some of the animals and growing things to guide them and protect them from the Children, who will hold these spirits in reverence. Chief among these spirits are the great Eagles of Manwë, and the Shepherds of the Trees.[34] This satisfies Yavanna, who is assured that the lesser creatures and plants are not defenseless against the coming Children who, as declared by Eru, will exercise dominion over the earth. This also indicates that conflict will exist between Children and the rest of the created world—strife between their *musica humana* and the *musica mundana*.

The freedom that Eru has given to the Ainur to adorn themes in the music is illustrated on the earth during the process of creation. One of the more poignant and moving events in all of Tolkien's legendarium is the creation of the race of dwarves. Aulë, responsible for the earth, the minerals, and the mountains, works at his forge, crafting the various substances that make up the physical world. Seeing that the world is beautiful, that it has room for many inhabitants, and also being impatient for the coming of the Children of Ilúvatar, Aulë secretly creates the dwarves. Eru sees this and confronts him:

> Why dost thou attempt a thing which thou knowest is beyond thy power and thy authority? For thou hast from me as a gift thy own being only, and no more; and therefore the creatures of thy hand and mind can live only by that being, moving when thou thinkest to move them, and if thy thought be elsewhere, standing idle. Is that thy desire?[35]

The beginning of this speech by Eru echoes the conversation between God and Adam in the Garden of Eden, but quickly changes focus and mood from the biblical story. Eru reminds Aulë that the ability and authority to create beings that think and act of their own will—made in the image of Ilúvatar—belongs solely to Eru. Beings made without Eru's divine spark are simple automatons, moving only when their creator wishes to move them. Aulë answers by saying that crafting such creatures is not his desire,[36] but rather he is impatient to have other beings to teach and love, and to enjoy the beautiful world that Eru has caused to be. Aulë then reminds Eru that "the making of things is in my heart from my own making by thee; and the child of little understanding that makes a play of the deeds of his father may do so without thought of mockery, but because he is the son of his father."[37] Aulë in his humility puts the fate of the dwarves in Eru's hands, and offers to destroy them with his great hammer. The dwarves shrink in fear of the hammer and beg for their lives, at which point Eru says, "Thy offer I accepted even as it was made. Dost thou not see that these things have now a life of their own, and speak with their own voices?"[38] Thus Eru adopts the race of the dwarves, giving them the spark of life, and full status as Children of Ilúvatar. He accepts the dwarves because their making comes from love and a desire for companionship, and to have others with whom to share the blessings of the created world. However, Eru warns Aulë that there will often be strife between the elves—the firstborn of the Children—and the dwarves: "the children of my adoption and the children of my choice."[39] Though dissonance does indeed occur between the elves and the dwarves, it is not particularly worse than what exists between and among the other created races. There are times and places where there is friendship between the two races, particularly the close bond between Legolas the elf and Gimli the dwarf in *The Lord of the Rings*. Ultimately, though Aulë's act is outside the will of Eru, it is not in itself *dissonant*.[40] The case of Melkor, as we have noted above, is entirely different.

Before the music, Melkor is impatient just as Aulë later becomes impatient. Melkor is aware of the divine spark of life, and often goes in search of it in the infinite emptiness of the void, but he is not able to find it, not realizing that the spark originates with and is integral to Eru himself. Melkor feels that Eru does not properly consider the void, and he is eager for it to be filled. However, while Aulë's yearning to create comes from a desire to imitate Eru, and is done out of love and admiration, Melkor's craving comes of a desire to exercise his own power and will, "fall[ing] prey to the desire to make his own Music instead of subsuming his creative powers to Eru's theme."[41] The act of adorning the themes with his own ideas and devices is not itself Melkor's downfall, as Eru had instructed the Ainur to do exactly that. Dissonance is possible, and even likely, when people of independent wills make music together.[42] However, dissonance can be mitigated if participants agree on a common direction or idea, placing their own creative impulses in the context of a larger group, and in deference to a common theme. Such attitudes result in well-tuned *musica humana*. However, Melkor absolutely refuses to do this; his part of the music is "loud, and vain, and endlessly repeated," and his purpose is to "drown the other music by the violence of its voice."[43] Thus we see Melkor's natural creative impulse transformed into a desire to dominate and destroy, which he effects when he and the other Ainur create the physical world. Melkor's precluded aspiration to create has its most destructive consequences in his many acts of corrupting what has already been created. One particularly egregious example occurs when he becomes aware of the awakening of the race of the elves, the firstborn of the Children of Ilúvatar. Melkor captures some of the elves. and through long years of agony and torment, he twists them from the perfectly tuned creatures they are intended to be into the terrible race of orcs, an act considered "the vilest deed of Melkor, and the most hateful to Ilúvatar."[44] Though the orcs serve Melkor, they hate him, seeing in him "the maker only of their misery." Ultimately, Melkor cannot create, but only twist and ruin—he cannot attune himself to others, but only serve as a source of dissonance.

WATER AS AN ECHO OF CREATION

As they go down to create and inhabit the world, the Ainur encounter the various materials of which the world is made. Among these elements is water, first observed in the roaring of the oceans, which makes the Ainur uneasy and disquieted.[45] Though initially disturbing, water becomes the element most praised among the Ainur, because it contains an echo of the music in greater measure than any other earthly substance,[46] acting as a kind of cosmic DNA bearing the imprint of the entire creation—the *musica mundana*. The immortal race of elves is awakened with the sound of running water in their ears,[47] though these earliest encounters are of innocuous lakes, placid streams, and gentle waterfalls. The elves' first encounter with the great, untamed sea occurs "in fear and wonder," and it is through the agency of Ulmo, the Lord of Waters, that "their fear of the sea [is] turned rather to desire."[48] At their later awakening, the mortal race of men is also enamored of the sound of water, and Tolkien notes that water exercises *musical* influence on some of them. Tuor, one of the early human heroes, grows up near a lake and becomes a famous musician, who "carefully pays attention to the music of the water."[49] The element of water seems to reciprocate, likewise paying attention to the music of Tuor. While on a journey, he finds himself in desperate need of guidance. Stopping to sing and play his harp, a spring of water bubbles up from the ground, forming a stream that points him in the direction he should take.[50] Tuor becomes the first mortal man to look upon the ocean, and, like the elves, he is initially dismayed by its furious sound and violence. However, after seeing it, "a great yearning [fills] his heart," and he is only willing to stay where he can hear the sound of the waves on the shore,[51] and "the sound of it and the longing for it [are] ever in his heart and ear."[52] For their part, even the lowly hobbits are not completely immune to the siren call of the sea. Most hobbits are averse to *any* body of water, and the sea is for them a token of death.[53] A few hobbits, however, grow to love the ocean, and we will discuss one case below.

Given that water holds within it the imprint and echo of the original music, it may be argued that Ulmo, who among the Ainur is most associated with water, has a special role to play in the legends and stories of Tolkien's world. Though he is Lord of Waters, Ulmo keeps the entire world in his thought, even when the minds of the other Ainur are occupied elsewhere. As one most intimate with the element of water, Ulmo best understands the music, which represents a design or pattern of the world's history. His knowledge of this pattern prompts him to keep in close contact with the different sentient races, communicating with them by stream and flood, though they often misunderstand or are not aware of his words, thinking them only the sound of mindless elements.[54] Elves are somewhat more attuned to Ulmo's messages, but men are much less perceptive, though both are moved and stirred to a love of water.[55] Among the elves, the branch calling themselves the Lindar—the Singers—are regarded as the finest musicians in the world. It is not a coincidence that the beings possessing the best *musica instrumentalis* are those who remain in constant contact with the *musica mundana* in the form of water, as the Lindar will live only on the shores of the sea.[56]

While encounters with water and the sea are generally considered positive after initial fear is overcome, they can also be dangerous, as the one encountering the sea may become "infected" by a yearning—a yearning that cannot be satisfied by anything but the sea, as in the case of Tuor. The elven-queen Galadriel warns the wood-elf Legolas of this same danger in the following poem:

Legolas Greenleaf long under tree
In joy thou hast lived. Beware of the Sea!
If thou hearest the cry of the gull on the shore,
Thy heart shall then rest in the forest no more.[57]

Galadriel's warning is justified when Legolas approaches the sea during a battle at night. Though unable to see the ocean in the darkness, he hears the seagulls on the shore and later laments: "Alas for the wailing of the gulls! Did not the Lady tell me to beware of them? And now I cannot forget them."[58]

Frodo the hobbit is also sensitive to the draw of the sea, though it is not until the final chapter of his journey. that he actually sees it in person. Before this, he often dreams of the sea and feels a yearning for it, especially after the many wounds, both physical and mental, he suffers in the course of his journey. After the destruction of the Ring and the peace that follows, Frodo and his companions rest in the magical valley of Rivendell, a place that offers healing for both body and mind. While Rivendell has "something of everything," such as forests, meadows, inns, and palaces, Frodo wistfully notes: "Yes, something of everything, [. . .] except the Sea."[59] Frodo is perceptive to the sound of water in music, and conversely to the sound of music in water. During an earlier visit to Rivendell, Frodo hears the singing and playing of elven-musicians, whose music is described in very water-like terms. While listening, he falls into a trance, "until he felt that an endless river of swelling gold and silver was flowing over him," and he is "drenched and drowned" in it. He drifts along in this trance for some time, in "a dream of music that turned into running water."[60] Later in the story, when entering the enchanted realm of the elven-queen Galadriel, Frodo and company rest near a stream. As they sit quietly, they listen to the sound of a waterfall, and "Frodo [fancies] that he [can] hear a voice singing, mingled with the sound of the water."[61] Water, especially the sea, becomes an element with different meanings for Frodo. In one sense, the sea acts as a barrier, separating him from the healing of the wounds he has received during his journey.[62] At the same time, it represents the very healing he desires and becomes the medium through—or *over*—which he may find it.

The voice of water calls to the inhabitants of Tolkien's world, reminding them unconsciously of the music, and of their status as Children of Ilúvatar. For beings of goodwill, the echo of creation in water—*musica mundana*—is an alluring, if often unnerving, call. For evil creatures, it is a terror. Among the elements of the created world, Melkor has a special hatred for water and the sea, and he attacks it with extremes of heat and cold. This hatred of water also extends to his servants, who shun it and avoid the sea except in dire need.[63] Clearly, they also hear the echo of the music in the sound of water, but this echo serves to expose their own fundamental dissonance, and it speaks to them of betrayal, and of their ultimate doom.

CONSONANT LIGHT, DISSONANT DARKNESS, AND THE UNMUSICAL VOID

Just as water is generally analogous to music in Tolkien's world, so also are light and darkness comparable to musical consonance and dissonance. John Gardner makes this point in his October 12, 1977 review of *The Silmarillion* in the *New York Times Book Review*: "Music is the central symbol and the total myth of 'The Silmarillion,' a symbol that becomes interchangeable with light (music's projection)."[64] In Tolkien's legendarium, "good," or consonant, music is associated with light, and "bad," or dissonant music, with darkness. Among Melkor's earliest concerns is the emptiness and darkness of the void, and his belief that Eru neglects it. Though Melkor craves light, he is not able to seize it for his own selfish uses and so rejects it—though still desiring it—and embraces darkness, which he uses for his evil works, filling it with fear.[65]

During the song of creation, music penetrates the void, which disappears as it is replaced by light and substance. Hence the void may be defined simply as a place containing no music, or light, which is "music's projection." Tolkien, like C. S. Lewis above, channels Milton in his early passages on creation. In *Paradise Lost*, God begins the process by approaching the turbulence of Chaos and commanding, "your discord end!"[66] This discord is not simply the absence of light or matter, it is an element entirely opposed to them, a kind of "anti-matter." For Milton, the chaotic, empty void is a place of menace and danger, even for Satan. Speaking to the other fallen angels, Satan describes Chaos: "If any pass, the void profound of unessential Night receives him next, Wide-gaping, and with utter loss of being Threatens him, plunged into that abortive gulf."[67] This is an intriguing passage, because we are told by

Milton that even the fallen angels know they remain immortal, though now subject to pain.[68] In spite of this retained immortality, the "abortive gulf" of the primordial Chaos still threatens the fallen angels with destruction, with "utter loss of being." Chaos is then an essence that is *unessential*, and a substance that is *insubstantial*. To Milton, Chaos is the only means through which Satan and the fallen angels—apart from the initiative of God himself—can be destroyed or unmade. In Tolkien's world, it seems the unmusical void is likewise hazardous to Melkor as he wanders through it in the deeps of time before the beginning of the music. Perhaps Melkor, through his many journeys through the void seeking the spark of creation, becomes poisoned or mistuned through extended immersion in this decidedly *unmusical* element.[69]

The idea of the void as the special province of evil and dissonance occurs in various places in Tolkien's legendarium. While much more will be said below and in chapters 5.5 and 6 about the nature and function of the Ring of Sauron,[70] it is nonetheless an evil object, with power to draw its possessor into various void-like states. Among other powers, the Ring can make its user invisible, taking them out of the world of light, but if it is used too often the wearer will fade, at length becoming permanently invisible. From the perspective of the wearer of the Ring, the world becomes a vague and shadowy place, where most forms and objects are unclear and obscured. As a shape and a form, the Ring may be visualized as a circle enclosing a void, or a portal leading into a void. Ultimately, the Ring represents utter emptiness.[71] This is illustrated when the hobbit Frodo looks into the magic mirror of Galadriel, where he is confronted by a vision of Sauron, the maker and master of the Ring:

> But suddenly the Mirror went altogether dark, as dark as if a hole had opened in the world of sight, and Frodo looked into emptiness. In the black abyss there appeared a single Eye that slowly grew, until it filled nearly all the Mirror. Frodo stood rooted, unable to cry out or to withdraw his gaze. The Eye was rimmed with fire [. . .] and the black slit of its pupil opened on a pit, a window into nothing.[72]

This description shows us a Sauron who is fully immersed in the void, the "black abyss" in which his eye is framed. Furthermore, he is *consumed* by the void, as we look with Frodo into the nothingness at the center of Sauron's eye. Various passages point to the eventual fate of Sauron and his minions. Gandalf the wizard,[73] confronting Sauron's most powerful servant, says the following:

> Go back to the abyss prepared for you! Go back! Fall into the nothingness that awaits you and your Master. Go![74]

Gandalf is not making empty threats. At Melkor's eventual defeat at the hands of the Ainur, he is pushed out of the world and into the timeless void,⁷⁵ an act Gandalf likely witnessed personally. A similar fate awaits Sauron and his servants.

Just as members of the Ainur are seduced by Melkor's dissonant themes during the music, and help to magnify them, many of the Ainur who go into the world are drawn into Melkor's orbit, and become his servants. Among these is Ungoliant, who is said to have been born out of the darkness of the void and corrupted by Melkor, and enters his service. Like Melkor, Ungoliant lusts after light while at the same time hating it, and takes the form of a huge spider, "suck[ing] up all light that she [can] find, and [spinning] it forth again in dark nets of strangling gloom."⁷⁶ When she and Melkor attack the Undying Lands of Valinor, these nets are able to block even the sight of Manwë, the most powerful and farsighted of the Ainur. Recalling descriptions of Milton's palpable Chaos in *Paradise Lost*, Ungoliant's webs are not made of simple darkness, but rather "an Unlight, in which things [seem] to be no more, and which eyes [can] not pierce, for it [is] void."⁷⁷ Tolkien later describes the nature and effect of this Unlight:

> [It] was more than loss of light. In that hour was made a Darkness that seemed not lack but a thing with being of its own: for it was indeed made by malice out of Light, and it had power to pierce the eye, and to enter heart and mind, and strangle the very will.⁷⁸

The Ainur who come to oppose Melkor and Ungoliant are blinded and scattered, "powerless and [beating] the air in vain." Even Melkor is unnerved by Ungoliant, as she "[belches] forth black vapours" and "[swells] to a shape so vast and hideous that Melkor [is] afraid." Significantly, at the approach of her darkness, "all song [ceases],"⁷⁹ as light and music are replaced by darkness and silence.

There are other relics of the unmusical void in Tolkien's legendarium. Many thousands of years after the events just described, the hobbits Samwise and Frodo encounter the last child of Ungoliant, the darkness-spinning spider Shelob. Shelob lives in a labyrinth of dark tunnels, through which the hobbits must pass in order to continue their quest to destroy the Ring. As they enter, Frodo and Samwise are immediately surrounded by an "utter and impenetrable dark" that seems almost tangible:

> [A] black vapour wrought of veritable darkness itself that, as it was breathed, brought blindness not only to the eyes but to the mind, so that even the memory of colours and of forms and of any light faded out of thought. Night always had been, and always would be, and night was all.⁸⁰

This darkness, like that produced by Ungoliant, enters the mind and erases *memory* of light, even as it blots out physical illumination. Fortunately for the hobbits, they possess a magical light source that temporarily dazzles Shelob, forcing her to retreat. As Frodo and Samwise attempt to escape, they are blocked by the strands of a huge, dark web. Even their powerful light source cannot illuminate *these* gray, blank threads, as they are made of "a shadow that being cast by no light, no light [can] dissipate."[81] These palpable voids of Ungoliant and Shelob have an opposite effect to that of the music. While the presence of the music creates matter where once there was void, this consumed and excreted light creates void where once there was matter. Such a "recreation" of void out of consumed light—which Tolkien calls Unlight—is likewise an *Unmusic*, an ultimate dissonance and anathema to all kinds of *musica*, whether *mundana, humana,* or *instrumentalis*.

This juxtaposition of primordial light and essential darkness finds a practical application in the following narrative. After the Ainur finish forming the world, and have healed what they can of the violence of Melkor, they withdraw to the west and establish the blessed realm of Valinor. On a green mound in the middle of the land, Yavanna sings "a song of power, in which [is] set all her thought of things that grow in the earth."[82] Two saplings spring forth and quickly grow into tall and shapely trees, glowing with their own radiance—one tree with silver light, the other golden. Each of the trees waxes and wanes in brilliance, but at different times, so that there are periods in which the silver and golden lights alternate in dominance. The most beautiful moment occurs when both lights are relatively dim, one waxing and the other waning, and the gold and silver lights intermingle. It is noteworthy that the two trees, created through music and shining in their own light—itself analogous to music—are most beautiful when blended together in equal measure. Sadly, this image of beauty and consonance does not last long. After the creation of the trees, the greatest craftsmen of the race of elves, Fëanor, fashions three jewels, the Silmarils, which hold within them the radiance of the trees' mingled light. These jewels are an unparalleled feat of craftsmanship, even among the Ainur, and like all other things of beauty and light, Melkor covets them. He allies himself with Ungoliant in order to destroy the trees and steal the Silmarils, so that the remnants of their light will belong to himself alone. Through the agency of Ungoliant and her ability to create darkness, Melkor stabs each tree with a spear and Ungoliant sucks them dry, killing them. Melkor seizes the Silmarils and escapes with Ungoliant under the cover of her void and the general darkness that falls over Valinor after the death of the trees and the extinguishing of their light.

Much evil comes of this theft of the Silmarils, but for the sake of brevity, one of the three jewels ends up in the possession of the mariner Eärendil, who is placed with his ship in the sky, becoming a star to comfort and give hope to the inhabitants of the world. The light of Eärendil's star proves to be of great value to Frodo and Samwise in their encounter with Shelob. When visiting the elven country of Lórien earlier in their journey, Galadriel gives each a gift to aid them in their quest. The gift she gives Frodo is a crystal phial filled with water that shines with a white light. Galadriel tells him that it contains "the light of Eärendil's star, set amid the waters of my fountain. [. . .] May it be a light to you in dark places, when all other lights go out."[83] Among other things, this phial possesses a very *musical* provenance, as it contains the light of a Silmaril, which holds the memory of the light of the two trees created through the power of music. Moreover, the light is set within water, which as an element is an echo of the music of creation. It is this "musical light" that causes Shelob to retreat from Samwise and Frodo—but the light is not all-powerful. It has no power to illuminate Shelob's light-eating webs, and later, when Samwise attempts to use it inside Mount Doom, the center of the evil power of Sauron, the light has little to no effect there. So often do the forces of dissonance and darkness appear to conquer those of consonance and light, at least for a time.

CONSONANT AND DISSONANT CHARACTERS—FRODO

Continuing the analogy between light and consonance on one hand, and darkness and dissonance on the other, we can identify the *musical* natures of various characters who populate the worlds of Lewis and Tolkien. Among Tolkien's many characters, among the most deep and well-rounded is the hobbit Frodo who, in *The Lord of the Rings*, is the individual that best personifies the struggle between light and darkness. Through a complex and circuitous chain of custody, Frodo comes into possession of the Ring. Thousands of years before Frodo obtained it, Sauron helped to craft rings of power to be given as gifts to various beings in Middle-earth: nine for mortal men, seven for dwarves, and three for elves. However, these rings were ultimately traps to enslave and dominate the minds of their wearers, as Sauron secretly forged the One Ring, placing a large amount of his own native power into it, in order to control the others. Created solely as an instrument of control, and filled with Sauron's evil power and nature, the Ring possesses a nearly sentient ability to corrupt its wearer and those around them, regardless of their initial intentions or good nature. Like Ungoliant's shadowy webs, the Ring acts as a focal point of darkness, consuming or tainting nearby light. As noted above, one of the effects of the rings is invisibility, but this ability comes at a high price. If one often uses a ring to become invisible, they begin to fade, until the invisibility becomes permanent, and the user is doomed to exist in a world of perpetual twilight. Like the Unlight of Ungoliant discussed above, the invisibility offered by a ring is not a simple parlor trick, but rather a passageway to dissonance and unbeing—into the void.

We can comfortably describe Frodo as a character with very consonant *musica humana*. However, throughout his quest he must constantly bear the dissonant weight of the Ring's influence, and though he rarely uses it to become invisible, its close proximity relentlessly pulls him toward dissonance and darkness. Additional influences contribute to Frodo's struggle. Early in his quest, he encounters several of the nine men who have been enslaved by Sauron's rings, and they urge Frodo, irresistibly, to put on the Ring. He does so, and he immediately enters their world of shadows and darkness. One of them stabs Frodo with a cursed knife, and while the wound does not immediately kill him, he is "infected with [. . .] darkness."[84] The wound draws Frodo toward the shadow world, and he slowly begins to fade, becoming less visible in the world of light, and progressively *more* visible in the world of darkness.[85] Only when his wound is properly treated does Frodo recover, though he still exhibits a slight transparency, as if the process of fading is only partially reversed. While Frodo's new state of being may be interpreted as one of permanent damage or corruption, not all observers see it this way. The wisest eyes, who can detect Frodo's transparency, feel that it will not ultimately lead to evil, but that it may serve to make him "like a glass filled with a clear light for eyes to see that can."[86] Instead of a figure defined by a fading into darkness, Frodo may become, like Galadriel's phial or one of the Silmarils, a medium that both contains and shares light.

Sadly, Frodo's adventures do not have an entirely happy ending. While his quest to destroy the Ring succeeds, he suffers many dreadful injuries along the way. Frodo is variously stabbed with a cursed blade, stung and poisoned by the spider Shelob, and his ring finger is bitten off, to say nothing of the extremes of hunger, dehydration, and exhaustion he endures over the course of the journey. His mental and emotional injuries are just as severe. The lure of the Ring is an intense and continuous mental battle as it pulls him further into the world of darkness, and also a physical battle, as it becomes unbearably heavy as he nears his goal. At the end of the quest, the Ring has so possessed his mind that darkness enters into his memory, but unlike Shelob's lair, there is no magical phial to banish these internal shadows. Frodo's friend and companion Samwise attempts to cheer him by recounting past experiences of food and beautiful landscapes, to which Frodo replies:

> No, I am afraid not, Sam. [. . .] At least, I know that such things happened, but I cannot see them. No taste of food, no feel of water, no sound of wind, no memory of tree or grass or flower, no image of moon or star are left to me. I am naked in the dark, Sam, and there is no veil between me and the wheel of fire. I begin to see it even with my waking eyes, and all else fades.[87]

Samwise responds, "then the sooner we're rid of it, the sooner to rest."[88] Unfortunately, this is not to be, as being rid of the Ring does not bring Frodo the rest he desires. Though the destruction of the Ring eliminates its potential for use as a focal point of darkness and dissonance, the damage it inflicts on his *musica humana* remains. During the years Frodo possessed the Ring, it became an integral part of his physical, mental, and emotional being, and he developed a strong dependence on it.[89] For Frodo, the loss of the Ring is like the loss of a loved one, and its absence produces in Frodo something very like withdrawal symptoms. The elven-queen Arwen recognizes this, and gives Frodo a white gem, together with this message: "When the memory of the fear and the darkness troubles you, [. . .] this will bring you aid."[90] Frodo and his companions look forward to returning to their own quiet and peaceful land, only to discover that dissonance has come there too. After defeating enemies in his own homeland and settling down to a "regular" life, Frodo is unable to reintegrate, and few others recognize or understand his internal and external injuries.[91] Despite the aid of Arwen's jewel, the memories of the darkness and the Ring still haunt him, and at one point he says, "it is gone for ever, [. . .] and now all is dark and empty."[92] Unfortunately for Frodo and his loved ones, the healing that he seeks cannot be found in their world, and he must set sail across the sea for Valinor, in the hope of finding it. Ultimately, only through immersion in the pure and harmonious light of the Ainur can Frodo hope to leave darkness and dissonance behind. Whether this attempt at healing is successful or not, Tolkien never reveals.

CONSONANT AND DISSONANT CHARACTERS—SMÉAGOL

A character with many similarities to Frodo is Sméagol, a hobbit who formerly possessed the Ring. In *The Lord of the Rings*, Sméagol represents Frodo's potential future if he were to keep the Ring indefinitely, allowing it fully poison his mind and pull him into a state of complete dissonance. Sméagol's own mind is nearly entirely dominated by the Ring, so that he has nothing left in life but his desire for it. This transforms him into a pale shadow of his former self: thin and shrunken, living long past his natural lifespan, and shunning all light. Yet Sméagol is not *entirely* fallen, and a small bit of himself remains: "There was a little corner of his mind that was still his own, and light came through it, as through a chink in the dark: light out of the past."[93] This little corner of his mind is the last consonant part of his *musica humana*, and it asserts itself from time to time in *The Lord of the Rings*. Perhaps the most important instance, and certainly the most poignant, is when Sméagol is about to betray Frodo and Samwise, by leading them into the dark lair of Shelob to be captured and slaughtered. Sméagol observes the two hobbits sleeping peacefully, and for an instant his *musica humana* and theirs are attuned: "for a fleeting moment, could one of the sleepers have seen him, they would have thought that they beheld an old weary hobbit, shrunken by the years that had carried him far beyond his time, beyond friends and kin, and the fields and streams of youth, an old starved pitiable thing."[94] Sméagol gently touches Frodo's knee and almost repents his treachery, but the touch wakes Frodo, the suspicious Samwise snaps at Sméagol, and the moment is lost. However, there is a pungent irony, in that Sméagol's surrender to dissonance creates the conditions for the success of the quest. In order to destroy the Ring, it must be thrown into the volcanic mountain where Sauron crafted it, but upon arriving there, Frodo fails and claims the Ring for his own. Sméagol attacks Frodo and bites off his ring finger, and while reveling in triumph, trips and falls over the edge of the chasm, destroying the Ring forever. Knowing the quest would have been lost but for this betrayal, Frodo insists that they forgive Sméagol.

CONSONANT AND DISSONANT CHARACTERS—THE AINUR

The study of the musical natures of the members of the Ainur is a curious proposition, and it brings up issues not present with other created races in Tolkien's world. As creatures who create the material universe through music, the Ainur can be thought of as incarnations of *musica mundana* itself. At the same time, they are beings with their own wills and personalities who live in community with one another, and thus possess a distinct *musica humana*. Lastly, their creative power is expressed through real, audible music, so they have a high degree of *musica instrumentalis* as well.[95] In a way, to be a member of the Ainur is to exist as a simultaneous personification of all three kinds of *musica*. Often, however, one or another of these transcend the others in accounts and stories, especially in the case of *musica instrumentalis*. Examples of this include Yavanna's song that causes the two trees to grow in Valinor, the fact that one of Manwë's gifts to created beings is song and poetry,[96] and that the beautiful voice of Melian teaches the nightingales in Valinor to sing.[97] It is natural that the Ainur often sing audibly: "having participated in the Great Music, [they] express themselves through music [. . .], for it is essential to the very nature of these divine beings."[98]

The Ainur are intrinsically *consonant* creatures, having the ability to encourage consonance on one hand, and to "cure" or counteract dissonance on the other—this is, ultimately, Frodo's hope in traveling to Valinor. Ulmo performs this function in a general way, as he presides over water and its echo of the music in the oceans, lakes, rivers, and streams, which awakens a desire for light and music among the Children of Ilúvatar. Olórin, among the wisest of the members of the angelic orders, and who is later incarnated as the beloved wizard Gandalf, is "the friend of all the Children of Ilúvatar, and [takes] pity on their sorrows; and those who [listen] to him [awake] from despair and put away the imaginations of darkness."[99] The music of the Ainur even gives musical ability to otherwise non-sentient growing things, as Yavanna explains to Manwë: "While thou wert in the heavens and with Ulmo built the clouds and poured out the rains, I lifted up the branches of great trees to receive them, and some sang to Ilúvatar amid the wind and the rain."[100]

Like consonance, any dissonance made by the Ainur can influence and be transferred to other beings. This is clear in all the works of Melkor and his followers, particularly their attempts to corrupt and twist what was previously pure and whole. Melkor especially hates the sea and the constant echo of the music, and he attempts to entice Ossë—a vassal of Ulmo, and in charge of waves and sea storms—into his service, promising him Ulmo's authority over the entire ocean. Ossë joins Melkor for a period of time, creating huge storms and damaging waves, but his spouse, Uinen—protector of sea creatures and plants—calms him, convincing him to return his allegiance to Ulmo.[101] Given the correspondence between music and light in Tolkien's world, it is understandable that Melkor hates light, choosing rather to commit his worst deeds under cover of darkness, as we saw in his killing of the trees and the theft of the Silmarils. The member of the Ainur most associated with light is Varda, the ruler of the stars and celestial bodies, who earns the special hatred of Melkor. Because the light of Eru perpetually shines from Varda's face, she has particularly penetrating vision, not only of physical bodies but also of the internal character of created beings, even the Ainur. She detects the darkness and dissonance within Melkor even *before* the music begins, and rejects him at even that early point. Thus, Melkor fears and hates her more than any other member of the Ainur.[102]

CREATOR AND CREATION

Though each of the Ainur has his or her province or element, over which they exercise authority, their power is not limitless or inexhaustible. For instance, after Melkor and Ungoliant destroy the two trees, Yavanna cannot simply sing them back to life or create new ones to replace them. The creation of the trees is something that can be done only once, and when they are gone their beauty disappears from the world forever. The case is similar with the three Silmarils crafted by the elven prince Fëanor, who knows that he can never make anything like them again, which explains his unquenchable wrath after

Melkor steals them.[103] Such limitations on power are not restricted to the more consonant members of the Ainur and the Children, but are rather more pronounced among Melkor and his servants. The power of the music and the beauty of the material universe exist because the Ainur put forth their natural abilities in cooperation, as those living in harmonious *musica humana* should do. As shown during the music itself, and in many subsequent dissonant acts, Melkor is not interested in this kind of consonance, rather, he uses his power to dominate, subsume, and consume the music and creative power of others. In short, he spends his power only on himself, but does not grow in power or ability as a result—in fact, quite the opposite.

Just as a single instrumentalist ruins the balance of a music ensemble by loudly drowning out the other members, so Melkor partially spoils the larger effect of the music by blasting out his own themes without regard for his fellow creators. Much of Melkor's own native power is consumed through such attempts at domination and control. By refusing to engage in the part of *musica humana* that works in harmony and community with others, he also sacrifices the part of *musica humana* that regulates the balance of elements within himself. The final result is a permanent diminishing of *all* parts of his *musica*, and ultimately his creative power. Similarly, Melkor's most powerful servant and successor, Sauron, forges the Ring to give himself the ability to dominate the minds of others. In order to exercise this ability, he transfers a large amount of his own power into the Ring, which greatly diminishes the power at his disposal when separated from it. This works much to the advantage of the free peoples of the world, who are thus able to survive due to Sauron's reduced power until the Ring can be destroyed. When Frodo and Samwise—with the accidental assistance of Sméagol—achieve the destruction of the Ring, Sauron is forever weakened to the point he can no longer exercise effective control or influence over others, and his power is ended.

As with Melkor and Sauron, one of the consequences for members of the Ainur and the Children who use their power to create, is that some of their power remains *within* their creations, whether a living creature or an object. Yavanna cannot recreate the trees, Fëanor cannot remake the Silmarils, and Sauron cannot remake the Ring, because they have used up a measure of their own power in the making. Sometimes, the fate of the maker and the fate of the creation are intertwined. Fëanor understands this, and when he is asked to break the Silmarils in the hope that their trapped light will revive the dead trees, he says, "If I must break them, I shall break my heart, and I shall be slain."[104] Sauron also understands this and puts forth all of his evil will—and the will of his most deadly servants—toward the single object of regaining the Ring, knowing that he will be forever diminished if it is destroyed. This concept of the connected fates of creator and creation is illustrated in a story Tolkien tells about a member of the race of men known as the Drúedain. Shorter and broader than other kinds of men, they have a number of powers, among them the ability to sit or stand still for hours or days at a time, so that anyone passing by might mistake them for carved statues. The Drúedain do, however, see and remember all that passes near them, and are highly sought after as guards. They are also skilled in carving images in stone, and make life-sized effigies of themselves to place as markers or as warnings to enemies, who believe that the power of the Drúedain is retained within the images. Such is the case with Aghan, a member of the Drúedain who lives near his friend Barach and family, keeping watch over their house at night. Evil creatures have been abroad in the area, and Barach and his family are dismayed when Aghan must leave them for a time. However, Aghan has a stone image brought and placed near the house. One night, Barach is awakened by the sound of orcs attempting to set fire to his house, and he prepares to fight them. Before he can do anything, a figure runs up, kills or disables the orcs, and stamps out the fire before disappearing. When Aghan returns, he searches the area and finds his carved image, sitting on a dead orc some distance away, with its legs blackened and burned, and a foot broken off. He then tells Barach, "Ah well! He did what he could. And better that his legs should trample Orc-fire than mine." Aghan shows Barach his own feet, which are blistered and bandaged, showing signs of having been burned just as those of the image. "Alas!" he said, "If some power passes from you to a thing that you have made, then you must take a share in its hurts."[105] This symbiotic relationship between creator and creation is a common theme throughout the works of Tolkien.

MUSIC OF HEALING AND RE-CREATION—MAIOR PERFECTUM AND THE FELIX PECCATUM ADAE

We examined the concept of the *maior perfectum* as an expansion of the capacity for perfection in medieval music treatises and theological works in chapter 1, as well as in Dante's journey through the heavenly spheres in chapter 2. The worlds of Tolkien and Lewis include new and novel illustrations of this concept. Ultimately, the authors' use of *maior perfectum* attempts to answer the question of why evil, death, and decay are allowed to exist in these created worlds—as well as in our own.

Lewis treads a thought-provoking path between two opposing points. On one hand, Lewis characterizes the fall into sin as a net negative, bringing pain and death, while on the other hand, he admits that the fall is an event that ultimately produces more good than evil. In the second book of *The Space Trilogy*, *Perelandra*, the protagonist Ransom is sent to the planet Venus, with the mission of preventing the newly created humans there from succumbing to temptation and falling into sin. However, the tempter in Venus is subtle—he is the Satan from *this* world, after all—and uses an argument designed to convince both the Venusian Eve and Ransom himself that breaking God's law is actually *better* than obedience.[106] The tempter uses the concept of *Felix peccatum Adae*, the "blessed sin of Adam," as mentioned in chapter 1. This doctrine argues that, because Christ came to Earth and became human, He created a unique bond between Himself and humanity, and so it was ultimately *better* for sin to have entered the world, than for this bond never to have been created. Without sin, there would have been no salvation *from* sin, and no greater good—no *maior perfectum*. In *Perelandra*, this is a very strong argument, as Ransom himself largely agrees with the doctrine. It is also partially true, at least on that particular world, as one of the angelic creatures confirms after temptation is resisted, and no fall takes place on Venus:

> It was never seen before. Because it did not happen [on Earth] a greater thing happened, but not this. Because the greater thing happened [on Earth], this and not the greater thing happens here [on Venus].[107]

This "greater thing" referred to is the coming of Christ to Earth to sacrifice himself, which will now not happen on Venus. Should the lack of a fall into sin on Venus then be considered negatively, since the plan of—indeed, the need *for*—salvation never occurs? Lewis answers this question from the mouths of both Ransom and the angelic creatures. In this passage, Ransom is responding to the tempter, who has suggested that good ultimately came of sin on Earth:

> Of course good came of it. Is [God] a beast that we can stop His path, or a leaf that we can twist His shape? Whatever you do, He will make good of it. But not the good He had prepared for you if you had obeyed Him. That is lost for ever. The first King [Adam] and first Mother [Eve] of our world did the forbidden thing; and He brought good of it in the end. But what they did was not good; and what they lost we have not seen. And there were some to whom no good came nor ever will come.[108]

Lewis, through Ransom, threads a conceptual needle, asserting that salvation did indeed happen on Earth, which was a great thing, but also that God's original plan was lost forever, and many creatures lost as well. Later in the story, one of the angelic creatures contributes to Ransom's argument: "For though the healing what was wounded and the straightening what was bent is a new dimension of glory, yet the straight was not made that it might be bent nor the whole that it might be wounded."[109] The angel confirms that, while the healing of harm is a glorious thing, the worlds and the creatures inhabiting them were not created be harmed, in order that they might then be healed.

In some ways, Tolkien's view of the *maior perfectum* agrees with that of Lewis, and in other ways it contrasts, but like the rest of Tolkien's legendarium it is intimately concerned with music. It is important to remember that some parts of the music of the Ainur, such as the rise of the Children of Ilúvatar, are known only to Eru, and are not fully comprehended by any of his created beings. Not only is the completeness of the music hidden, even the seeming discords are conceived by Eru as part of the whole. After the music has finished, he tells the dissonant Melkor:

> And thou, Melkor, shalt see that no theme may be played that hath not its uttermost source in me, nor can any alter the music in my despite. For he that attempteth this shall prove but mine instrument in the devising of things more wonderful, which he himself hath not imagined.[110]

Another passage supporting Tolkien's acceptance of the *Felix peccatum Adae* is a conversation between Eru and Ulmo, the Lord of Waters. While the rest of the Ainur enter the newly created world to take up the elements and provinces assigned them, Melkor comes to meddle with and destroy all they create. Noting this, Eru speaks to Ulmo:

> Seest thou not how here in this little realm in the Deeps of Time Melkor hath made war upon thy province? He hath bethought him of bitter cold immoderate, and yet hath not destroyed the beauty of thy fountains, nor of thy clear pools. Behold the snow, and the cunning work of frost! Melkor hath devised heats and fire without restraint, and hath not dried up thy desire nor utterly quelled the music of the sea. Behold rather the height and glory of the clouds, and the everchanging mists; and listen to the fall of rain upon the Earth![111]

Ulmo's answer confirms Eru's explanation:

> Truly, Water is become now fairer than my heart imagined, neither had my secret thought conceived the snowflake, nor in all my music was contained the falling of the rain.[112]

Melkor's violence in Ulmo's province of water definitively creates things of beauty that are "more wonderful, which he himself hath not imagined." Michael Cunningham notes that in his conflict with the rest of the Ainur, Melkor unwittingly supports Eru's purpose:

> The natural elements of fire, ice and storm were now resident in the world and in constant friction; through their collisions destructive forces were unleashed yet these very forces would also have been creative through their fury; a chaotic landscape of destruction and regeneration.[113]

Keith W. Jensen puts it another way when hypothesizes what Tolkien's created world would be like without Melkor's dissonance:

> Yes, Melkor is evil, and does evil things to mar the world, but the world wouldn't be what it becomes without it. Arda [the earth] would be beautiful and carefree, almost Eden-like, but there would be no growth and no reason to grow. Life would be boring.[114]

While the idea that the Earth would be a boring place if not subject to death and decay is somewhat debatable,[115] it is clear that the Earth becomes what it is through Melkor's dissonance, and this is part of Eru's plan for the world. Reuven Naveh makes the following provocative statement in support of this concept: "Evil is not a deviation from perfection but part of it, and it has a role in the divine activity."[116] Validation of this statement comes from the mouth of Manwë himself, during a time in which many elves are forsaking Valinor in order to pursue Melkor in an attempt to regain the Silmarils: "Thus even as Eru spoke to us shall beauty not before conceived be brought into [the world], and evil yet good to have been."[117]

Cunningham's use of the world "regeneration" above is serendipitous, as it speaks to the idea of growth after decay, or of life after death. Ultimately the question remains: How are wrongs righted, and the wounded made whole, in the worlds of Tolkien and Lewis? In *The Space Trilogy*, Lewis speaks of the fundamental difference between unfallen Venus and fallen Earth. The Venusian Adam describes his planet's resistance to temptation as a *beginning*, while the fall into sin on Earth was "a failure to begin."[118] After the true beginning, God's purposes for the planets and their resident creatures can *begin* to be realized. However, this is not a waiting for, or a delay in the consummation of, perfection. One of the angels tells Ransom that the concept of heaven—called the Great Dance—does not require the participation of the planet-bound creatures to make it perfect. It has *always* been perfect, but it is clear that the addition of planetary creatures will increase its *capacity* for perfection—a *maior perfectum*. Lewis echoes this sentiment at the end of the final book in *The Chronicles of Narnia*, where he describes the experience of heaven—Aslan's Country—for those who enter:

> But for them it was only the beginning of the real story. All their life in this world and all their adventures in Narnia had only been the cover and the title page: now at last they were beginning Chapter One of the Great Story which no one on earth has read: which goes on for ever: in which every chapter is better than the one before.[119]

For the children who have visited Narnia, all their lives in their own world, and all their visits to Narnia, do not even amount to a beginning. The different universes they have experienced are only pale reflections, what Lewis calls "shadowlands," in comparison with the "real countries" that exist within Aslan's Country.

In Tolkien's legendarium, it is not clear if the end of the world includes a restoration, which would render the pain and sorrow of previous existence moot and unworthy of remembrance. Eru takes Melkor's loudest and most brazen dissonances and weaves them into his own theme, but this may seem a mere "patching up" of what has already been sullied and stained. For Tolkien, the remedy is a second music at the "end of days." This music will be creative, like the original music, but will include not only the Ainur, but also the Children of Ilúvatar. Here, the musical themes will be played correctly, without dissonance, and rather than being reflections of things to be made at some point in the future, the creative ideas will come to immediate and full fruition. This time, all of the singers will be perfectly attuned in their *musica humana*—knowing perfectly their own parts in the music, as well as the parts of all the others. Consonance will not merely prevail over dissonance—dissonance will not even begin or be conceived of. The result of this perfect *musica humana* will be a *musica mundana* that is not only perfect, but *more* than perfect—another *maior perfectum*—and an eternal paradise for all.

NOTES

1. Genesis 1:3 (KJV).
2. John Milton, *Paradise Lost* (London: Suttaby, Evance & Fox, 1812), 164.
3. I will stretch the concept of *musica humana* somewhat in this chapter, as the created worlds of Tolkien and Lewis are filled with creatures that are not human, but nonetheless possess human characteristics. Whether they are angelic creatures, races of immortal elves, dwarves, or anthropomorphized animals, all are written well within a "human" purview, and can be analyzed in terms of *musica humana*.
4. This was the sixth book to be published, but is the earliest story in the Narnian chronology.
5. Though Lewis does not name the hymn in *The Magician's Nephew*, I feel fairly confident that he is referring to the popular hymn, "Come, Ye Thankful People, Come," written by English clergyman Henry Alford in 1844. The first stanza is as follows:

> Come, ye thankful people, come,
> Raise the song of Harvest-home!
> All is safely gather'd in,

Ere the winter storms begin:
God our Maker doth provide
For our wants to be supplied:—
Come to God's own temple, come,
Raise the song of Harvest-home!

    Henry Alford, *Psalms and Hymns* (London: Francis & John Rivington, 1844), 147.

    6. Lewis, *The Magician's Nephew*, 108–9. I like to imagine this moment as somewhat similar to the musical depiction of the first sunrise during the biblical third day of creation in Joseph Haydn's 1799 oratorio *The Creation*. Haydn's setting of this scene is one of the great musically descriptive moments in Western music.

    7. Lewis, *The Magician's Nephew*, 112–13.

    8. John Milton, *Paradise Lost* (Minneapolis: First Avenue Editions, 1984), 176–7.

    9. Lewis, *The Magician's Nephew*, 122–3.

    10. More will be said about Jadis and her background in chapter 6.

    11. Lewis, *The Magician's Nephew*, 148.

    12. Ibid.

    13. This name, in one of the languages devised by Tolkien, means "he who is alone, the father of all."

    14. Readers familiar with Tolkien's works may know that the members of the Ainur who enter the created world become known as *Valar* and *Maiar*. To avoid confusion for those not initiated into the deeper levels of Tolkien esoterica, I will retain the use of Ainur throughout.

    15. J.R.R. Tolkien, *The Silmarillion* (Boston and New York: Houghton Mifflin Company, 1998), 15.

    16. Ibid.

    17. Sam McBride, *Tolkien's Cosmology: Divine Beings and Middle-earth* (Kent, OH: The Kent State University Press, 2020), 7.

    18. Tolkien, *The Silmarillion*, 16–17.

    19. Ibid., 17–18.

    20. Ibid., 20. When the Ainur go down into the world, they become Eru's vice-regents, as Eru himself rarely interferes or intervenes. The Ainur's practical position is similar to that of the ancient Greek or Norse gods, and some of the Children of Illúvatar, especially Men, (mistakenly) worship them instead of Eru. Sam McBride describes this reality as "polytheistic monotheism." McBride, *Tolkien's Cosmology*, 10–16.

    21. Tolkien, *The Silmarillion*, 20.

    22. Ibid., 22.

    23. Ibid., 15.

    24. Ibid.

    25. Chiara Bertoglio, "Polyphony, Collective Improvisation, and the Gift of Creation," in Julian Eilmann and Friedhelm Scheidewind, eds., *Music in Tolkien's Work and Beyond* (Zurich and Jena: Walking Tree Publishers, 2019), 23.

    26. Ibid.

27. Sadly, Melkor could have had both, like the rest of the Ainur. However, his selfishness and pride cause him to value the individually focused *musica instrumentalis* over the collective *musica humana*. Ultimately, he retains neither.

28. Verlyn Flieger, *Splintered Light*, rev. ed. (Kent and London: The Kent University Press, 2002), 127.

29. Ibid., 58.

30. Ibid., 109.

31. Tolkien, *The Silmarillion*, 49.

32. Ibid., 41.

33. Verlyn Flieger, *Interrupted Music* (Kent and London: The Kent University Press, 2005), xiii.

34. Tolkien, *The Silmarillion*, 45–6.

35. Ibid., 43.

36. As Sam McBride notes, Eru's question, "Is that thy desire?" is not entirely rhetorical. McBride, *Tolkien's Cosmology*, 150. Were the same question asked of Melkor, he would likely be *very* interested in beings that he could dominate, and that had no will but his own. We see throughout the legendarium that Melkor, as well as his successor Sauron, exercise mental control over large numbers of their servants and slaves, and who are left witless when that control is loosened or broken.

37. Tolkien, *The Silmarillion*, 43.

38. Ibid., 44.

39. Ibid.

40. I want to acknowledge my former student Isabel Serrano, who mentioned in a music history paper that an action by a character in a certain opera was "an atonal thing to do." This planted the seed in my mind that dissonance does not only refer to states of being, but can define actions as well.

41. Flieger, *Splintered Light*, 109.

42. Keith W. Jensen, "Dissonance in the Divine Theme: The Issue of Free Will in Tolkien's *Silmarillion*," in Bradford Lee Eden, ed., *Middle-earth Minstrel: Essays on Music in Tolkien* (Jefferson, NC and London: McFarland & Company, Inc., Publishers, 2010), 104.

43. Tolkien, *The Silmarillion*, 17.

44. Ibid, 50.

45. This seems to be the common *initial* reaction to water for all creatures inhabiting the earth, from the most powerful angelic spirit to the humblest hobbit.

46. Tolkien, *The Silmarillion*, 19.

47. Ibid., 49.

48. Ibid., 57.

49. Elizabeth A. Whittingham, "The Power of Music and Song in Tolkien's Legendarium," in Eilmann and Scheidewind ed., *Music in Tolkien's Work and Beyond*, 148.

50. J. R. R. Tolkien, *Unfinished Tales of Númenor and Middle-Earth* (New York: Ballentine Books, 1980), 22–3.

51. Ibid., 27.

52. Tolkien, *The Silmarillion*, 238.
53. J. R. R. Tolkien, *The Fellowship of the Ring* (Boston and New York: Houghton Mifflin, 2002), 7.
54. Tolkien, *The Silmarillion*, 26–7.
55. Ibid., 103–4.
56. Flieger, *Splintered Light*, 99.
57. J. R. R. Tolkien, *The Two Towers* (Boston and New York: Houghton Mifflin, 2002), 507.
58. J. R. R. Tolkien, *The Return of the King* (Boston and New York: Houghton Mifflin, 2002), 885.
59. Ibid., 999.
60. Tolkien, *The Fellowship of the Ring*, 234.
61. Ibid., 340.
62. The sea separates the mortal realm of Middle-earth from the Undying Lands of Valinor, and Frodo eventually makes the journey over this sea in search of healing. The relationship between Middle-earth and Valinor will be explored further in chapter 6.
63. Tolkien, *The Silmarillion*, 120.
64. John Gardner, "The World of Tolkien," *New York Times Book Review* (October 23, 1977), quoted in Flieger, *Splintered Light*, xviii.
65. Tolkien, *The Silmarillion*, 31. Darkness is not always associated with fear and danger. For many ages, most elves lived in a Middle-earth under perpetual starlight, before the appearance of the sun or the moon. When the hobbits meet the ancient and enigmatic Tom Bombadil, he tells them that he "knew the dark under the stars when it was fearless." Tolkien, *The Fellowship of the Ring*, 132.
66. Milton, *Paradise Lost*, 170.
67. Ibid., 38. Ovid describes this primordial chaos as "strife," in which "nothing had any lasting shape, but everything got in the way of everything else . . . cold warred with hot, moist with dry, soft with hard, and light with heavy." Innes, *The Metamorphoses of Ovid*, 29.
68. Milton, *Paradise Lost*, 149.
69. Melkor's journeys within the void certainly have the effect, intended or not, of mistuning his *musica humana*, as he undertakes these journeys alone, "neglect[ing] the comradeship of the Ainur." McBride, *Tolkien's Cosmology*, 7.
70. Sauron is Melkor's chief lieutenant, and becomes the new "dark lord" after his master's eventual defeat.
71. Christine Chism, "Middle-earth, the Middle Ages, and the Aryan nation: Myth and history in World War II" in Jane Chance, ed., *Tolkien the Medievalist* (New York: Routledge, 2003), 80.
72. Tolkien, *The Fellowship of the Ring*, 367.
73. Gandalf is actually a member of the Ainur, but appears in Middle-earth as an elderly wizard.
74. Tolkien, *The Return of the King*, 838.
75. Tolkien, *The Silmarillion*, 254.
76. Ibid., 73.

77. Ibid., 74.
78. Ibid., 76.
79. Ibid., 76–7.
80. Tolkien, *The Two Towers*, 725.
81. Ibid., 729.
82. Tolkien, *The Silmarillion*, 38.
83. Tolkien, *The Fellowship of the Ring*, 379.
84. Flieger, *Interrupted Music*, 141.
85. Flieger, *Splintered Light*, 150.
86. Tolkien, *The Fellowship of the Ring*, 223.
87. Tolkien, *The Return of the King*, 947.
88. Ibid., 948.
89. This was the case with both Sméagol and Frodo's uncle Bilbo, both of whom possessed—or were possessed *by*—the Ring for many years. It was not safe for either of them to see the Ring, or be in close proximity to it.
90. Tolkien, *The Return of the King*, 987.
91. Flieger, *Interrupted Music*, 14. Flieger notes that Frodo is suffering from a textbook case of post-traumatic stress disorder, something that Tolkien, a veteran of World War I who lost many close friends in the fighting, would have understood only too well.
92. Tolkien, *The Return of the King*, 1036.
93. Tolkien, *The Fellowship of the Ring*, 54.
94. Tolkien, *The Two Towers*, 722.
95. Sam McBride notes that the Music of the Ainur takes place before material creation, and before the creation of time, both of which are necessary for music as we experience it to exist. McBride, *Tolkien's Cosmology*, 5. I agree with McBride that these essential elements are indeed missing, but will add that whatever physical or temporal realities may have existed—or not—the music is described by Tolkien in terms both audible and temporal. Though it is entirely possible, and even probable, that Tolkien intended the story of the music to be taken allegorically, I will accept the literal reading if for no other reason than it better supports my own argument.
96. Tolkien, *The Silmarillion*, 40.
97. Ibid., 55.
98. Whittingham, "The Power of Music and Song in Tolkien's Legendarium," 144.
99. Tolkien, *The Silmarillion*, 31.
100. Ibid., 45–6.
101. Ossë does again submit himself to Ulmo, but his love for storms remains, and sailors often call upon the assistance of Uinen to restrain his violence. As for Ossë himself, the Children hold him in reverence; however, "those who dwell by the sea or go up in ships may love him, but they do not trust him." Ibid., 30.
102. Ibid., 26.
103. Ibid., 78.
104. Ibid., 78.
105. Tolkien, *Unfinished Tales*, 393–8.

106. Lewis, *Perelandra*, 103–4.
107. Ibid., 169.
108. Ibid., 104.
109. Ibid., 184.
110. Tolkien, *The Silmarillion*, 17. A similar passage from Milton's *Paradise Lost* belongs here, where the demons of Hell are plotting destruction in the newly created Earth, and the new race of men:

> So deep a malice, to confound the race
> Of mankind in one root, and Earth with Hell
> To mingle and involve, done all to spite
> The great Creator? But their spite still serves
> His glory to augment.

    Milton, *Paradise Lost*, 36.

111. Tolkien, *The Silmarillion*, 19.
112. Ibid.
113. Michael Cunningham, "An Impenetrable Darkness: An Examination of the Influence of J.R.R. Tolkien on Black Metal Music," in Heidi Steimel and Friedhelm Schneidewind, eds., *Music in Middle-earth* (Zurich and Jena: Walking Tree Publishers, 2010), 217.
114. Jensen, "Dissonance in the Divine Theme," 106.
115. I, for one, would welcome the ability to live—on a strictly trial basis—in such a perfect world for a few millennia.
116. Reuven Naveh, "Tonality, Atonality and the Ainulindalë," in Steimel and Schneidewind ed., *Music in Middle-earth*, 39.
117. Tolkien, *The Silmarillion*, 98.
118. Lewis, *Perelandra*, 182.
119. Lewis, *The Last Battle*, 210–11.

Chapter Vignette 3.5

Powerful Music

Horns, Trumpets, Voices, and Other Magical Instruments in Tolkien and Lewis

The trumpet shall be heard on high,
The dead shall live, the living die,
And Musick shall untune the sky.[1]

In the previous chapter, we examined the music of the Ainur, and other accounts of creative music in terms of singing. We have not as yet treated the sounds of musical instruments, or of voices used in other than creative capacities. Some of this music will be epic in scale and scope, but there will also be much to say about individuals and their own voices and instruments. These latter cases are no less meaningful or magical, but operate at more personal and local levels. We will look at the magical properties of various instruments and voices, their power to transport the hearer, tempt the listener, and even break the wheel of fate.

POWERFUL TRUMPETS AND HORNS

Trumpets and horns have a long history of use in military and signaling contexts, due to their portability and large volume of sound. In the Western imagination, including in the works of C. S. Lewis and J. R. R. Tolkien, there are many such instruments that possess both earthly and cosmic powers. References to these instruments are found in the Bible: trumpets signal to Moses and the Israelites that God is ready to speak to them from Mount Sinai, trumpets are used to inaugurate important religious festivals, the noise of trumpets and shouting voices causes the walls of Jericho to collapse, seven angels are given trumpets to signal disasters and plagues, and the sound of a trumpet causes the dead to wake at the second coming of Christ at the end of the world. John Dryden, in his 1687 poem *A Song for St. Cecilia's Day*, describes the force of this final trumpet:

So, when the last and dreadful hour
This crumbling pageant shall devour,
The trumpet shall be heard on high,
The dead shall live, the living die,
And Musick shall untune the sky.[2]

The power of the last trumpet is not to be underestimated, as it has the ability to wake the dead, and to destroy the very fabric of nature and the cosmos. A similar "untuning" of the sky exists in Lewis' world of Narnia. Just as Narnia is created through Aslan's singing, so also music signals the end of that world. In *The Last Battle*, the seventh and final book of *The Chronicles of Narnia*, the children, who at various times have visited that land, find themselves in Aslan's Country, next to a closed door leading back into Narnia.[3] Aslan arrives and shouts "Time!" at the door, which flies open, revealing a starlit night beyond, in stark contrast to the broad daylight in which they are standing. At length the children observe the silhouette of a huge figure against a background of stars: the outline of the giant Father Time. Two of the children, Eustace and Jill, had seen him sleeping in a cave deep underground during a previous visit to Narnia, and were told that Father Time would awake at the end of the world. The children see the giant raise a horn to his lips, and then hear the blast, "high and terrible, yet of a strange, deadly beauty." Immediately the stars begin falling to the earth, until the sky becomes a dark and empty void. All the creatures of Narnia rush in a mass toward the door,[4] great beasts arrive to tear up and destroy the trees and vegetation, and a great wave covers the land with water. The sun and the moon rise together and collide, Father Time reaches out his hand and squeezes them, and all light goes out. Finally, the door is shut and Narnia is no more.[5] All of the destruction, the "untuning," not only of the sky, but of the entire universe of Narnia—its *musica mundana*—is initiated by the music of Father Time's great horn.

This destructive blast is not the last time we hear a horn in the story. The children explore the land around them, and discover that it is actually the *true* Narnia. All that was good has come through the door leading from the old Narnia, and lives forever and uncorrupted in the true Narnia in Aslan's Country. At length, the children approach a hilltop garden, surrounded by high walls and a golden gate. They hesitate, feeling that such a solemn and beautiful place cannot be intended for such as *them* to enjoy. However, they hear another horn, "wonderfully loud and sweet," which signals the gate to open and let them into the garden, where they meet the friends they have made in Narnia during their many visits over the years. This juxtaposition of Father Time's horn with the one heard in Aslan's Country is significant, given that only a few pages separate the two accounts in *The Last Battle*. The first horn is one of destruction, signaling the *shutting* of the door to an entire universe. In contrast, the second horn *opens* the door into a new world and a higher mode of existence, where there is no longer any death, decay, or sorrow.[6]

There are also horns with various powers and functions in Tolkien's legendarium. Ulmo, the Lord of Waters, plays on a set of horns made from white shells. At times he plays them on lonely seashores, and at others he travels along inlets of the ocean, and anyone who hears the music of his horns are forever drawn to the sea.[7] Oromë, the Huntsman of the Ainur, also uses a horn, the sound of which is compared to the rising of the sun, or of lightning splitting the clouds. The blast of this horn acts as a signal to Oromë's followers to hunt and destroy the servants of Melkor.[8] Its sound causes all evil creatures and spirits to flee, and even Melkor himself cowers in fear at its sound.[9] However, as we observed in the previous chapter, Oromë's horn is not omnipotent. When Melkor and Ungoliant flee Valinor after having killed the two trees and stolen the Silmarils, Oromë and other members of the Ainur pursue them, but upon entering the dark void of Ungoliant, they are blinded, and the sound of the horn falters and fails.

MUSIC OF TRANSPORT

The horns and trumpets above have power to tear the heavens apart, or to encourage good creatures, while striking fear into evil ones. Other instruments—and voices—possess different powers, among them the ability transport the minds and imaginations of hearers to other places, or even other times. The horns of Ulmo, besides having power to inspire sea-longing, can also prompt visions beyond mortal experience, and such is the experience of the human hero Tuor. He is summoned by Ulmo to the shore to be given an important mission, and as a storm rages around him, the Lord of Waters blows a single, long note:

> And as heard that note, and was encompassed by it, and filled with it, it seemed to Tuor that the coasts of Middle-earth vanished, and he surveyed all the waters of the world in a great vision: from the veins of the lands to the mouths of the rivers, and from the strands and estuaries out into the deep. The Great Sea he saw through its unquiet regions teeming with strange forms, even to its lightless depths, in which amid the everlasting darkness there echoed voices terrible to mortal ears. Its measureless plains he surveyed with the swift sight of the [Ainur] [. . .], until remote upon the edge of sight, and beyond

the count of leagues, he glimpsed a mountain, rising beyond his mind's reach into a shining cloud, and at its feet a long surf glimmering. And even as he strained to hear the sound of those far waves, and to see clearer that distant light, the note ended, and he stood beneath the thunder of the storm, and lightning many-branched rent asunder the heavens above him. And Ulmo was gone . . .[10]

Through the power of Ulmo's horn, Tuor is given a brief moment of vision as it is experienced by the Ainur.[11] He observes the depth and breadth of Ulmo's ocean province, filled with unnamed creatures, and finally catches a glimpse of a towering peak, the mountain in Valinor from which Manwë and Varda rule the skies and stars. This power of music to transport hearers occurs in many other places in the worlds of Tolkien and Lewis, although the medium through which it is accomplished is most often the sound of a voice in song.

One such incidence occurs when the elven king Finrod, journeying alone at night, hears singing in the woods. Not recognizing the language of the singers, he waits until they are asleep before approaching them. This is the first time that elves from Valinor encounter the race of men. Finrod goes down among the sleeping forms, picks up a simple harp that had been laid aside by one of them, and begins to play and sing. The men awake, feeling that they are in some kind of dream, because of the beauty and power of the music. Finrod's song brings unbidden to their eyes visions of the making of the world, and the splendor and beauty of Valinor. Though they do not understand Finrod's elven language, the power of the music opens their minds, showing images of things they have never before experienced, and allowing them to receive new wisdom.[12] Here, music transports the listeners with visions of other places, back in time even to creation, while expanding their capacity for wisdom and learning.

Another example involves the elven queen Galadriel, who sings as Frodo and his companions depart her magical land of Lórien. Though the words of her song are in an ancient elvish language, they remain forever "graven" in Frodo's memory, so that he later remembers and translates them, allowing him to share in the images of Galadriel's imagination.[13] The land of Lórien itself is a very musical place—full of singing minstrels with harps—but there is something about the land itself, apart from the more obvious instances of *musica instrumentalis*. Samwise puts it very succinctly when he exclaims to Frodo, "I feel as if I was *inside* a song."[14] Perhaps he is, for Lórien is a time capsule of sorts, where sights and sounds are experienced that should be impossible, as in a living dream:

> Frodo stood still, hearing far off great seas upon beaches that had long ago been washed away, and sea-birds crying whose race had perished from the earth.[15]

Not only is Frodo able to hear what no longer exists, his very presence in this enchanted land is enough to make him a permanent part of its living history:

> Though he walked and breathed, and about him living leaves and flowers were stirred by the same cool wind as fanned his face, Frodo felt that he was in a timeless land that did not fade or change or fall into forgetfulness. When he had gone and passed again into the outer world, still Frodo the wanderer from the Shire would walk there, upon the grass among *elanor* and *niphredil* in fair Lothlórien.[16]

In Lórien, a magical power prevents death and decay, or change of *any* kind, so that the land is frozen at a nearly perfect point in time.[17] Lórien enjoys an endless moment of perfect *musica mundana*, where visitors may experience a strengthening or tuning of their own *musica humana*.[18]

Frodo and his hobbit companions encounter another, even more powerful singer early in their adventures—the mysterious and strange Tom Bombadil. Though Tom appears to be a merry and cheerful human of some kind, he is identified by the immortal elves as "Eldest," the most ancient being in the world. His language is unique: he sings as much as he speaks, and his talk is full of playful rhymes and nonsense syllables. While spending a few days in his house, this musical language of Tom's rubs off on the hobbits, who find themselves "suddenly aware that they [are] singing merrily, as if it [is] easier and more natural than talking."[19] Later, Tom teaches them all about the lives of the plants and animals in the woods, and his songs transport them far afield as well as far back in history, to the ages before the sun and the moon were created, when only the stars shone in the sky. The hobbits feel as if they are being enchanted by these musical tales, and many hours or days pass unnoticed while listening to them.

Something of the same kind happens to Frodo's uncle Bilbo in *The Hobbit*. Thirteen dwarves and the wizard Gandalf visit Bilbo's home to convince him to join them on an adventure, and while there, the dwarves begin to sing and play various instruments. This dwarvish music is powerful, so much so that Bilbo forgets his fear, "and [is] swept away into dark lands under strange moons."[20] This vision, prompted by music, together with a certain amount of prodding from Gandalf, eventually convinces Bilbo to undertake the journey.

Finally, a poignant and beautiful example of the power of music to transport the listener comes from Lewis' *Out of the Silent Planet*, the first book in *The Space Trilogy*. Ransom is kidnapped by two other humans, and forcibly taken to Mars in a spacecraft. After escaping from them, he befriends many of the non-human inhabitants of the planet. On Mars, death exists, and is accepted as a natural part of life,[21] but it is not considered an event of great fear or sorrow, for the creatures know that death is simply a gateway into a higher plane of existence. When they die, Martians are taken to the angelic ruler of the planet, who releases their souls while others sing. Ransom observes one of these ceremonies, and when he hears the music, he perceives "great masses moving at visionary speeds, of giants dancing, of eternal sorrows eternally consoled." The words of the song speak of releasing the soul from the body, entering "the second life, the other beginning," and the music "[bows] down his spirit as if the gate of heaven had opened before him."[22] The music transports Ransom spiritually as he briefly sees the true structure of the universe, just as Dante sees the *musica mundana* from below and above in his own heavenly journey. It also transports the deceased being in a literal sense, separating the dead body from the living soul, and sending the soul onward into its next life.

MUSIC OF TEMPTATION AND EVIL

Though music is a tool of creation and destruction, and can impart wisdom and beatific visions to the hearer, it can also be used to tempt a hearer toward evil, to fatal inaction, or the denial of reality. Music can even be used as a weapon of offense or defense.

In Lewis' *The Silver Chair*, the children Jill and Eustace are on a journey to find and rescue the Narnian prince Rilian, who disappeared without a trace some years before. While traveling through desolate country, they encounter a beautiful lady dressed in green, who is ultimately the witch who kidnapped and enslaved the prince. Among her many powers, which include shapeshifting into the form of a huge green serpent, she can weave enchantments through music. When the children meet her, her voice is "as sweet as the sweetest bird's song," and when she laughs, it is "the richest, most musical laugh you can imagine."[23] Later, Jill and Eustace discover prince Rilian in a vast underground kingdom ruled by the witch, and they deliver him from the enchanted silver chair used to make him forget his identity and former life. They confront the witch, who quickly charms them with the aid of her sweet, musical voice, and with a mandolin that she steadily strums as she speaks. In a masterpiece of gaslighting, the witch proceeds to convince them that there is no Narnia, no England, no lands open to the sky, no sun, and no Aslan—indeed, nothing except her own dark underground realm. The companions agree that reality must be as the witch describes it, and only when she is killed are the effects of her deception undone.

Two episodes from *The Lord of the Rings* illustrate the connection of music to temptation, as well as resistance to and victory over evil. The first occurs as Frodo and his companions travel through the Old Forest, an ancient place full of dark and seemingly sentient trees, where paths curiously shift, and branches and roots seem to grasp at and trip up unsuspecting travelers. Frodo attempts to cheer up his companions with a song, but the hot, stifling air beneath the trees smothers his voice. Later, the hobbits enter a river valley filled with willow trees. As they pass beneath the shade of one particularly large willow, the hobbits suddenly feel an overwhelming urge to lie down and sleep. Two of them lie against the great trunk of the tree to rest, while Frodo hears "a gentle noise on the edge of hearing, a soft fluttering as of a song half whispered," before he too gives in to sleep. Samwise becomes suspicious, saying, "I don't like this great big tree. I don't trust it. Hark at it singing about sleep now! This won't do at all!" He turns around to see that the tree has pushed Frodo into the water, and is holding him down with one of its roots. Pulling him out, Samwise and Frodo notice that the trunk of the tree has closed over their other two companions, trapping them inside. Unable to help his friends and feeling utterly overwhelmed, Frodo runs back along the path, yelling for help, but a great wind rises and spreads through the forest, blowing away the sound of his voice in a massive rustling of willow leaves.[24] Fortunately for the hobbits, they meet Tom Bombadil dancing and singing along the pathway toward them. At the sound of Tom's voice, the wind immediately ceases, and the forest becomes still. Frodo and Samwise ask him for help to free their friends, and Tom identifies the tree, Old Man Willow, emphasizing his own musical power over it:

"What?" shouted Tom Bombadil, leaping up in the air. "Old Man Willow? Naught worse than that, eh? That can soon be mended. I know the tune for him. Old grey Willow-man! I'll freeze his marrow cold, if he don't behave himself. I'll sing his roots off. I'll sing a wind up and blow leaf and branch away. Old Man Willow!" [25]

Tom then sings to the tree in a low voice, and Old Man Willow relents and releases the trapped hobbits. After they are safe in Tom Bombadil's house, he tells them that Old Man Willow is an ancient, black-hearted tree, the most dangerous creature in the Old Forest. The tree is "a master of winds, and his song and thought [run] through the woods," until it holds nearly all of the trees in the forest under its control.[26] Old Man Willow's influence forced the hobbits to travel toward the focal point of his evil power, where they were tempted through song to lie down and sleep—assumedly forever—abandoning their quest. The old tree's actions were based on his implacable hatred of "things that go free upon the earth,"[27] and he uses the power of music to attack those he hates. Ultimately, however, he is no match for Tom Bombadil's more ancient and more powerful music, which, in the nature of *musica mundana*, seems to have influence over the weather, as well as the living things in the forest.

The second episode also features Tom Bombadil. After the events described above, the hobbits leave his house to continue their quest, and

Tom teaches them a song to sing, if they should happen to get into trouble as they travel over the grassy downs on the other side of the Old Forest. Many of these downs are topped by barrows: ancient tombs haunted by evil spirits. Cheerfully continuing their journey, the hobbits take a midday nap much longer than they intended, and find themselves trapped among the downs at night in a heavy fog. Becoming separated from the others in the dark, Frodo attempts to find his way, but ends up near a haunted barrow, where he is seized by an evil spirit—known as a Barrow-wight—and loses consciousness. Upon waking and finding himself trapped inside the barrow, Frodo sees his companions lying asleep on a stone floor, clad in white robes and adorned with jewels, rings, gold chains, and other rich ornaments. A song begins, at first a distant and ghostly "cold murmur," filled with "grim, hard, cold words, heartless and miserable."[28] This song resolves into an incantation—a sacrificial song prepared for the killing of Frodo and his companions:

Cold be hand and heart and bone,
and cold be sleep under stone:
never more to wake on stony bed,
never, till the Sun fails and the Moon is dead.[29]

The power of this song makes Frodo feel as if he has been turned to stone, and in his terror he begins to think of escape. He wonders if he can put on the Ring, and through its power of invisibility escape the Barrow-wight and the horrible fate awaiting his companions. However, his own innate courage and conscience overcomes this temptation, and he attacks the Barrow-wight instead. Suddenly, Frodo remembers the song Tom taught them, and sings it loudly inside the barrow:

Ho! Tom Bombadil, Tom Bombadillo!
By water, wood and hill, by the reed and willow,
By fire, sun and moon, harken now and hear us!
Come, Tom Bombadil, for our need is near us![30]

Only a moment later, though Tom is assumedly many miles away from the barrow, Frodo hears an answering voice, singing:

Old Tom Bombadil is a merry fellow,
Bright blue his jacket is, and his boots are yellow.
None has ever caught him yet, for Tom, he is the master:
His songs are stronger songs, and his feet are faster.[31]

Then one of the walls of the barrow caves in, and Tom enters the chamber, still singing:

Get out, you old Wight! Vanish in the sunlight!
Shrivel like the cold mist, like the winds go wailing,
Out into the barren lands far beyond the mountains!
Come never here again! Leave your barrow empty!
Lost and forgotten be, darker than the darkness,
Where gates stand for ever shut, till the world is mended.[32]

Immediately, the inner part of the barrow collapses with a crash, and Frodo hears a long, inhuman shriek that trails away into silence. After singing the Barrow-wight out of earthly existence, Tom sings Frodo's companions out of their own deep enchantment. As the words of Tom's song suggest, his songs are indeed stronger than the deadly incantations of the Barrow-wight, just as they were stronger than the sleepy allure of Old Man Willow's whispered music. In the case of the Barrow-wight, Frodo's proximity to its malevolent music tempts him to commit two evil acts. The first, putting on the Ring, is inherently dangerous, as using the Ring may well reveal himself to the servants of Sauron, some of whom are nearby. The second, abandoning his friends to be sacrificed by the Barrow-wight, is unthinkable for Frodo from the standpoint of his kinship[33] and friendship with the other hobbits, and also because the quest to destroy the Ring would not be possible without them. In both cases—the encounter with Old Man Willow, and their capture by the Barrow-Wight—it is Tom Bombadil's music, together with Frodo's quality of character—his good *musica humana*—that are the means by which temptations are resisted and conquered.

Tom Bombadil's songs illustrate the power of music that is in some way analogous to a weapon of war. In a great battle that takes place in *The Silmarillion*, music is used overtly as a weapon of both good and evil. The elven king Finrod, whose musical proficiency we have discussed above, is captured and interrogated by Sauron while on a secret mission. During this encounter, Finrod and Sauron fight each other with competing songs of power. Sauron begins:

He chanted a song of wizardry,
Of piercing, opening, of treachery,
Revealing, uncovering, betraying.[34]

Finrod attempts to resist the power of Sauron's song with his own musical response:

[He] sang in answer a song of staying,
Resisting, battling against power,

Of secrets kept, strength like a tower,
And trust unbroken, freedom, escape;
Of changing and of shifting shape,
Of snares eluded, broken traps,
The prison opening, the chain that snaps.[35]

These dueling songs of Sauron and Finrod continue back and forth, becoming louder and more powerful on each side. As potent a musician as Finrod is, Sauron is a member of the Ainur, who took part in the singing of the music of creation, and has by far the greater power, even in his evil, fallen state. In the end, his music proves mightier, and "Finrod [falls] before the throne," eventually dying in the dungeons of Sauron. While the account in the story does not specify what particular effects the contending songs have, it is clear that they occur in both the physical and mental realms, with competing images that affect the physical, psychological, and spiritual power of both singer and listener.

LÚTHIEN—THE ORPHEUS OF MIDDLE-EARTH

One of the most powerful musicians in Tolkien's legendarium, apart from Eru and the Ainur, is the elven princess Lúthien Tinúviel.[36] Her musical abilities, as well as the events of her life, are highly suggestive of the legend of Orpheus, whose story I will briefly summarize.[37] Orpheus is a demigod with great skill in music and lyric poetry, which he sings to the accompaniment of his magic lyre. He has just been married to the beautiful Eurydice, but as she and her companions walk through the fields, a snake bites her on the foot and she dies. Orpheus, stricken with grief, vows to travel to the land of the dead in an attempt to bring Eurydice back with him. He gains access to the underworld through the power of his songs, using music to eliminate all barriers to his entry. When he finally appears before Hades and Persephone, the king and queen of the dead, he is able to move even their implacable hearts to pity. They agree to allow Eurydice to return with Orpheus to the land of the living, on the condition that he does not look behind him until both have exited the underworld. Orpheus is not able to do this, and looks back at Eurydice, who is immediately, and permanently, drawn back into the land of the dead. Orpheus is eventually torn to pieces by a group of women who are weary of hearing him lament for his lost bride, and upset at his unwillingness to marry one of them in her place. Only after his death is he reunited with Eurydice in the afterlife. The Orpheus story illustrates the power of music to eliminate physical and spiritual obstacles, and even to conquer death.[38]

Lúthien's story is somewhat more complex, but contains many of the same contours and events as that of Orpheus, with a similarly bittersweet ending. Lúthien is the daughter of the elven king Thingol and his wife Melian. Melian is a member of the Ainur, famous in Valinor for the beauty and power of her voice, where she taught the nightingales to sing. Much of Melian's power is transferred to her daughter Lúthien, whose voice has various magical effects, including the ability to release the hold of winter on the land. In this way, her voice seems to retain some of the creative, elemental power that characterizes her mother, who participated in the music of the Ainur.[39] Lúthien lives in a kingdom ruled by her father, which is shielded and protected from the outside world by the enchantments of her mother. A mortal man, Beren, breaks the enchantment, and observes Lúthien as she dances and sings in the forest, and is struck by her grace and beauty. At length they fall in love, though such a thing had never happened between elves and men because of their separate fates.[40] Lúthien's father will only allow Beren to have her hand in marriage if he can retrieve and bring back a Silmaril from Melkor's iron crown. Despite the impossibility of a mortal man challenging a member of the Ainur, Beren accepts the terms, and departs. It is at this point that Lúthien begins to "weaponize" her Orpheus-like powers of song.

Lúthien perceives that Beren has been captured by Sauron during his quest, and to prevent her from going to his rescue, her father confines her to a house in a tall tree. Rapunzel-like, she sings to make her dark hair grow to a great length, from which she weaves a magic cloak of invisibility and a rope that charms the guards to sleep. Lúthien reaches Sauron's fortress, and sings a song that penetrates to the depths of the dungeons, where Beren hears it. This song comforts Beren, and transports his imagination into a forest where stars are shining and nightingales are singing. Following up with a song of power that shakes the fortress and fills its evil inhabitants with dread, she defeats Sauron in a battle and demolishes the fortress.[41] Lúthien's actions recall those of Orpheus, as she sings away the physical barriers between herself and her beloved, who is languishing in the "underworld" of Sauron's dungeons.

Now together again, Beren and Lúthien come to the terrible stronghold of Melkor. They approach his throne, where Lúthien identifies herself and offers to sing before the dark lord. Melkor looks on her with lustful malice and allows her to sing, but Lúthien's song is of such power that Melkor and his entire court are put to sleep, allowing Beren to cut a Silmaril from the dark lord's crown. Beren eventually gives the Silmaril to Lúthien's father, but only after suffering a mortal wound. Beren's soul departs to the halls of Mandos, through which all human souls must transit on the way to their unknown fate beyond the confines of the world. There he lingers, waiting for his beloved. Lúthien, though immortal, nevertheless dies of grief, and her soul follows Beren. There, she kneels before Mandos and sings to him a "song most fair that ever in words was woven, and the song most sorrowful that ever the world shall hear." This song moves even Mandos to pity, who like Hades had never before or since been so moved. Mandos gives Lúthien a choice: to be released from death and dwell forever in bliss in Valinor, or to return with Beren to Middle-earth, but as a mortal. She chooses mortality, and by doing so, her ultimate destiny is separated from that of the entire race of elves, to their great sorrow.[42]

Lúthien's choice adds an intriguing element to the story, and beyond what Orpheus and Eurydice experience. Regardless of whether Orpheus is reunited with Eurydice immediately or later after his death, their naturally mortal fates will bring them together, and also their families, ancestors, and friends. Lúthien's choice, however, is seemingly an eternal one, between her love on the one hand, and her family and her people on the other.[43] In spite of her eventual choice, Lúthien serves as one of the focal points in the construction of Tolkien's musical universe. She has the ability to create, destroy, restore, and to cheat death and fate. In many ways she is like the Ainur, who have musical power, possessing simultaneous perfection in *musica mundana*, *musica humana*, and *musica instrumentalis*. However, Lúthien goes beyond the Ainur in other respects, through the power of her music to influence the *fate* of created beings, a power otherwise possessed only by Eru.

The worlds of Tolkien and Lewis are full of powerful, magical instruments. Whether trumpets, horns, or voices, they are concentrated vehicles for the expression of power, both personal and universal. These instruments are tools of creation and of destruction—they open doors and shut them, cause growth and promote decay, bind things together and release them, and are weapons for good and for evil.

NOTES

1. John Dryden, *Alexander's Feast, MacFlecknoe, and St. Cecilia's Day* (New York: Charles E. Merrill Co., 1883), 30.
2. Ibid.
3. Most of the members of this group have actually been killed in a railway accident in England, and it is their deaths that draw them into Aslan's Country.
4. The creatures who run toward the door have two fates. Some, those who see and love Aslan, pass through the door and into Aslan's Country. The others, those who hate him upon seeing him, veer off and disappear into his shadow, never to be seen again.
5. Lewis, *The Last Battle*, 171–81.
6. Horns are present in two other books in the *Chronicles*—*The Lion, the Witch, and the Wardrobe* and *Prince Caspian*. In *The Lion, the Witch, and the Wardrobe*,

Susan is given a horn that has power to summon help when sounded. In *Prince Caspian*, it is Susan's horn that pulls all four of the siblings out of England and back into Narnia—this horn is able to move people between *universes*.

7. Tolkien, *The Silmarillion*, 27. This is similar to the sea-longing prompted by the sounds of water, waves on the shore, and sea gulls, as explored in the previous chapter.

8. Ibid., 29.

9. Ibid., 41.

10. Tolkien, *Unfinished Tales*, 33.

11. This again recalls Dante, as his senses are upgraded when ascending through the heavenly spheres.

12. Tolkien, *The Silmarillion*, 140–1.

13. Jörg Fündling, "An Imperialist Battle Cry behind the Lament for Boromir," in Eilmann and Schneidewind ed., *Music in Tolkien's Work and Beyond*, 116.

14. Tolkien, *The Fellowship of the Ring*, 351. An older name for Lórien was Laurelindórenan, which translates as "Land of the Valley of Singing Gold," illustrating the musical pedigree of that realm. Tolkien, *The Two Towers*, 470.

15. Tolkien, *The Fellowship of the Ring*, 353.

16. Ibid.

17. Lórien is preserved in this perfect moment through the power of Galadriel, assisted by one of the three rings made with the aid of Sauron. Unfortunately, with the destruction of Sauron's Ring, Galadriel's ring loses its power, and the land of Lórien is doomed to fade, being now subject to the ravages of time.

18. An example of collective *musica humana* that is incubated by time spent in Lórien, is the friendship between Legolas the elf and Gimli the dwarf. However, as for individual *musica humana*, Boromir, prince of the human kingdom of Gondor, has already become subject to the temptation of the Ring. Galadriel may be powerful, but she is nothing compared to Sauron, a member of the Ainur. The strength of her ring to "tune" places and people cannot overcome the lure of Sauron's Ring, which has a much greater dissonant power.

19. Tolkien, *The Fellowship of the Ring*, 125.

20. J. R. R. Tolkien, *The Hobbit* (Boston and New York: Houghton Mifflin Company, 1994), 13.

21. Ransom is told that God does not intend any world or race of beings to live forever.

22. Lewis, *Out of the Silent Planet*, 130.

23. Lewis, *The Silver Chair*, 88.

24. Tolkien, *The Fellowship of the Ring*, 111–19.

25. Ibid., 119.

26. Tolkien, *The Fellowship of the Ring*, 130.

27. Ibid., 130–1.

28. Ibid., 140.

29. Ibid., 141.

30. Ibid., 142.

31. Ibid.

32. Ibid.
33. Two of Frodo's three companions are his cousins.
34. Tolkien, *The Silmarillion*, 171.
35. Ibid.
36. Tinúviel means "nightingale" in elvish, illustrating Lúthien's natural proclivity for singing.
37. There are many versions of the Orpheus story, but the account from Ovid's *Metamorphoses* is perhaps best-known, and I will adapt that account.
38. The story of Orpheus and Eurydice fits well within a system of imperfection, as outlined in chapter 1. In spite of the power of Orpheus' voice and lyre, death *is* the ultimate winner in the story, as both he and Eurydice die, though reunited. Later audiences adapted the story when needed, to fit into a system of *perfection*. Such was the case in 1600, when one of the very first operas was produced in Florence, for the marriage celebrations of Henry IV of France and Maria de' Medici. In this treatment of the Orpheus story, the musical hero successfully brings Eurydice out of the underworld, and they live happily ever after. Admittedly, this was rather a more appropriate ending for a wedding entertainment.
39. Whittingham, "The Power of Music and Song in Tolkien's Legendarium," 150.
40. Elves are forever bound to the world and tied up with its fate. Though they are naturally immortal, they can be killed and after death go to the halls of Mandos, the doomsman of the Ainur—roughly equivalent to Hades in Greek mythology. There they wait until the end of the world, or at times are reincarnated and return to the land of the living. Men have a different fate, which was at first considered a gift from Eru, that they are mortal and not tied to the world, but have a fate beyond it. Melkor, Sauron and other evil beings pervert this gift and make it a curse, filling it with fear and dread.
41. In the account in *The Silmarillion*, is not clear if Lúthien destroys the fortress through the power of her voice, though it is probably safe to assume that she does.
42. Tolkien, *The Silmarillion*, 165–87.
43. Tolkien does not say for whether the fates of elves and men are forever separate. Tolkien speaks of a second music of the Ainur, in which *all* created beings will take part, which may point to a future reunification.

Chapter 4

When the Celestial Laws Change

No fixed rule should guide the creative artist:
rules are established by works of art, not for works of art.[1]

The motions of the celestial bodies were, for untold millennia of human history, the image of stability and perfection, written on the sky for all to see. The consistency of the heavens, with their parts moving with seeming mathematical simplicity, was considered the highest form of music, the *musica mundana*. In chapter 1, we explored several theoretical texts that described the heavenly music, and how practical, audible music—*musica instrumentalis*—should imitate its elegance. This practical music could in turn help regulate the "tuning" of the human body and mind, the *musica humana*. However, as methods for measuring and calculating the movements of the sun, moon, and planets became more precise, the idea of a simple and elegant cosmos was largely lost.[2] Not only were celestial mechanics found to be infinitely more complex, with the Earth ignominiously thrust from its privileged position at the center of the universe, but more planets were discovered, disrupting traditional numerological parallels between heavenly bodies and musical concepts. For many early music theorists, the number of planets related directly to the number of consonant intervals, so practical applications to *musica instrumentalis* were affected. To be fair, some theorists had always doubted whether patterns in the *musica mundana* corresponded to actual musical forms. Aurelian of Rêóme hedged his bets somewhat in the ninth century, when comparing the heavenly harmony to astronomical observations: "Whether such music holds to the aforementioned rules [of astronomy], however, is not mine to say."[3] Reading between the lines, one can see that Aurelian is quite aware of the potential incongruities, but is willing to let them be.

Milton provides a novel perspective on this growing celestial complexity in the pages of *Paradise Lost*. When Raphael is sent by God to the Garden of Eden to describe the created universe to Adam, the archangel is aware of the many things that humanity, with its inborn desire to explore the nature of things, will have difficulty understanding. Among them is the position of the Earth, and the precise nature and motions of the celestial bodies. Raphael does not blame humanity for its curiosity:

To ask or search, I blame thee not; for Heaven
Is as the book of God before thee set,
Wherein to read his wonderous works, and learn
His seasons, hours, or days, or months, or years:
This to attain, whether Heaven move or Earth,
Imports not, if thou reckon right; the rest
From Man or Angel the great Architect
Did wisely to conceal, and not divulge
His secrets to be scanned by them who ought
Rather admire;[4]

According to Raphael, studying the heavens to understand such elementary patterns as the passing of the seasons and the dividing of time, is a reasonable occupation for mankind. However, some things have not been—and *will not be*—revealed to man or even to angels, and it is better to simply admire them than to attempt to unlock their secrets. Raphael goes on for some time describing the lengths to which future humanity will go to comprehend celestial motion, but he warns Adam simply: "Sollicit not thy thoughts with matters hid; Leave them to God above; him serve, and fear!"[5]

Just as mathematics and astronomy have changed the way humans relate to the heavens, so have innovations in music composition altered the perspectives of theorists and practical performers alike. We saw in chapter 1 that composers began using rhythms and intervals outside those that could be defended numerologically. Additionally, the three "perfect" consonances—perfect octave, perfect fifth, and perfect fourth—elegantly aligned with ancient mathematical views of *musica mundana*, but did not satisfy the needs of evolving musical tastes and practice. Other rhythms and intervals were added to those considered acceptable for use and, for a time, there were attempts to support them through theological and numerological means. In allowing for the division of meters and rhythms into sets of two—instead of the accepted *perfectio* of three—music theorists referred to the dual nature of Christ as both human and divine as justification. Seeking to validate the use of more intervals than the perfect three, theorists found sufficient philosophical cover to allow for other numerical ratios. Richard Crocker notes that, for theorists as late as the sixteenth or eighteenth century, the ability to find the form of music in the realm of numbers and physical phenomena, "somehow made music more real or more true."[6] Such a connection between natural law and musical practice reinforced the integral connection between *musica mundana* and *musica instrumentalis*. However, this reliance on *musica mundana* to rationalize musical practice was not of interest to all composers, or even all theorists. For many, the standard of judging musical practice was not the motions of the celestial bodies or specific mathematical proportions, but rather the extent to which music pleased the senses—the realm of *musica humana*.

MUSICA HUMANA AND THE JUDGMENT OF THE EAR

The primacy, or at least the importance, of the human ear was not a particularly new concept for medieval music theorists. Boethius takes the ear into account, noting that it is the means by which music is "taken in" to the mind, in order to be subjected to reason.[7] However, many theorists were suspicious of the ear—as they were of all human sensory organs—due to the fundamentally sinful and imperfect nature of the body, and they noted the ear's tendency to be "tricked" into accepting theoretically suspect intervals. Walter of Odington, writing around the turn of the fourteenth century, argues that the *apparent* consonance of the intervals of the (non-perfect) major and minor third is the result of defects in human *perception*, and not any actual *consonance* possessed by the intervals.[8] A later treatise notes that not all *ears* are equal, and that individual disposition and training, as well as age, may lead to various "errors." Rather, one must rely on "reason—to discern by proportions of numbers."[9] In the end, such attempts at holding the line against intervals, otherwise approved by the ear, was a losing proposition, and the practical needs of the human ear triumphed over other, strictly theoretical, demands.

Such a change was not merely the result of the passage of time and the evolution of musical styles. Several surviving theoretical treatises from as far back as the ninth century seem little concerned with theoretical foundations, and focus rather on actual musical practice. According to Sarah Fuller, authors of such treatises described music that was *already* customary in the geographical regions in which they were living and working, and they viewed their task as follows: "To devise [a] reasonable and relatively coherent doctrine to fit what was already happening."[10] This is seen in copies and later editions of earlier theoretical works. The ca. 1100 *Ad organum faciendum* lists the well-known consonances acceptable for use in polyphonic music: perfect octave, perfect fifth, and perfect fourth. However, a later copy of the same treatise adds the major and minor thirds to the list, with no reason given for their inclusion. The later *Montpellier treatise* allows for the addition of major and minor sixths, again without theoretical defense. The *Montpellier* author's reasoning for the use of certain intervals is simple and yet revolutionary, especially in the context of an environment that still valued strong connections between *musica mundana* and *musica instrumentalis*. Describing why certain intervals are more commonly used than others, *Montpellier* simply states that intervals such as the second and seventh are less common because they sound bad, and intervals like the perfect fourth and perfect fifth are more common because they sound good.[11] The thirteenth-century scholar Johannes de Garlandia, whose hierarchy of consonant and dissonant intervals we examined in chapter 1, adds an important argument challenging the celestial and numerological models of identifying consonances. Rather than the ear simply confirming what reason has first determined is consonant, Garlandia argues that mathematical ratios found in consonances confirm what the ear already "knows" through its own perception.[12] Understood this way, the *musica humana* is no longer guided by reason "up" toward the patterns defined by *musica mundana*; rather it is guided by the sense of hearing "down" toward *musica instrumentalis*, to determine what is pleasurable.[13]

CAST OUT OF HEAVEN—THE CASE OF THE PERFECT FOURTH

In chapter 1, we saw that perfect intervals were so called because their mathematical ratios are limited to the numbers of the *tetractys*, in which the 2:1 ratio creates the perfect octave, the 3:2 ratio the perfect fifth, and the 3:4 ratio the perfect fourth. The use of these intervals in simple, practical harmony is illustrated in Figure 4.1. On the top line are a series of fifths, and on the bottom, a series of fourths. Note that in each of the two series, there is an instance of the interval being imperfect: the seventh interval in the series of fifths is a *diminished fifth*, while the fourth interval in the series of fourths is an *augmented fourth*.[14] As it was relatively easy to avoid the diminished fifth, it was not discussed much, if at all, in early treatises. However, the position of the augmented fourth—right in the middle of the melodic scale—made it highly problematic in actual practice. Theorists and practical musicians found ways to detour around this imperfection, but that did not spell the end of trouble for the interval of the fourth, even in its perfect form.

The perfect fourth began to fall out of favor during the early fourteenth century. Before then, it was included in lists of consonances together with its other perfect siblings. However, it started to disappear from the lists, at first excluded from the consonances, and then categorized as a *dissonance*. For authors of practical treatises, whose purpose was simply to show readers

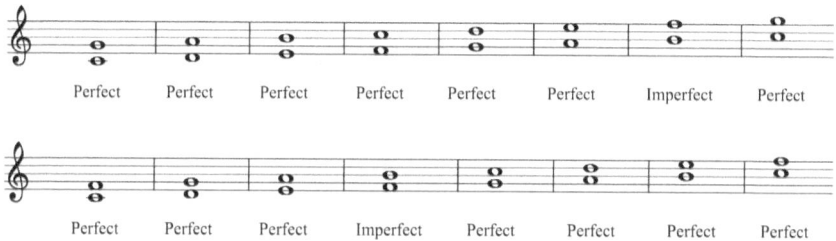

Figure 4.1 Melodic Dispositions of Fifths and Fourths. *Source*: Author.

how to compose music, this change was not important, as it reflected what was happening in practice, and needed no theoretical backing. But for authors of speculative, theoretical treatises, this posed a real difficulty: the perfect fourth is one of the perfect consonances, its numerical ratios are within the *tetractys*, and it *sounds* like a consonance.[15] Regardless of its theoretical and numerological pedigree, it was nonetheless treated as a dissonance, in both practical treatises and musical compositions of the fourteenth century.[16]

It may be that practical theorists were wary of committing open blasphemy by consigning the perfect fourth *entirely* to the ranks of the dissonances. At times, it was categorized as the *least* dissonant of the dissonances, and at other times it held an intermediate position *between* consonance and dissonance, but belonging to neither.[17] René Descartes called the fourth *infelicissima consonaniarum omnium* ("unhappiest of all consonances"), because it would not stay in a single category.[18] Notwithstanding such theoretical equivocation, by the sixteenth century the perfect fourth had been so long out of favor that its place among the dissonances was unquestioned. Even the eminent theorist Gioseffo Zarlino, of whom more will be said below, considered the fourth *theoretically* perfect but admitted that "musical practice placed it . . . among [the] dissonances."[19] Other theorists were less ambivalent. Franchino Gaffurio placed the perfect fourth among the intervals "which are rightfully and naturally banished from sweet harmony,"[20] and Francesco Bianciardi considered it "an insipid thing, namely of no value."[21]

The reclassification of the perfect fourth from perfect consonance to dissonance is illustrative of changes that occurred in music theory and practice over the course of the late medieval and Renaissance periods. While not in itself a repudiation of the idea of *musica mundana*—of divine patterns that reveal themselves in *musica instrumentalis*—it was perhaps the recognition of an *expanded* cosmic system with new and novel elements. Not everyone, however, was willing to abandon the old cosmological models in favor of new ones, as we will see in the following section.

SPEAKING OF THE DEVIL—THE TREATMENT OF DISSONANCE

In this and in previous chapters we have surveyed various discussions on dissonance, including its arithmetical properties, and the practical steps taken to avoid or mitigate their effect in performance. However, we have not yet looked closely at the *idea* of dissonance, and what it meant to early speculative music theorists. The title of this section foreshadows the fundamental discomfort with the presence of dissonance because, like "speaking of the devil," speaking of dissonance acknowledges its existence, and the system of imperfection that ultimately enables it.

Boethius was among the first to highlight a sharp distinction between consonance and dissonance. David Cohen notes that Boethius "treats consonance and dissonance as two entirely distinct phenomena defining classes whose members are absolutely different."[22] Consonance exists due to its proximity to, and a partaking of, *essential unity*—a Platonic concept that would have been understood by a Christian like Boethius as *essential divinity*, the perfect *musica mundana*. In contrast, dissonance exists as a state of fundamental duality and difference—distinctly undesirable elements in the metaphysics of antiquity.[23] Boethius' rejection of dissonance is achieved "via a rhetoric of violence, obstinacy, conflict, harshness, and separation." He uses language like "harsh and unpleasant," "[refusing] to be blended," "collid[ing]," "unwilling to be mixed together," and "each one interfer[ing] with the other."[24] Though the English translation blunts some of the effects, Boethius' Latin is particularly and unusually intense, as he uses "vivid [and] personified images of clash and conflict," that "present dissonance as the embodiment in sound of a duality and difference that are intrinsically, irredeemably oppositional, antithetical, allergic, [and] conflictual."[25] These descriptions are visceral and evocative, calling to mind images of human conflict and violence with which Boethius' readers could relate.

Later theorists, such as the ninth-century author of the *Musica Enchiriadis*, accepted the three perfect intervals on the authority of Boethius. Their treatment of dissonance was also similar in that they refer to it only obliquely, as *not-consonance*. It is only when performing musicians and practical treatises began *using* dissonance, that speculative theorists began to expand the number of consonances, categorizing and ranking both consonances and dissonances. Despite an acknowledgment of the existence of dissonance, it was never placed in a position of equality with consonance. As Cohen notes, "consonance is always self-sufficient and self-evident, [and] the presence of dissonance always requires justification, which is to say that it is ultimately dependent on consonance for its 'grounds of existence' and thus always, no matter how prominent it may be in a given texture, secondary."[26] To put it another way, dissonance may be *undesirable*, but it is necessary as a referent back toward consonance.[27] A number of theorists and musicians noted that the use of too many perfect intervals made a musical composition static and uninteresting. A solution to this problem was the cautious and controlled use of dissonance, which, like a diner first consuming a bitter dish, makes subsequent savory and sweet flavors more pleasurable. For instance, though the intervals of the third and the sixth were considered dissonances in early music, they could still be used as "harbingers" of subsequent perfect fifths and octaves, serving as their "heralds and maidservants," that would "allure the ear" lest it "cease its attention."[28] This piquantly illustrates the fundamentally subservient nature of dissonance. Though permitted to exist in music, dissonance serves merely to announce the arrival of consonance—in short, its *presence* is contingent upon its own *absence*. Eventually, dissonance as a distinct entity was subsumed by and incorporated into consonance. Theorists and musical practitioners began to identify the movement from dissonance to consonance—from tension to release—as a *single* event, identified as a consonance. In this sense, the dissonance was "virtually fused with its hierarchically superior companion."[29] If we are to consider this element of *musica instrumentalis* in light of the greater *musica mundana*, we can think of the relationship as one of conflict and victory. Consonance "fights against," "vanquishes," and "reabsorbs" dissonance, making the ensuing consonance even sweeter than it would have been without the conflict, an example of *maior perfectum*. To use an appropriate passage from the Bible: "Death has been swallowed up in victory."[30]

CELESTIAL WARFARE?—THE ARTUSI-MONTEVERDI CONTROVERSY

The decades around the turn of the seventeenth century represented a high-water mark of sorts for subservience of dissonance to consonance in Western music. Though the traditional practice of musical counterpoint reached its highest levels of refinement at this time, it was also an era of experimentation, with the emergence of new styles and genres of music, of which opera was arguably the most important. In such a time of simultaneous refinement and innovation, it is understandable that supporters and practitioners of conservative and progressive styles will come into conflict—this occurs during any major generational change. That the conflict was indeed generational, equal in intensity and vitriol to any other in the reader's living memory ("you young people and your music!"), is clear through the controversy that erupted between the innovative young composer Claudio Monteverdi and Giovanni Maria Artusi, a practitioner of the older, established style. This controversy focused on the proper treatment of dissonance, and how it should proceed toward its necessary resolution to consonance.

The commonly accepted rules and techniques for approaching dissonance and proceeding to consonance in vocal music, were set down by Gioseffo Zarlino in his 1558 treatise *Le institutioni harmoniche*. This treatise was widely published during the second half of the sixteenth century, and one of its leading defenders was Giovanni Maria Artusi. While Artusi himself was not slavish in his devotion to his teacher and mentor—he relaxed a few of Zarlino's more stringent rules—he did feel that the foundation of the graceful and polished discipline of counterpoint was under attack.[31] Artusi considered modern musical innovations, like those of Monteverdi, a threat to the rational, stable, and balanced musical system—the *musica mundana* as he saw it.

Claudio Monteverdi's particular transgression, in Artusi's eyes, was an improper treatment of dissonance in his compositions. When writing vocal music, Monteverdi did not always approach dissonances according to the established conventions. For instance, he would often move to a dissonant interval by means of a melodic leap instead of by step, or would place a dissonance on a strong beat instead of a weak one. To be fair, Monteverdi did not originate these techniques, but was simply systematizing a practice that had been current among composers for some time.[32] His reasoning for treating dissonances contrary to the traditional rules of vocal music was quite simple: the words demanded it. Monteverdi argued that the primary purpose of music when used to set a poem or other text, was to support and enhance the meaning of the words. He and other progressive composers were attempting to express the more extreme emotional states, such as anger, disgust, revulsion, and despair, and to accomplish this, new harmonic tools were necessary.[33] Monteverdi would be the first to admit the pungency and bitterness of his harmonies, but asserted that such sonorities were *required* by the sentiments expressed in the texts of his vocal works.[34]

In opposition to Monteverdi, Artusi published two treatises in 1600 and 1603, each of them subtitled *Delle Imperfettioni Della Moderna Musica* ("On the Imperfections of Modern Music"). We will examine a part of the first treatise, which is in the form of an extended conversation between two invented characters: "Luca," a young amateur music lover, and "Vario," an older music master. In a widely read passage—meaning, "widely assigned in undergraduate music history courses"—Luca describes to Vario a recent experience, in which he was invited to listen to a new kind of music. Luca recognizes that this music makes use of several innovations, and he brings a number of interesting musical passages that he has transcribed to show to Vario. The elder musician is no Luddite—rejecting innovation simply because it is new—and he is happy to hear that composers are devising new ways of writing music, and asserts that "discovering new things is not merely good but necessary."[35] However, Vario is *not* happy that the new compositions are guilty of breaking the old, established rules handed down by the masters.[36] Luca notes that the musical innovations are fascinating, and appeal strongly to the ear. Vario agrees that this may very well be so, and explains the cause:

> Sensuous excess corrupts the sense, meaning simply that the ear is so taken up ... that it does not perceive the offense committed against it [. . .], while reason, which knows and distinguishes the good from the bad, perceives right well that a deception is wrought on the sense.[37]

Luca agrees, saying "it is known that the ear is deceived," and that composers writing such music "seek only to satisfy the ear," not perceiving that "what the[ir] instruments tell them is false." Rather, the correct method is to compose music that is approved "by means of reason, [and] seconded by the ear."[38] Luca and Vario agree that reason must ultimately rule over the senses, and one must be wary of being deceived. If a person's *musica humana* is to remain well-tuned, it must be guided *from above,* by the eternal patterns of the *musica mundana*, as they exist in established rules and methods, rather than being deceived *from below* by the changeable practices of *musica instrumentalis*.[39] Such practices are ultimately artificial, and being thus unnatural, they cannot properly stimulate and move the emotions of the listener.[40]

In a 1605 introduction to a published group of songs, Monteverdi defends his innovative use of dissonance. He simply states that there are *two* ways of composing vocal music. One is what he calls "First Practice," referring to traditional counterpoint and all its rules and conventions, as described by Zarlino and defended by Artusi. Monteverdi acknowledges that this style is well-suited to conservative forms of sacred and liturgical music, and should be used in them. The other method of composition he calls "Second Practice," and this is applicable for modern secular music with expressive texts that embrace various extremes of emotion.[41] Monteverdi argues that each practice is appropriate in its own sphere, and does not campaign for the elimination of one in favor of the other. He does, however, take issue with Artusi's method of criticism. In Artusi's first treatise, Luca shows Vario some musical passages that he has jotted down, which Vario disparages for breaking the rules of dissonance treatment, calling the passages "barbarisms."[42] Monteverdi criticizes this analysis because the musical passages Vario examines—the passages are printed in Artusi's treatise—do not include the underlying texts. Monteverdi argues that by including the texts, it is clear that the points at which he breaks the rules of the "First Practice" are precisely where he is emphasizing a strong word or emotion, as per the "Second Practice."

However, Artusi does not admit the existence or validity of any such "Second Practice," so there is no reason for him to include the texts in his analysis.[43]

Artusi uses a two-pronged approach in defense of the refined counterpoint style of Zarlino: appeal to nature, and appeal to authority. Firstly, he argues that the rules of dissonance treatment are based on the balances and proportions found in nature. Secondly, the rules are tried and true, having been perfected and handed down by the great and celebrated musical masters of the past. Interestingly, Monteverdi and his supporters counter with the same appeals. To Monteverdi, nothing could be more natural than for music and text to support one another, which allows the listener to hear and move in sympathy with the emotional message of the words. As for authority, all great artists of the past were known for their innovations, and not simple imitation of others.[44] Monteverdi does not claim to be the inventor of the "Second Practice," but rather takes a position similar to that of Zarlino, identifying and codifying a new text-centered approach for the needs and purposes of modern music.[45] Monteverdi's ultimate trump card against Artusi's appeal to authority, is the assertion that the necessity for music to be subservient to the text derives from Plato himself.[46] Even a direct quote from the scriptures or the Church Fathers would be unlikely to hold higher authority among music theorists.

This controversy is at its heart a duel between different musical cosmologies—differing concepts of *musica mundana*. Monteverdi may be considered the initial winner of this contest, as his "Second Practice" becomes the dominant method of composition in the seventeenth century, especially in opera. However, by the late seventeenth century, Zarlino's rules are further codified, becoming the model for the "severe" traditional style of counterpoint, common in sacred and liturgical music of that time. This highly conservative style has survived to the present as a pedagogical tool for students to learn the rules of counterpoint and dissonance treatment. So, while Monteverdi's particular views on dissonance and the textual treatment of music have largely come and gone—though immortalized in peerless operas and vocal works—music students to this very day are subjected to exercises in "First Practice" counterpoint. Through a long process of attrition, Artusi may have won the argument, though he likely would not be pleased to see his valued methods and techniques reduced to mere academic formulas.

EMANCIPATING DISSONANCE

Despite significant differences of opinion between Artusi and Monteverdi, they were in full agreement on at least one point about dissonance—it was inferior to, and should be subsumed by, consonance. This basic principle was current from Boethius in the sixth century until the beginning of the twentieth, and still dominates much of the music of the last century, especially in popular genres of music. The fundamental superiority of consonance over dissonance, manifested through ignoring the existence of dissonance, categorizing it, controlling its motion, or using it as a tool to illustrate poetic texts, has been central to the concept of *musica mundana* for almost the entirety of the Western musical tradition.

Such a view of consonance and dissonance is integral to the practice of tonality. Until the sixteenth century, the primary method of controlling melody, and thus harmony, was the system of *church modes*—a collection of melodic scales with different sounds and characteristics. These church modes were gradually phased out in favor of the tonal system, which contains only two modes, major and minor.[47] This reduction in modes allowed for the systematization of harmony, just as Zarlino codified the rules of counterpoint and dissonance treatment. In fact, these two systems are intimately related. The theory and practice of tonality sets rules for harmonic progression, from moments of tension and anticipation—often using dissonance to create tension—to moments of release and stability, using consonances. One practical result of the tonal system is that one particular pitch, known as the *key*, takes a principal position among the other pitches. For example, if a piece of tonal music is in the key of D, then "D" and the harmonies built on that pitch become the primary focus of the composition, acting as the "home" to which the music will return. Other pitches and harmonies may be used, but their ultimate purpose is to lead the listener back to the key of D. Dissonances are used to create a sense of tension and anticipation, so that the return to the home key is more satisfying. This is fairly simple and straightforward. However, as with Monteverdi and his followers, later composers experimented with tonal materials to make their music more expressive and innovative—adapting *musica instrumentalis* to serve their own evolving concepts of *musica mundana*.

The tonal system served Western music well for centuries, and the concept of the home key remained—and generally still remains—the dominant musical language. However, the system holds within itself the seeds of its own destruction. Since there are only twenty-four keys available to the composer (twelve in the major mode and twelve in the minor), there are clear limits on how far one can depart from the home key. Just how far one could go was controlled at any given time by generally accepted conventions of "good taste." These conventions were always subject to review and revision, and a pioneering or revolutionary composer might push the limits, departing ever further from the home key, often including more pungent dissonances as well. Eventually, composers reached the furthest possible distance from the home key, and though they created other methods of building tension, such as delaying the return to the home key and using the strongest possible dissonances, many composers by the turn of the twentieth century felt that nothing more could be said within the confines of the tonal system. Claude Debussy declared that music should not be considered major *or* minor, undercutting one pillar of the tonal system, adding also that harmonies don't need to resolve to anything: "One can travel where one wishes and leave by any door."[48] Anton Webern agrees, noting that for quite a long time "major and minor have no longer existed!"[49] He also notes that the practice of moving further and further away from the home key, and for longer periods of time, blunts the effect of tension and release common in tonal music: "In the end one found it was no longer so necessary to return to the keynote."[50] Once blunted, it was eventually eliminated altogether, so that "relation to a keynote—tonality—has been lost."[51] This was, in Webern's opinion, the result of an attempt to defend the tonal system: "precisely because we took steps to preserve tonality—we broke its neck!"[52] While many composers agreed that tonality had come to the end of its useful life, the question of where to go next was an open one, and musicians experimented widely. Much of the inspiration for this experimentation was, interestingly enough, derived from very traditional views of *musica mundana*.

Nostalgia for music that partakes of "nature," and a desire to return to it, is palpable in the writings of musicians and theorists of the early twentieth century. Claude Debussy pined for the spirit of Bach's time, two centuries prior, "when music was subject to laws of beauty inscribed in the movements of Nature herself."[53] He disparagingly describes his own era as the "age of veneer."[54] Closer communion between *musica humana* and *musica mundana* was touted as a cure for such decadence: "To see the sun rise does one far more good than hearing the *Pastoral* Symphony [of Beethoven]," and "listen to no one's advice except that of the wind in the trees."[55] Ferruccio Busoni describes the shortcomings of the tonal system in the following way: "What we now call our Tonal System is nothing more than a set of 'signs'; an ingenious device to grasp something of the eternal harmony; a meagre pocket-edition of that encyclopedic work; artificial light instead of the sun."[56] Busoni later muses on how "music may be restored to its primitive, natural essence," ending with a statement that could stand beside Boethius and the other ancients:

> *let Music be naught else than Nature mirrored by and reflected from the human breast*; for it is sounding air and floats above and beyond the air; within Man himself as universally and absolutely as in Creation entire; for it can gather together and disperse without losing in intensity.[57]

Debussy concurs, and suggests one of the ways to access such natural purity—one that can be mirrored by the *musica humana*—is to look to the music of other cultures that have *not* experienced the strictures of Western theory. Speaking from his experiences of Javanese and Vietnamese music,[58] he notes:

> There used to be—indeed, despite the troubles that civilization has brought, there still are—some wonderful peoples who learn music as easily as one learns to breathe. Their school consists of the eternal rhythm of the sea, the wind in the leaves, and a thousand other tiny noises, which they listen to with great care, without ever having consulted any of those dubious treatises.[59]

Debussy places the responsibility on musicians in the West to lead the way in restoring nature to the arts, because "only they can re-create Nature's atmosphere."[60] Charles Ives agrees in principle, noting that these natural materials and devices are available to everyone. Though it may be difficult at first for those used to music created in the tonal system, "that needn't keep anyone from trying to find out how to use a few more of the myriads of sound waves nature has put around in the air . . . for man to catch if he can."[61]

The desire for a return to nature is clear, but what would it sound like in practice? We have already noted composers abandoning the major and minor modes, as well as other concepts underpinning the tonal system. What replaced it? There is no complete answer to this question—or rather, no room *here* for a complete answer—as the twentieth century saw the proliferation of many different "schools" of composition, based on various philosophical and aesthetic systems, which were themselves influenced by practical considerations of economics, technology, politics, and social change. One could describe the musical twentieth century as an age of "isms": modernism, symbolism, primitivism, expressionism, minimalism, neoclassicism, postmodernism, and so on. However, there are a few major currents we can point to that have exercised a high degree of influence. Debussy outlined such an aesthetic principle during a conversation with one of his former professors at the Paris Conservatoire. The professor played a dissonant chord on the piano, noting that such a chord needed to resolve to a consonant one. When Debussy replied that he didn't see why it should, the professor played a string of parallel chords and asked, rhetorically, "well, do you find this lovely?" When Debussy answered with an emphatic "yes," the professor responded: "I am not saying that what you do isn't beautiful, but it's theoretically absurd." Debussy's answer, quoted at the head of the chapter, is timeless: "There is no theory. You merely have to listen. Pleasure is the law."[62] This sentiment asserts, among other things, that dissonance is not required to resolve to anything—provided that the ear perceives it as beautiful.

Perhaps the most influential among those attempting to create and clarify a new set of rules and practices for non-tonal—or *atonal*—music, was the group of Austrian composers known as the Second Viennese School.[63] Arnold Schoenberg, in a 1909 letter to Ferruccio Busoni, notes his intentions: "I have long been occupied with the removal of all shackles of tonality. And my harmony allows no chords or melodies with tonal implications any more."[64] Schoenberg later developed and adopted the "twelve-tone method," in which tonality was not only rejected, but its *absence* was systematized. In twelve-tone music, all notes of the scale are equal, and none of them may be repeated until each of them has been sounded. If one of the notes is repeated too early or too often, it takes on the characteristics of a home key, and sounds tonal. Schoenberg argues that the fundamental equality of pitches "depriv[es] one single tone of the privilege of supremacy."[65] This denunciation of pitch hierarchy applied also to consonance and dissonance. As I argued above, one of the foundations of *musica mundana*, as practiced in the Western world, is the dominant position of consonance in relation to dissonance. Schoenberg eliminates this distinction, in what he coins the "emancipation of the dissonance." He notes that human ears have become used to a wide range of dissonances in music,[66] allowing for compositions in which any harmony can follow any other harmony, "as if there were no dissonance at all."[67] Schoenberg argues that the difference between what is heard as dissonance and what is heard as consonance, is not due to any essential beauty, or nearness to a mathematical or heavenly pattern, but simply the level of comprehensibility of the sound to the human ear. It is *because* dissonances have been avoided or tightly controlled that the ear perceives them differently than consonances, which one hears more often in tonal music.[68] To Schoenberg and his followers, all sounds were, ultimately, consonances. In some ways, this idea returns to—or even surpasses, in a kind of *maior perfectum*—the position of Boethius and other early theorists and musicians. However, rather than admitting the existence of only three "perfect" sounds that reflect celestial truths in the *musica mundana*, now *all* sounds are perfect.

Clearly, such a cosmic shift did not go unnoticed by audiences. Although the music-loving public had gradually grown accustomed to a wide range of pungent sonorities, this final abandonment of the tonal system, and the rejection of the dissonance-consonance relationship, was for many a bridge too far. Schoenberg describes his first major atonal work, the *Five Pieces for Orchestra*, in the following way: "completely unsymphonic, devoid of architecture or construction, just an uninterrupted change of colors, rhythms and moods," which is "built upon none of the lines that are familiar to us," so that "we cannot grasp or analyze them nor can we trace its themes."[69] If this is how the *composer* described the nature of his own work, the responses of the public and the critics must have been fascinating indeed. The *Five Pieces* premiered in London in 1912, and a correspondent for the *London Times* described it as follows: "it was like a poem in Tibetan; not one single soul could possibly have understood it at a first hearing," and "there was not a single consonance from beginning to end."[70] Those present at the concert did not know what to make of it, and attendees reported that the audience was either hissing, laughing, or simply stupefied. A similar performance of the music of Schoenberg and his students in Vienna the next year was an unmitigated disaster, today remembered as the *Skandalkonzert*. As Schoenberg conducted, the Viennese audience began to boo, shout, and hiss, while others applauded, so that the music was almost inaudible. Though the concert organizer appealed for calm, fistfights eventually erupted in the audience, and the matter ended up in the courts. One witness, a physician, testified that "for a certain section of the public, [the music was] so nervewracking, and therefore so harmful for the nervous system, that many who were present already showed obvious signs of severe attacks of neurosis."[71] Instead of a pure expression of *musica mundana*, this new music was perceived as entirely antithetical to the public concept of what music should be, and if the testifying doctor is to be believed, it had a decidedly negative effect on the listener's physical and mental health, their *musica humana*.

There is much more to be said about how the celestial and natural bases of music have evolved, but this chapter may be considered representative of the varied ways in which composers sought to stay true to their aesthetic, and *cosmic*, imperatives. We have investigated the development of number of hierarchical systems, and have also spent time exploring the importance of text settings in vocal music. The next chapter will combine these two issues, particularly ways in which words and texts illustrate the human understanding of the relationship between itself—the *musica humana*—and the created universe of the *musica mundana*.

NOTES

1. This quote is ascribed to Claude Debussy. Felix Borowski, *The Theodore Thomas Orchestra: Eighteenth Season 1908–1909* (Chicago: Orchestral Association, [1909]), 187.
2. The motions of the heavens remain elegant, but are far, far from simple.
3. Ponte, *Aurelian of Réôme*, 22.
4. Milton, *Paradise Lost*, 189.
5. Ibid., 192.
6. Richard L. Crocker, *Studies in Medieval Music Theory and the Early Sequence* (Aldershot, Hampshire: Variorum, 1997), 20.
7. John L. Snyder, "Theinred of Dover on Consonance: A Chapter in the History of Harmony," *Music Theory Spectrum* V (Spring 1983): 113–14.
8. Ibid., 116.

9. Ellsworth, *The Berkeley Manuscript*, 221.
10. Fuller, "Theoretical Foundations of Early Organum Theory," 60.
11. Ibid., 66–7.
12. Crocker, *Studies in Medieval Music Theory*, 4.
13. To be clear, not all music theorists abandoned reason, or the observation of celestial and natural phenomena, as we will see later in the chapter. However, they did not attempt a return to the three perfect consonances or the older rhythmic restrictions—that genie was already out of the bottle—but rather used natural phenomena to defend whichever practice happened to be in vogue. It is quite a nice thing to have one's own musical preferences confirmed by the senses *and* by universal law. Much more will be said about this in chapter 7.
14. In today's commonly used equal tempered tuning system, the diminished fifth and augmented fourth sound exactly the same. However, in the Pythagorean tuning assumed by most early theorists, the augmented fourth has a 729/512 ratio, and the diminished fifth an even uglier ratio of 1024/729.
15. Crocker, *Studies in Medieval Music Theory*, 5–7.
16. Carl Schachter, "Landini's Treatment of Consonance and Dissonance: A Study in Fourteenth-Century Counterpoint," *The Journal of Musicology* 7 (Summer 1989): 131.
17. Ibid., 136.
18. Ernest Trumble, "Dissonance Treatment in Early Fourxbourdon," in Bryan Gillingham and Paul Merkley, eds., *Beyond the Moon: Festschrift Luther Dittmer* (Ottawa: Institute of Mediaeval Music, 1990), 244.
19. Garrett, *Adriano Banchieri*, 26.
20. Ibid.
21. Ibid., 27.
22. David E. Cohen, "Metaphysics, Ideology, Discipline: Consonance, Dissonance, and the Foundations of Western Polyphony," *Theoria: Historical Aspects of Music Theory* 7 (1993): 59.
23. I find two foundational difficulties with Boethius' arguments as presented in Cohen's work. First, the very nature and definition of consonance must include the existence of *two* separate pitches, that then blend smoothly together. Even if the result shares in unity, it is still comprised of separate, and separable, components—a fundamental duality. Second, Boethius does not provide any particular reason for accepting only the three perfect consonances. He does not use the argument, as others do, of the efficacy of the *tetractys* or the *dekad*. In fact, he gives no reason at all, but accepts the consonances just as they are. In contrast, earlier theorists like Ptolemy allowed for a continuum between more- and less-perfect consonances, which provided for the use of many more intervals. Ibid., 56–9.
24. Ibid., 60–1.
25. Ibid., 61.
26. Ibid., 3.
27. Ibid., 6.
28. Sarah Fuller, "Tendencies and Resolutions: The Directed Progression in *Ars Nova* Music," *Journal of Music Theory* 36 (Fall 1992): 229–30.

29. Ibid., 230.

30. 1 Corinthians 15:54 (NIV). Scripture quotations marked (NIV) are taken from the Holy Bible, New International Version®, NIV®. Copyright © 1973, 1978, 1984, 2011 by Biblica, Inc.™ Used by permission of Zondervan. All rights reserved worldwide. www.zondervan.com. The "NIV" and "New International Version" are trademarks registered in the United States Patent and Trademark Office by Biblica, Inc.™

31. Claude Palisca, "The Artusi-Monteverdi Controversy," in Dennis Arnold and Nigel Fortune, ed., *The New Monteverdi Companion* (London: Faber and Faber, 1985), 127–8.

32. This was particularly true in instrumental music, where these kinds of dissonance treatments were more widely used and accepted, likely because of the quick decay of sound natural to many instruments. Palisca, "The Artusi-Monteverdi Controversy," 135.

33. Ibid., 140.

34. Ibid., 129.

35. Leo Treitler, gen. ed., *Source Readings in Music History – Vol. 4: The Baroque Era*, Margaret Murata, ed. (New York and London: W.W. Norton and Co., 1998), 24.

36. Ibid., 19.

37. Ibid., 24.

38. Ibid.

39. This is precisely the opposite position than that taken by fourteenth-century theorist Johannes de Garlandia, as discussed earlier in the chapter.

40. Palisca, "The Artusi-Monteverdi Controversy," 151.

41. Ibid., 128.

42. Treitler, *Source Readings in Music History – Vol. 4: The Baroque Era*, 23.

43. Palisca, "The Artusi-Monteverdi Controversy," 128.

44. Ibid., 150.

45. Ibid., 153.

46. Ibid., 153–5.

47. This is a gross simplification of the transition between modal and tonal systems, an analysis of which could, and does, occupy multiple volumes.

48. Weiss and Taruskin, *Music in the Western World*, 418.

49. Ibid., 433.

50. Ibid.

51. Ibid.

52. Ibid., 434.

53. Leo Treitler, gen. ed., *Source Readings in Music History – Vol. 7: The Twentieth Century* (New York and London: W.W. Norton and Co., 1998), 161.

54. Ibid.

55. Weiss and Taruskin, *Music in the Western World*, 420.

56. Ibid., 421.

57. Ibid., 423.

58. Debussy had the opportunity to hear this music during a number of World's Fairs held in Paris during the late nineteenth century. He was particularly enamored

of the Javanese *gamelan* ensembles he heard there, and some of his works reflect this inspiration.

59. Treitler, *Source Readings in Music History – Vol. 7: The Twentieth Century*, 165.
60. Ibid., 162.
61. Weiss and Taruskin, *Music in the Western World*, 424.
62. Ibid., 418.
63. The members of this group are Arnold Schoenberg, and his students Alban Berg and Anton Webern. The name "Second Viennese School" is used to distinguish them from what is known as the First Viennese School, which includes the composers Joseph Haydn, Wolfgang Amadeus Mozart, and Ludwig van Beethoven (sometimes Franz Schubert is included in this group).
64. Treitler, *Source Readings in Music History – Vol. 7: The Twentieth Century*, 18.
65. Weiss and Taruskin, *Music in the Western World*, 436.
66. Luigi Russolo argued that the widespread use of machinery in the wake of the Industrial Revolution made mankind accustomed to noise, which dissonance imitates. He suggested a new kind of music made up only of various classes of noise, indicative of humanity's new sonic reality. Treitler, *Source Readings in Music History – Vol. 7: The Twentieth Century*, 59–64.
67. Ibid., 87.
68. Ibid.
69. Weiss and Taruskin, *Music in the Western World*, 428.
70. Ibid.
71. Ibid., 430.

Chapter 5

To Conserve, Exploit, or Embrace?
The Human and the Non-Human in Christian Hymnody

> For You have made him a little lower than the angels, And You have crowned him with glory and honor. You have made him to have dominion over the works of Your hands; You have put all things under his feet, All sheep and oxen—even the beasts of the field, The birds of the air, And the fish of the sea That pass through the paths of the seas.[1]

Until now, our analysis of *musica mundana* has focused largely on the celestial bodies, and the mathematical concepts that underpin our understanding of reality. In this chapter, we will spend time with the part of the *musica mundana* most accessible to humans, namely the earthly elements, and the flora and fauna. Though *musica humana* remains a function of the internal, spiritual attunement of humankind, I will emphasize the balance that occurs as a by-product of mankind's *material* relationship with the *musica mundana*. This includes human relationships with, and concern for, the physical world, including the life and value of the flora and fauna itself, and to a certain extent the elements. We examine this relationship largely through the lens of Christian hymnody though, as has been the case throughout the book, I will include other lenses. The Christian church possesses an enormous trove of hymns and texts for chanting and singing. These texts have many purposes: praise, exhortation, marking seasons and celebrations in the liturgical year, marking important events in the life of the believer, instruction and education, accompanying specific sacraments of the church, and evangelization and conversion. These texts are (usually) relatively short, and are often poetic and metrical. As such, hymns and liturgical texts represent a parallel tradition for the transmission of Christian theology—alongside the teachings of the Church Fathers and theologians—from the early Christian church until the present.

The particular subset of texts from hymnody we will examine focuses on the relationship between mankind and the created world, particularly those parts of creation humanity has traditionally exercised some measure of "dominion" over. As mankind's ability to access, affect, and alter its environment has increased over time, the conceptual scope of this dominion has also increased. However, for much of the history of Christianity, humanity did not exercise much effective control over the elements, such as air, water (especially the oceans), and to a lesser extent, land. Technological advances over the past few centuries have given mankind the capacity to explore the limits of these elemental realms, and also to gravely damage and pollute them—dominion of the worst sort. However, most of the hymnody in this chapter will treat the parts of the creation "nearest to hand," particularly those parts that provide physical sustenance and comfort to humankind, and to some extent, aesthetic sustenance as well.

To facilitate an analysis of this hymnody, I propose a number of categories and subcategories into which we can place hymns and texts that recognize the wide spectrum of relationships between humanity and the natural world. They are illustrated for ease of reference in Figure 5.1.

While I have suggested three major categories and six minor categories, they should not be thought of as of defining strict or absolute boundaries. Indeed, the categories will tend to bleed into one another. For example, Aesthetic Value is placed under Acknowledgment, but in some cases will contain traces of Subjugation, while Stewardship is as often a part of Conservation as it is a part of Subjugation. However, all of the categories exist along a single value axis. While value can be a difficult concept to define, being caught up in questions of value *to* whom and *for* whom, I will simply say that as we move along the axis, the categories represent increasing value to humanity, together with the evolution of how humanity determines what *is* valuable.

The first major category, Acknowledgment, generally confirms the created world—and often the celestial spheres as well—as a system of stand-alone and objective identities, not metaphorically or symbolically linked to humanity, a Deity, or anything outside itself. While this may seem a very low bar to clear, references to the created world in hymnody that do *not* point, directly

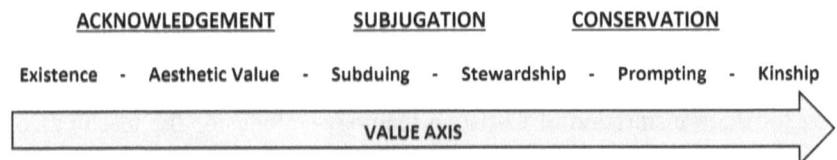

Figure 5.1   Value Axis. *Source*: Author.

or indirectly, to humanity or to God are much less common than one might think. For example, the commonly sung passage from Psalm 42, "As the deer pants for the water brooks, so pants my soul for You, O God,"[2] is not about a deer's physical need for water, but rather uses animal imagery to describe a human spiritual need. The common Latin hymn "Ave Maris Stella" is not about stars or seas, but uses them as images to describe the Virgin Mary, just as references to the Lion of Judah and the Lamb of God have little to do with actual lions or lambs, but act as symbols of Jesus Christ. Thus, I do not include in the categories references to the created world that are strictly metaphorical or symbolic.

Within the category of Acknowledgment, I offer two subcategories: Existence and Aesthetic Value. Existence means simply that humanity acknowledges that creation, or individual members of creation, exist with their own identities, and are neither images nor metaphors. This ethic is placed lowest on the value axis, because acknowledging existence does not imply any relative value, apart from the ability to be noticed. Hymns of Existence often note that non-human members of creation have the capacity to praise their creator through their essential or primary actions, such as stars shining or birds singing. Such texts go no further than this acknowledgment, and there is no overt prompting of humanity to likewise praise the creator, though this is often implied. The second subcategory, Aesthetic Value, *does* suggest an increased value from a human point of view. Mankind realizes that the created world is beautiful, and that it pleases the senses, realizing also that God has created and sustains this beauty, which prompts humans to praise God as the maker of good things.

The second major category, Subjugation, is a logical—from a human perspective—extension of Aesthetic Value. If God has made and maintains beautiful things that please the aesthetic sensibilities, these things must have been expressly created for humanity to meet its need for aesthetic gratification. Subjugation takes this a step further by emphasizing the value of the created world from the point of view of human *physical* sustenance. In this case, members of the created world retain their individual value and identity, but in a more impersonal and calculating manner. Trees are esteemed, but in terms of the fruit they can offer for human consumption, or wood for heating and shelter. Animals are valued, but in terms of the caloric content of their milk or meat, or the utility of their wool or skin for clothing. It is not surprising that the celestial bodies are largely absent from hymns and texts of this type, with the important exception of the sun, which gives warmth, light, and some protection from the physical dangers of nighttime darkness.

The Subduing subcategory is primarily concerned with mankind's dominion over creation. There is certainly strong backing from the biblical narrative for such a position, which I will describe in more detail below. Hymns of this kind tend to focus on the fact that humanity has been "put in charge" of creation, but without any specific instructions, injunctions, or restrictions related to this charge. The subcategory of Stewardship *does* provide such instructions to a greater or lesser extent. While maintaining the principle of human dominion, as well as creation's value as a consumable resource, Stewardship admits the notion of creation as a gift, with a tacit—and at times, explicit—expectation that God expects it to be used and managed wisely. The baseline of creation's value to humanity increases between Subduing and Stewardship, because natural resources become something that, through proper administration and attention to sustainability, can be increased to support a larger human population, and over a longer period of time. It may seem then that the Stewardship ethic belongs in the category of Conservation, and to a certain extent it does. However, the operative difference is not in the *how* of stewardship, but in the *why*.

The *why* is found within the final major category of Conservation, which is again connected to the inherent value of creation, but not in the human-centered value systems of the previous categories. In those categories, human aesthetic enjoyment and physical sustenance are the primary objectives of creation. In contrast, Conservation provides an intrinsic value for the created world, which is both outside and independent of human desires and needs, or even recognition. This ethic asserts that members of the non-human creation have identities and values in and of themselves, and even a purpose and a destiny imbued to them by God, entirely separate from human interests.

The first subcategory of Conservation, Prompting, is related to the earlier subcategory of Existence, and in some ways they parallel one another. However, while Existence does not urge mankind to do anything apart from acknowledging the reality of creation—which requires no self-reflection—the Prompting ethic tells humanity that it should follow the example of the created world in praising God, and importantly, that the non-human world possesses a spiritual dimension that humanity does not have. In this ethic, humanity admits that the creation is able to relate to God in ways that it does not, or *can*not. Nature is thus valuable as a model for imitation, and such imitation improves humanity, making its *musica humana* "better-tuned." The final subcategory is Kinship. Kinship makes the revolutionary assertion that individual members of creation have their own individuality, their own needs and desires, and maintain their own value, not only independent of humanity, but in ways equal to and interconnected with those of mankind. This suggests a familial association, one in which all members relate to one another in an extended, interdependent, and mutually beneficial kinship relationship. In this case, humanity values the created world, not as something that beautifies the landscape or provides for physical and spiritual wants, but that values creation in the same way it values itself.

DOMINION AND PILGRIMAGE

Before moving on to a closer examination of the various categories, I feel that the concept of value in creation bears a deeper examination. The Bible does not provide many statements about humanity's relationship with the created world, and those that exist are largely statements of dominion, as in the following passages:

> Then God said, "Let Us make man in Our image, according to Our likeness; let them have dominion over the fish of the sea, over the birds of the air, and over the cattle, over all the earth and over every creeping thing that creeps on the earth." So God created man in his own image, in the image of God created he him; male and female created he them. And God blessed them, and God said unto them, Be fruitful, and multiply, and replenish the earth, and subdue it: and have dominion over the fish of the sea, and over the fowl of the air, and over every living thing that moveth upon the earth.[3]

> Then God blessed Noah and his sons, saying to them, "Be fruitful and increase in number and fill the earth. The fear and dread of you will fall on all the beasts of the earth, and on all the birds in the sky, on every creature that moves along the ground, and on all the fish in the sea; they are given into your hands. Everything that lives and moves about will be food for you. Just as I gave you the green plants, I now give you everything."[4]

Many hymns and texts reinforce the concept of dominion using the language and imagery of the above Old Testament passages, but an important contributing factor is the notion of *pilgrimage* that appears in the New Testament. Such passages emphasize that humans do not belong to, or are not of, the earth, which is ephemeral and doomed to fire and destruction. Our "true home" is elsewhere:

> For our citizenship is in heaven, from which we also eagerly wait for the Savior, the Lord Jesus Christ.[5]

> For this world is not our permanent home; we are looking forward to a home yet to come.[6]

This notion of temporary pilgrimage through an undesirable or transitory environment is common in hymn texts, including the following two examples:

I'm but a stranger here, Heaven is my home:
Earth is a desert drear, Heaven is my home:
Danger and sorrow stand Round me on every hand;
Heaven is my father-land, Heaven is my home.

What though the tempest rage! Heaven is my home:
Short is my pilgrimage; Heaven is my home:[7]

This world is not my home, I'm just passing by,
My treasures and my hopes are all laid up on high;
Where many friends and kindreds are gone on before,
I can't feel at home any more.
O Lord, you know I have no friend like you!
If heaven's not my home, Lord what shall I do?
Loved ones beckon me from heaven's welcome door,
And I can't feel at home in this world any more.[8]

Clearly the purpose of these texts is to attract attention to heavenly things, with the hope of a future devoid of trouble—such as the sorrow, danger, and raging tempests mentioned above. Such a desire for a future, better world is a familiar theme in Christian theology and eschatology, but it has a number of potentially harmful side effects. For example, if the earth is impermanent, and one is simply passing through on the way to a more preferred destination, what particular mandate does humanity have to care for it in a way that allows it to remain a home—even a temporary one—for generations of future wayfarers? On the one hand, an attitude emphasizing the impermanence of the earthly environment may be considered positive among Christians, (sometimes) countering tendencies toward avarice and rampant materialism. On the other hand, the view that "it's all going to burn anyway" does not tend to prompt actions that ensure a viable and sustainable ecosystem for all.

The concept of a temporary home under the dominion of mankind looms large in Christian theology and hymnody. However, many hymns and texts also proclaim and affirm the beauty and the value of the created world, and I will treat them in order as we return to the categories introduced at the beginning of the chapter.

THE ETHIC OF ACKNOWLEDGMENT: EXISTENCE

Acknowledging the existence of the created world does not require a stretch of the imagination, though, as noted above, references to the created world are often made only metaphorically in hymns. In the subcategory of Existence, members of the created world are not described as being "like" anything else, but are distinctly and uniquely *themselves*. To admit that something has an identity implies that it possesses a kind of personhood, and perhaps even a form of agency and independence, though not always in a strictly human sense. The first six verses of Isaac Watts' 1715 paraphrase of the first chapter of Genesis[9] capture this essence:

I sing th'Almighty Pow'r of God,
That made the Mountains rise,
That spread the flowing seas abroad,
And built the lofty Skies.

I sing the Wisdom that ordain'd
The Sun to rule the Day;
The Moon shines full at His Command,
And all the Stars obey.

I sing the Goodness of the Lord,
That fill'd the Earth with Food;
He form'd the Creatures with his Word,
And then pronounced them good.

Lord, how thy Wonders are display'd,
Where're I turn my Eye,
If I survey the Ground I tread,
Or gaze upon the Sky.

There's not a Plant or Flower below
But makes thy Glories known;
And Clouds arise, and Tempests blow
By Order from thy Throne.

Creatures (as numerous as they be)
Are subject to thy Care;
There's not a Place where we can flee,
But God is present there.[10]

Watts' hymn illustrates the *what* of the created world: mountains, seas, skies, the sun, moon, and stars, creatures, plants, flowers, clouds, tempests, the land, and the air. It also identifies *who* provides these things, namely God. As might be expected from a work initially intended for children, the hymn reads as a kind of mnemonic device to aid in recalling major components of creation. While some passages do speak of the love and power of God in creating all of these wonderful things, the hymn is, ultimately, a list. It is a hymn of Existence, which does not suggest that any of these things are *like* any other thing, but simply are what they are, and doing what they do.

Another hymn acknowledging the existence of creation, and the unique identity of each part—specifically planned and designed by God—is a setting of an 1848 poem by Cecil Frances Alexander, "All Things Bright and Beautiful." This text has remained popular through Martin Shaw's 1915 hymn adaptation, Sir John Rutter's excellent modern choral version, and the use of phrases from the poem as titles for the American omnibus editions of the beloved animal stories of James Herriot. I will include the stanzas most commonly included in modern hymnals:

All things bright and beautiful,
All creatures great and small,
All things wise and wonderful,
The Lord God made them all.

Each little flower that opens,
Each little bird that sings,
He made their glowing colours,
He made their tiny wings.

The purple-headed mountain,
The river running by,
The sunset and the morning
That brightens up the sky,

The cold wind in the winter,
The pleasant summer sun,
The ripe fruits in the garden,
He made them every one.

The tall trees in the greenwood,
The meadows where we play,
The rushes by the water,
We gather every day;–

He gave us eyes to see them,
And lips that we might tell,
How great is God Almighty,
Who has made all things well.[11]

Again, this is largely a list of members of the created world, and a reminder that God created them. However, the final verse brings us a step further than a simple recitation of the wonders of creation, by noting a particularly *human* element that takes us into the next subcategory.

THE ETHIC OF ACKNOWLEDGMENT: AESTHETIC VALUE

Note the first line of the final verse of "All Things Bright and Beautiful" above. Here, we see that God not only created things of astounding beauty and variety, but that "He gave us eyes to see them." Certainly, all creatures have some means of sensory perception—not always eyes—through which they react to stimuli and survive in their various environments, but here, humans are given eyes precisely for the purpose of seeing and enjoying the other members of creation. This assumes a greater value for creation from a human standpoint: creation not only exists, but it is *good* for something, namely the pleasing of human senses. The first two lines of "Praise We the Lord," a hymn written in 1928 by Sir James Steuart Wilson, makes this point rather succinctly:

Praise we the Lord, who made all beauty
For all our senses to enjoy.[12]

Wilson's hymn makes it clear that beauty exists for the purpose of mankind's enjoyment. While this compels humankind to acknowledge the existence and beauty of creation, it also prompts humanity to understand that each created being has physical needs, that can only be supplied by God. The first two verses of Cecilia M. Caddell's 1853 hymn, "Behold the lilies of the field," illustrates this latter point:

Behold the lilies of the field,
They neither toil nor sow;
Yet God doth all things needful yield,
That they may bud and blow.

Not Solomon in glory shone
Like one of these poor flowers,
That look to God, and God alone,
For sunshine and for showers.[13]

This hymn demonstrates God's singular position of responsibility ("to God, and God alone") for the care of creation. Humankind has, as yet, no burden of responsibility, except to "behold." Aesthetic beauty, as seen in celestial objects, has additional usefulness to humanity, namely the reminder of mankind's own place in the cosmic hierarchy, and the sense of wonder—perhaps even humility—that such a realization should inspire. We observe this reminder in the second verse of "The Duteous Day Now Closeth" by the seventeenth-century composer Paul Gerhardt, here in an 1899 paraphrase translation by Robert S. Bridges:

Now all the heav'nly splendour
Breaks forth in starlight tender
From myriad worlds unknown;
And man, the marvel seeing,
Forgets his selfish being,
For joy of beauty not his own.[14]

As I mentioned above, the recognition of something, even the perception of its beauty, is not the same as giving it real and tangible value.[15] Of course, the concept of *tangibility* is fraught with tendencies toward exploitation and abuse, unless other values are also considered. It is to this often-unfortunate reality of exploitation that we now turn.

THE ETHIC OF SUBJUGATION: SUBDUING

In the previous section, we saw hymns demonstrating God's care for created beings by providing for their physical needs. It follows that, if mankind is the foremost member of creation, there will be an abundance of hymns and texts noting God's particular provision for humanity. This is illustrated by the many hymns that treat the non-human creation as a source of necessary, material sustenance.[16] Texts about harvesting and gathering supplies of food are common, such as the first verse of the 1844 hymn "Come, Ye Thankful People, Come" by Henry Alford:

Come, ye thankful people, come,
Raise the song of Harvest-home!
All is safely gathered in,
Ere the winter storms begin:
God our Maker doth provide
For our wants to be supplied:–
Come to God's own temple, come,
Raise the song of Harvest-home![17]

While Alford's hymn does not *directly* suggest that humanity's needs, as supplied by God, are greater than the needs of the other members of creation,[18] other texts imply this by emphasizing mankind's distinctly privileged position. "God of the Earth, the Sky, the Sea," a hymn by Samuel Longfellow—younger brother of the American poet Henry Wadsworth Longfellow—begins with a statement of divine regard for the entire creation, followed by a declaration of its aesthetic properties, ending with a verse emphasizing humankind's higher and privileged relationship, both to God above and to the created world below:

God of the earth, the sky, the sea!
Maker of all above, below!
Creation lives and moves in Thee,
Thy present life through all doth flow.

Thee in the lonely woods we meet,
On the bare hills or cultured plains,
In every flower beneath our feet,
And even the still rock's mossy stains.
[. . .]
But higher far, and far more clear,
Thee in man's spirit we behold;
Thine image and Thyself are there,–
The Indwelling God, proclaimed of old.[19]

This is a clear statement of hierarchy with mankind in an honored position, one that provides humanity with the authority necessary to subdue the rest of creation. However, this illuminates only a part of the hierarchical "ladder," that which exists on earth. A similar "ladder" is found in the fourth verse of John Ellerton's 1871 hymn, "The Day of Praise is Done," but this illustrates mankind's position within the *divine* hierarchy:

Yet, Lord, to Thy dear will
If Thou attune the heart,
We in Thine angels' music still
May bear our lower part.[20]

There is much to unpack in this single verse. First, there is a reference to "attunement," the tuning of the *musica humana* through submission to God, the personification of *musica mundana*. This *musica humana* is connected to *musica mundana* through humanity's participation in the music of the angels, but at a specific level, the "lower part" that mankind occupies, even when otherwise attuned to God's will. While this verse may not appear, at first glance, to support an ethic of human subjugation vis-à-vis the earthly created orders, the placing of humanity *here*, with one hand grasping the lower rungs of the divine hierarchy, is of paramount importance in maintaining a system of dominion over "lower" orders. Although mankind plays only a minor role in the divine harmony, none of the other members of creation participate in the "angels' music." This special position, as part of the earthly *and* heavenly hierarchies, places humanity in a kind of viceregal capacity, with prerogatives similar to those exercised by royalty. The fourth verse of an 1893 hymn by Emily F. Seal, "What is thy birthright, man," makes this clear:

Take then the charmed rod;
Thou art not error's thrall!
Thou hast the gift of God
—Dominion over all.[21]

The following poem by Rudyard Kipling, written in 1897 during the Victorian Diamond Jubilee, extends the concept of royal domination by mankind. The words and images are very much a product of their time:

God of our fathers, known of old,
Lord of our far-flung battle-line,
Beneath whose awful Hand we hold
Dominion over palm and pine—
Lord God of hosts, be with us yet,
Lest we forget, lest we forget![22]

Humanity's position as representatives of the divine power is clearly stated in the third line, where it is described as the very hand of God. "Dominion over palm and pine" is a literary device intended to encompass the entire natural world in the form of two kinds of trees, that indicate vastly different ecosystems and biomes. One could read this line as "dominion from north to south," or some other sweeping geographical generalization. Such dominion is not limited to the natural, non-human world, but extends into the human sphere, as might be expected in a poem written by Kipling during a period of massive British imperial expansion, with its attendant patriotic and nationalistic fervor. For Kipling, (white, male, and British) dominion is a part of the divine blueprint, with the rest of humankind variously described as "lesser breeds without the law," and "heathen heart that puts her trust in reeking tube and iron shard." It should not be lost on us, as it was not lost on

Kipling's readers, that such "heathens" and "lesser breeds" were considered not *quite* human, and thus did not possess a place on the divine side of the hierarchy.

Not every text of the Subduing type is as egregiously jingoistic as Kipling's.[23] "O How Glorious, Full of Wonder," a 1958 hymn by the minister Curtis Beach, certainly maintains a position of subjugation, as the passage below illustrates:

Thou hast given man dominion
O'er the wonders of thy hand,[24]

However, a later portion of the hymn is of particular interest, and is relatively unique in hymnody of this ethic, because it confesses the darker side of human dominion over the created world:

Soaring spire and ruined city,
These our hopes and failures show.[25]

Here, we are given examples of both the success and the failure of the human subjugation of the earth: the "soaring spire" as a symbol of hope, and the "ruined city" illustrating our negligence and carelessness. The solution for such human failure is the following:

Teach us more of human pity,
That we in thine image grow.[26]

Beach's hymn ultimately calls on mankind to practice humility in its dominion of the earth and, as the next section will illustrate, to exercise wise stewardship while exercising that dominion.

THE ETHIC OF SUBJUGATION: STEWARDSHIP

The practice of treating the created world as a consumable resource can serve humanity's physical needs only when the population is maintained at a level the natural world can support. From the perspective of the writers of the biblical accounts, living at a time when the human population is much lower, and the earth more dangerous and less "subduable," stewardship may seem a curious concept. The last few centuries of human history, however, characterized by steep population surges and increased stresses on limited natural resources, have opened our minds to the concept of sustainability, even if for strictly human ends. An ethic of Stewardship has the effect of *increasing* the inherent value of creation so that, through proper management and planning, the subjugation of the natural world can be maintained, allowing for maximum utility for the largest possible human population.

Just as the stewardship parables of Jesus illustrate the consequences of poor management—usually in the form of some awful punishment for the incompetent or faithless steward—so too do hymn texts warn of the practical and spiritual dangers of mankind's mismanagement of creation. The final verse of Charles Kingsley's 1871 hymn, "From Thee All Skill and Science Flow," looks forward to a time of proper stewardship:

When ever blue the sky shall gleam,
And ever green the sod;
And man's rude work deface no more
The Paradise of God.[27]

A large number of Stewardship hymns and texts are similar to those of the Subduing ethic—in that humanity is the divinely appointed overseer of the created world—but they include additional language, warning mankind against taking an attitude of *direct* ownership over creation, with the rampant greed and waste that invariably results. The following passage from the 1893 hymn, "Son of God, Eternal Saviour" by Somerset Corry Lowry, concisely sets up humanity's position in this ethic. Mankind's stewardship of the world exists in a larger context of *divine* ownership, where humanity is directed to imitate God in selflessness, and commanded to avoid abusing the creation for which it has been given responsibility:

As Thou, Lord, hast lived for others, so may we for others live.
Freely have Thy gifts been granted, freely may Thy servants give.
Thine the gold and Thine the silver, Thine the wealth of land and sea,
We but stewards of Thy bounty, held in solemn trust for Thee.

Come, O Christ, and reign among us, King of love, and Prince of peace;
Hush the storm of strife and passion, bid its cruel discords cease:
By Thy patient years of toiling, by Thy silent hours of pain,
Quench our fever'd thirst of pleasure, shame our selfish greed of gain.[28]

In Lowry's hymn, humans are enjoined to wisely manage the bounty of creation, but for the ultimate purpose of sustaining humankind. While avoiding greed and strife, and fairly distributing the blessings of creation to other humans, is good *musica humana*, it still fails to consider the created world as valuable for its own sake.

As I mentioned near the beginning of the chapter, lines between categories and subcategories sometimes blur, and such is the case with the ethic of Stewardship. Thus far, we have not seen any indication that the non-human members of creation have any particular value or worth, apart from their ability to be beautiful, to sustain mankind's physical needs, or as property to be maintained by divine command. However, the following hymns stray into such territory, where the inherent self-worth of created beings begins to be hinted at. It is no coincidence that these hymns are relatively modern. The first is Fred Pratt Green's "God in His Love for Us," written in 1973:

God in His love for us lent us this planet,
Gave it a purpose in time and in space:
Small as a spark from the fire of creation,
Cradle of life and the home of our race.

Thanks be to God for its bounty and beauty,
Life that sustains us in body and mind:
Plenty for all, if we learn how to share it,
Riches undreamed of to fathom and find.

Long have our human wars ruined its harvest;
Long has earth bowed to the terror of force;
Long have we wasted what others have need of,
Poisoned the fountain of life at its source.

Earth is the Lord's: it is ours to enjoy it,
Ours, as His stewards, to farm and defend.
From its pollution, misuse, and destruction,
Good Lord, deliver us, world without end![29]

This hymn has brief moments that value the non-human creation as something with "a purpose in time and in space," but it is still largely one of subjugation, and the exhortations are ultimately in the service of "our race," and "what [humans] have need of." A similar example is a 1969 hymn by Walter Farquharson, "For Beauty of Meadows":

For beauty of meadows, for grandeur of trees,
For flowers of woodlands, for creatures of seas,
For all You created and gave us to share,
We praise You, Creator, extolling Your care.

As stewards of beauty received at Your hand,
As creatures who hear Your most urgent command,
We turn from our wasteful destruction of life,
Confessing our failures, confessing our strife.

Teach us once again to be gardeners in peace;
All nature around us is ours but on lease;
Your name we would hallow in all that we do,
Fulfilling our calling, creating with You.[30]

At the very least, this hymn *names* some of the non-human members of creation, with a veiled hint that "our wasteful destruction of life" is bad for them, as well as for us. However, it is in the next ethic, Conservation, that we begin to see a true change of focus, from human-centered to creation-centered.

THE ETHIC OF CONSERVATION: PROMPTING

There are many hymns and texts that speak of the creation praising the creator. However, nearly all of them are calls for creation to imitate *humanity* in praising God, which assumes that such praise is natural to mankind, but not to the rest of the created world. In this section, we will see that this is not always the case, and mankind is rebuked for being the *only* member of creation that does not naturally praise its creator. This is illustrated in the first two verses of a 1940 hymn by Douglas Albert Raoul Aufranc, "Far From All Care":

Far from all care we hail the Sabbath morning;
O'er waving fields and from the distant sea
Swell notes of praise in harmony resounding
As all creation turns her heart to Thee.

Though man alone, Lord, of Thy great creation
Fails now to laud Thee for Thy love and power,
Yet still a remnant love Thee and remember
Thy holy law and each sweet Sabbath hour.[31]

The subcategory of Prompting is related to, and often moves together with, the earlier subcategory of Existence. However, the Prompting ethic differs in showing that members of the non-human creation have something humans lack—not a physical lack, but a spiritual one. While humanity easily perceives physiological differences between itself and the world, wherever such differences are obvious and not particularly noteworthy—birds have wings, trees have branches, humans have neither—any realization of the *spiritual* dimension of the non-human creation is indeed worthy of note. While mankind may be excused for considering itself the only spiritual being in the world, it may be shocked to observe that other members of creation also have spiritual properties, including intimate contact with the creator. A well-loved example in Christian hymnody is "Joyful, Joyful, We Adore Thee," by Henry van Dyke, known widely in its 1907 musical setting to one of the major themes of Ludwig van Beethoven's Ninth Symphony. The second verse below demonstrates the Prompting ethic:

All Thy works with joy surround Thee,
Earth and heaven reflect Thy rays,
Stars and angels sing around Thee,
Centre of unbroken praise:
Field and forest, vale and mountain,
Blooming meadow, flashing sea,
Chanting bird and flowing fountain
Call us to rejoice in Thee.[32]

Here, all creation instinctively rejoices and praises their creator—except for humanity, which must be *called* to participate in the spiritual festivities. The other members of creation need no reminder to praise, but mankind does. Going further, the Prompting ethic urges humanity, as it makes its observations of the natural world, to imitate the harmony between and among the members of the different created orders. This is again a call for mankind to "tune" its *musica humana*, through and by its proximity to *musica mundana*. One such example is found in the third verse of "O Peace of the World," written in 1932 by Irving Clinton Tomlinson:

As stars in their courses never contend,
As blossoms their hues in harmony blend,
As bird-voices mingle in joyful refrain,
So God's loving children in concord remain.[33]

Tomlinson's hymn uses "as . . . so" clauses—strengthening the effect by using "as" three times in succession—to illustrate the harmony to which humanity should aspire. Another example is the 1836 hymn, "O Lord! How Happy Should We Be," by Joseph Anstice. The following verses illustrate positive attitudes and qualities that are innate to members of the non-human creation, and that humans should imitate:

We cannot trust him as we should,
So chafes fallen nature's restless mood
To cast its peace away;
Yet birds and flowerets round us preach,

And all, the present evil, teach
Sufficient for the day.

Lord, make these faithless hearts of ours
Such lessons learn from birds and flowers,
Make them from self to cease,
Leave all things to our Father's will,
And taste, before him lying still,
E'en in affliction, peace.[34]

We must note that "weak nature's restless mood" does not refer to nature as a whole, but rather human nature—the hymn is not indicting *musica mundana*, but rather *musica humana*. Other hymns suggest that God created the world with its changing seasons in order to teach humanity valuable lessons. The following hymn, originally written in Latin in the late sixteenth century as "Tempus Adest Floridum," appears in a 1928 translation by Percy Dearmer. It begins with a description of the winter sleep of herbs and plants, and their transition to springtime:

Now bestirring, green and strong,
Find in growth their pleasure:[35]

The use of the word "pleasure" here is telling, as it ascribes to plant life the ability to experience emotion. This continues and is expanded on in a subsequent passage:

Flowers make glee among the hills,
Set the meadows dancing.[36]

This affirms that the creation—even the *flora*—has the capacity, not only for pleasure, but for exuberant emotions like "glee." Importantly, from the standpoint of the Prompting ethic, these capacities are meant to teach humanity something, namely to be mindful of its own spiritual condition:

In His grace of glad new birth
We must seek revival.[37]

To a certain extent, Dearmer's hymn uses anthropomorphic language to describe the work of nature, but it should also give us pause to consider the nature of anthropomorphism itself. Why is it that expressing happiness and enjoying the pleasures of life is so often considered a strictly *human* phenomenon, that other creatures must by needs imitate? If all of created nature relishes life, and in many of the same ways, then we have much more in common with the created world than otherwise. It may be that humanity, while busy pursuing its own affairs, is depriving itself of these commonalities.[38]

THE ETHIC OF CONSERVATION: KINSHIP

The highest point of the proposed value axis is Conservation expressed through Kinship. We have seen how humanity values the created world, from acknowledging its existence, to recognizing its worth as an aesthetic and physical resource, to the perception of nature's spiritual dimensions. The final step is one in which mankind identifies a familial relationship between itself and the rest of creation. Many hymns and texts call on humankind to show pity, compassion, and brotherly love to other humans, but hymns in the Kinship subcategory challenge mankind to widen the scope to include the entire world and everything in it.[39] The fourth verse of Laurence Housman's 1919 hymn, "Father Eternal, Ruler of Creation," lightly touches on this ethic:[40]

How shall we love thee, holy, hidden Being,
If we love not the world which thou hast made?
O give us brother-love for better seeing
Thy Word made flesh, and in a manger laid:
Thy kingdom come, O Lord, thy will be done.[41]

Somewhat obscured in the language of the first three lines is a revolutionary suggestion, that humanity *cannot* love God, unless it also regards the created world with "brother-love." Though not a hymn, Johann Wolfgang von Goethe's *Faust* is a poem, and the author puts beautiful words into the mouth of his eponymous protagonist, as he observes nature in the wilderness giving thanks to the creator spirit.

Erhabner Geist, du gabst mir, gabst mir alles,	Sublime Spirit, you gave me everything, gave me all I ever asked.
Warum ich bat. Du hast mir nich umsonst Dein Angesicht in Feuer zugewendet.	Not in vain you turned your fiery countenance on me.
Gabst mir die herrliche Natur zun Königreich, Kraft, sie zu fühlen, zu genießen. Nicht	You gave me glorious Nature for my kingdom, the strength to feel and to enjoy Her.
Kalt staunenden Besuch erlaubst du nur, Vergönnest mir, in ihre tiefe Brust, Wie in den Busen eines Freunds, zu schauen.	You gave me more than a visit merely of cold wonderment; you granted that I peer into Her boundless depths as I peer into a friendly heart.
Du führst die Reihe der Lebendigen Vor mir vorbei, und lehrst mich meine Brüder In stillen Busch, in Luft und Wasser kennen.	And you pass the ranks of living creatures before me, and you acquaint me with my brothers in silent bush, in airy heights and water.[42]

While earlier parts of this passage, such as "You gave me glorious Nature for my kingdom," may align with the ethic of Subjugation, the poem goes on to describe the natural world as something that can be understood like the heart of a friend, and the living creatures as members of one's own family.[43]

Perhaps the greatest hymn illustrating the familial relationship between humankind and non-human creation was written in 1224 by St. Francis of Assisi.[44] Composed in Umbrian-Italian nearly a full century before Dante's *Comedia*, it is among the first pieces of literature written in any Italian dialect. Paraphrases and glosses of the text are common in hymnals, especially William H. Draper's 1919 paraphrase, "All Creatures of Our God and King." For sake of clarity, I eliminate some of the repetitions:

All creatures of our God and King,
Lift up your voice and with us sing:
O burning sun with golden beam
And silver moon with softer gleam:

Thou rushing wind that are so strong,
Ye clouds that sail in heav'n along,
Thou rising morn, in praise rejoice,
Ye lights of evening, find a voice,

Thou flowing water, pure and clear,
Make music for thy Lord to hear,
Thou fire so masterful and bright,
That givest man both warmth and light,

And all ye men of tender heart,
Forgiving others, take your part,
Ye who long pain and sorrow bear,
Praise God and on Him cast your care,

Let all things their Creator bless,
And worship Him in humbleness,
Praise, praise the Father, praise the Son,
And praise the Spirit, three in one,[45]

This is a beautiful hymn, especially when set to the melody "Lasst uns erfreuen," with Ralph Vaughan Williams' peerless harmonization. However, St. Francis' original has something that modern paraphrases leave out, and that is the kinship relationships that pervade the original text. For St. Francis, the non-human creation is not only aesthetically pleasing, useful for human sustenance and comfort, and spiritually uplifting—though it is indeed all of those things—it is also a member of his family, "blood-related" by having its being in the mind of the same creator:

Altissimu, onnipotente bon Signore, Tue so' le laude la gloria e l'onore, e onne benedictione. A te solo, altissimu, se konfanno, e nullu homo ene dignu te mentovare.	Almighty, most high, good Lord God, thine are the glory, praise, honor, and all blessing! To Thee alone, Almighty, do they belong and no man is worthy to speak Thy name.
Laudato si, mi Signore, cum tucte le tue creature, spetialmente lu messor frate sole, lu quale lu iorno, et allumeni per nui; E ellu è bellu e radiante cum grande splendore; de te, altissimo, porta significatione.	Praise be to Thee, O Lord, for all Thy creatures and especially for our brother the sun who gives us the day and who shows forth Thy light. Fair is he and radiant with great splendor. To us he is the symbol of Thee, O Lord.
Laudato si, mi Signore, per sora luna e le stele; in celu l'ài formate, clarite e pretiose e belle.	Praise be to Thee, O Lord, for our sister the moon and for the stars. Thou hast set them clear, beautiful and precious in the heaven above.
Laudato si, mi Signore, per frate ventu e per aere e nubilo e sereno e onne tempu, per le quale a le tue creature dài sustentamentu.	Praise be to Thee, O Lord, for our brother the wind, for the air and the clouds, for the clear sky and for all weathers by which Thou givest life and the means of life to all Thy creatures.
Laudato si, mi Signore, per sora aqua; la quale è multo utile, e humele e pretiosa e casta.	Praise be to Thee, O Lord, for our sister water who is so serviceable to us, humble also, precious and chaste.
Laudato si, mi Signore, per frate focu, per lu quale n'allumeni la nocte; e ellu è bellu e iucundu e rubustosu e forte.	Praise be to Thee, O Lord, for our brother fire, by whom Thou givest us light in the darkness; he is beautiful and bright, courageous and strong.
Laudato si, mi Signore, per sora nostra matre terra,la quale ne sustenta e governa, e produce diversi fructi et colorati flori e herba.	Praise be to Thee, O Lord, for our mother the earth who sustains us and nourishes us, bringing forth divers fruits, flowers of many colors and the grass.
Laudato si, mi Signore, per quilli ke perdonano per lo tuo amore e sostengo infirmitate e tribulatione; Beati quilli ke le sosterrano in pace, ka da te, altissimu, siranno incoronati.	Praise be to Thee, O Lord, for all those who are forgiving one to another for His love's sake and who endure weakness and tribulation; blessed are they who shall endure peaceably, for Thou, O Most Highest, shall give them a crown.

Laudato si mi Signore, per sora nostra morte corporale, da la quale nullu homo vivente po' skampare: guai a quelli ke morrano in peccato mortale; beati quelli ke trovarà no le tue sanctissime voluntati, ka la morte secunda no li poterà far male.	Praise be to Thee, O Lord, for our sister the death of the body whom no man can escape. Woe unto him that dieth in mortal sin. Blessed are they who are found walking according to Thy most holy will for the second death shall be powerless to do them harm.
Laudate et benedicete lu mi Signore et rengratiate e servite a lui cum grande humilitate.[46]	Praise ye and bless ye the Lord and give thanks unto Him and serve Him with great humility.[47]

St. Francis' profound devotion to God, and his deep affection for the created world, is clear for all to see in his hymn. Such fraternal affection and regard for the non-human creation is rare, even in contemporary hymnody that has arisen in the wake of the environmentally conscious movements of the later twentieth century. It is even more remarkable to find such an example from the early thirteenth century, though St. Francis was clearly remarkable in many ways. But perhaps most significantly, St. Francis did not consider the created world a place of temporary pilgrimage, merely to be used, enjoyed, consumed, and ultimately destroyed, but rather akin—to be regarded, loved, and treated as family.

Just as we discovered with Dante in chapter 2, humanity—and by extension, its *musica humana*—cannot come away from contact with the *musica mundana* unscathed or unchanged. As the hymns and texts we have explored in this chapter show in part, mankind does not "come away" from this contact at all—humankind lives *within* the *musica mundana*, and is subject to its elements and seasons, just as the rest of the created world. The question follows, what kind of influence does humanity allow *musica mundana* to exert on itself? It is not absolute. Humans may choose to ignore the *musica mundana* completely, or otherwise acknowledge it, exploit it, sustain it, or claim it as part of its own family. All of these actions, or inactions, have an effect on the *musica humana*, for better or for worse, making humanity more, or less, attuned to the universe it calls home.

NOTES

1. Psalm 8:5–8 (NKJV). Scriptures marked (NKJV) are taken from the New King James Version®. Copyright © 1982 by Thomas Nelson. Used by permission. All rights reserved.

2. Psalm 42:1 (NKJV).

3. Genesis 1:26–28 (KJV). Scripture quotation from The Authorized (King James) Version. Rights in the Authorized Version in the United Kingdom are vested in the Crown. Reproduced by permission of the Crown's patentee, Cambridge University Press.

4. Genesis 9:1 (NIV)

5. Philippians 3:20 (NKJV).

6. Hebrews 13:14 (NLT). Scripture quotations marked (NLT) are taken from the Holy Bible, New Living Translation, copyright © 1996, 2004, 2007 by Tyndale House Foundation. Used by permission of Tyndale House Publishers, Inc., Carol Stream, IL 60188. All rights reserved.

7. W. S. Matthews, *Memoirs and Select Remains of the Rev. Thomas Rawson Taylor* (London: Westley and Davis, 1836), 242.

8. *Joyful Meeting in Glory Song Book No. 1*, 93.

9. This hymn also includes bits of Job and the Psalms.

10. Isaac Watts, *Divine Songs Attempted in Easy Language for the Use of Children* (London: M. Lawrence, 1715), 2–4.

11. Cecil Frances Alexander, *Hymns for Little Children* (London: Joseph Masters, 1852), 27–8. I have omitted the third verse, which is never used in modern hymn settings. It reads:

> The rich man in his castle,
> The poor man at his gate,
> God made them high and lowly,
> And ordered their estate.

This verse is ripe for social, political, and economic analysis, but is ultimately outside the scope of this book.

12. Martin Shaw, Percy Dearmer, and Ralph Vaughan Williams, eds., *The Oxford Book of Carols* (Oxford: Oxford University Press, 1928), 201.

13. *Catholic Hymns* (London: Burns and Lambert, 1853), 51.

14. Robert S. Bridges and H. Ellis Woolridge, eds., *The Yattendon Hymnal* (Oxford: B. H. Blackwell, 1905), 83.

15. In *Perelandra*, the second book of C. S. Lewis' *Space Trilogy*, the protagonist Ransom travels—on the back of a fish—over a vast ocean on Venus. The planet is in its "human infancy," meaning the planet and its oceans, plants, and animal life have existed for millions of years, but its first humans have been only recently created. Ransom muses about this Venusian reality, and wonders, what was the purpose of this planet full of teeming life, so long before the rise of humanity? What if all of this life has existed solely for *itself*? Ransom realizes that, "it was strange that he to whom a wood or a morning sky on earth had sometimes been a kind of meal, should have had to come to another planet in order to realise Nature as a thing in her own right." Lewis, *Perelandra*, 136. Ransom recognizes the aesthetic beauty and physical bounty of Venus, and that it does not exist merely for human consumption. As in Gerhardt's hymn, Ransom experiences "joy of beauty not his own."

16. I have never been entirely satisfied with placing Subjugation ahead of Aesthetic Value on the Value Axis. If we are considering the hierarchy of human

physical needs, it seems obvious to place aesthetics much lower than the physical needs of food, clothing, and shelter. As a musician, I place a high value on aesthetics, but Aesthetic Value has a lower *intrinsic* value in a strictly utilitarian sense—one could physically survive with access to food and not music, though with a dramatically reduced quality of life. However, when we turn to the larger Conservation ethic, human needs will not always be paramount, so I admit that my categorization system is not always easy to maintain.

17. Henry Alford, *The Poetical Works of Henry Alford: in Two Volumes*, vol. 2 (London: Francis & John Rivington, 1845), 160.

18. In chapter 3, we explored this hymn as it (likely) appears in C. S. Lewis' *The Magician's Nephew*, just before the creation of Narnia by Aslan. Digory, Polly, Uncle Andrew, Jadis, the cab driver, and his cab-horse have been transported by magic into Narnia, which is at this time dark, empty, and formless. Thinking they have perhaps fallen into a subway tunnel under construction, the cabby suggests they pass the time by singing a hymn. That this hymn is "Come, Ye Thankful People Come" is, according to Peter J. Schakel, perhaps a bit of a joke for Lewis, since they are singing about harvesting in a pre-created world in which nothing has ever grown. However, I argue that the hymn *predicts* the creation of Narnia, as a world in which all physical needs are met. Peter J. Schakel, *Imagination and the Arts in C. S. Lewis: Journeying to Narnia and Other Worlds* (Columbia: University of Missouri Press, 2002), 93–4. We can, however, analyze the use of this hymn in the context of Subjugation. The cab driver will, in just a few pages, be crowned King of Narnia and Aslan, the creator, will put him in charge of the newly created world, in much the same way God puts Adam and his descendants in charge of creation on our own earth. Though it is Aslan who sings Narnia into being, it is almost as if the cab driver sings *his* position in the Narnian hierarchy into being, with a hymn about subduing the created world for the good of humanity. Fortunately for the talking beasts, and the rest of the flora and fauna about to be created, the cab driver is a very decent, humble, and kindly man, and does not abuse his divinely delegated authority.

19. Samuel Longfellow and S. Johnson, eds. *Hymns of the Spirit* (Boston: Ticknor and Fields, 1864), 229.

20. Robert Brown-Borthwick, ed., *Select Hymns for Church and Home* (Edinburgh: Edmonston and Douglas, 1871), 34.

21. "The Seal of Love," *The Christian Science Journal* VIII/1 (April, 1890): 97.

22. Rudyard Kipling, *The Five Nations* (New York: Charles Scribner's Sons, 1903), 201.

23. We will, however, explore other aspects of this sort of jingoism in chapter 7.

24. *Pilgrim Hymnal* (Boston: The Pilgrim Press, 1958), 74.

25. Ibid.

26. Ibid.

27. *Charles Kingsley: His Letters and Memories of His Life*, vol 2, 11th ed. (London: C. Kegan Paul & Co., 1878), 371.

28. *Hymns Ancient and Modern* (London: William Clowes and Sons, Ltd., 1904), 696.

29. Words: Fred Pratt Green © 1973 The Hymn Society (Admin. Hope Publishing Company, www.hopepublishing.com). All rights reserved. Used by permission.

30. Words: Walter Farquharson © 1971 and this trans. © 2019 Walter Farquharson (admin. Hope Publishing Company, www.hopepublishing.com). All rights reserved. Used by permission.

31. *The Church Hymnal* (Takoma Park, MD: Review and Herald Publishing Association, 1941), 468.

32. Henry van Dyke, *The Poems of Henry van Dyke* (New York: Charles Scribner's Sons, 1914), 332.

33. *Christian Science Hymnal* (Boston, MA: The Christian Science Publishing Society, 1932), 236. Words by Irving C. Tomlinson. Reproduced from the *Christian Science Hymnal* with permission. © 1932 The Christian Science Board of Directors.

34. *The Child's Christian Year* (Philadelphia: Lea and Blanchard, 1842), 107–8.

35. Shaw, *The Oxford Book of Carols*, 125.

36. Ibid.

37. Ibid.

38. We are certainly aware of the positive effects of sounds and smells of nature—witness the brisk sales of "nature recordings" and nature-scented household products. Much of this book was written while I played recordings of ocean waves breaking on the shore, in an attempt (only partially successful) to eliminate distractions. Taking it several steps further, the practice of Forest Bathing, developed in Japan, immerses the human subject in the sights, sounds, and smells of nature. This has been linked to improvements in the health and well-being of the subjects. Many thanks to my student Chloe Hegstad for bringing this to my attention.

39. Leonardo Boff goes so far as to identify the earth and humanity as a single, indivisible whole. He imagines a time when "human beings come to understand that they and the Earth are one unit; and that this unit belongs to an even greater unity, that of the solar system; and that this unity in turn belongs to another, even greater unity, the galaxy; and that this belongs to the entire universe, which in the end belongs to the Mystery, and the Mystery to the Creator." Leonardo Boff and Robert H. Hopke, tr., *Toward an Eco-Spirituality* (Pearl River, NY: The Crossroad Publishing Company, 2015), 8–9.

40. The 1919 composition date for this hymn is important, as much of the world was reeling from the massive destruction caused by the Great War—disastrous to humans and the environment alike—to say nothing of the influenza pandemic simultaneously raging across the globe.

41. *American Student Hymnal* (New York: Fleming H. Revell Co., 1928), 64.

42. Johann Wolfgang von Goethe, and Peter Salm, tr., *Faust, Part 1*, rev. ed. (New York: Bantam Books, 1962), 220–1.

43. In C. S. Lewis' *Perelandra*, an angelic being gives the first two human inhabitants dominion over the planet Venus. As in the Biblical account of Adam and Eve, they are told to exercise authority over the rest of the created world. However, the terms are quite different than those found in Genesis, and support a dual subjugation/kinship reading of the text. The two first Venusian humans are told that all creation belongs to them, that they are to name and rule all things, and that they should fill the world with their children. In addition, they are commanded to *teach* the animals, "mak[ing] the nobler of the beasts so wise that they will become *hnau*

[rational beings] and speak: their lives shall awake to a new life in us." C. S. Lewis, *Perelandra*, 181. For these new humans, the created world of Venus acts not only as a source of sustenance, but is treated in the same way that parents raise and train their own children—as members of a family—causing them to grow and evolve into their own full potential. Interestingly, Ransom, who sees this happen on Venus, works to train and uplift animals back on Earth in *That Hideous Strength*, the final book of the trilogy.

44. The final passages praising "Sister bodily death" are said to have been composed by St. Francis on his deathbed in 1226.

45. *The Public School Hymn Book with Tunes* (London: Novello, 1919), 104–5.

46. Corrado Zacchetti, *Francesco d'Assisi e Le 'Laudes Creaturarum'* (Assisi: Tipografia Metastasio, 1904), 34–5.

47. *The Canticle of the Sun of St. Francis of Assisi* (New York: Duffield and Company, 1907)

Chapter Vignette 5.5

"Still, It May Be Useful"
The Ring of Sauron and the Value Axis

In the previous chapter, we examined various hymns and texts treating the relationship between the human and non-human spheres. While it may be possible to perform a similar investigation of relationships between the human (or human-equivalent) and the natural worlds in the works of Tolkien, such a treatment would largely rehash what has been done in a number of other excellent analyses. A different, and potentially useful, perspective is an examination of Sauron's Ring in terms of the value axis proposed in chapter 5. As with hymns and texts, we can use the value axis to determine the Ring's value to, and effect on, the *musica humana* of those who come into close contact with it.

Like the non-human created world, the Ring is an object that exists, possesses a measure of consciousness or sentience, has aesthetic value, can ostensibly be subjugated and used for one's own benefit, and is ultimately better "conserved," or left unused. Better yet, it should be destroyed, which is, somewhat ironically, an ultimate act of conservation. I will treat the major categories and subcategories of the value axis in a manner similar to the previous chapter, with the goal of highlighting the relationships between the human and non-human worlds, through Tolkien's creative lens.

The significance of the Ring is made clear in many of Tolkien's published works about Middle-earth, having its existence formally declared by the Ring spell included in the front matter of most modern editions of *The Lord of the Rings*:

Three Rings for the Elven-kings under the sky,
Seven for the Dwarf-lords in their halls of stone,
Nine for Mortal Men doomed to die,
One for the Dark Lord on his dark throne

In the Land of Mordor where the Shadows lie.
One Ring to rule them all, One Ring to find them,
One Ring to bring them all and in the darkness bind them
In the Land of Mordor where the Shadows lie.[1]

While such a basic acknowledgment of the Ring's existence is important (though obvious), it is the *aesthetic* value of the Ring that generally captures the attention of those who first encounter it. There are no accounts of how Sauron feels about his Ring as an object of beauty, and it is likely that he never considers it in such a light, being himself concerned solely with its practical uses of domination and control. However, the proximate possessor of the Ring, Isildur, does indeed note its aesthetic value:

> But for my part I will risk no hurt to this thing: of all the works of Sauron the only fair. It is precious to me, though I buy it with great pain.[2]

Isildur records this passage some months after achieving the defeat of Sauron, by cutting the Ring from his hand. It is not clear whether the physical beauty of the Ring itself is what initially tempts Isildur to keep it, against the advice of a number of wise elves, when it could have been destroyed with ease in the fires of nearby Mount Doom. However, it is clear that the *next* possessor of the Ring is instantly tempted by its beauty.[3] The hobbit Sméagol goes fishing in the river one day with his cousin Déagol. Déagol hooks a large fish, which pulls him out of the boat and into the water, where he sees something sparkling on the bottom of the riverbed. Grabbing at it, he resurfaces, and discovers that he has found a shining golden ring. Sméagol observes this:

> And he caught Déagol by the throat and strangled him, because the gold looked so bright and beautiful.[4]

In this case, Sméagol is enticed by the beauty of the Ring at first sight,[5] so much so that he immediately murders a close relative in order to possess it. A later possessor, Frodo, also observes the aesthetic value of the Ring after he becomes aware of its true identity:

> The gold looked very fair and pure, and Frodo thought how rich and beautiful was its colour, how perfect was its roundness. It was an admirable thing and altogether precious.[6]

Interestingly, when Frodo's uncle Bilbo encounters the Ring, he is unable to make any aesthetic observation at all, due to the fact that it is pitch dark when he first stumbles across it:

[Bilbo] guessed as well as he could, and crawled along for a good way, till suddenly his hand met what felt like a tiny ring of cold metal lying on the floor of the tunnel. It was a turning point in his career, but he did not know it. He put the ring in his pocket almost without thinking; certainly it did not seem of any particular use at the moment.[7]

We can assume that Bilbo comes to appreciate the aesthetic value of the Ring, as do nearly all its other possessors.[8]

The bearers of the Ring soon find other, more pragmatic uses for it, namely subjugating it for their own purposes and desires. Sméagol discovers some of these practical uses almost immediately:

But Sméagol [. . .] found that none of his family could see him, when he was wearing the ring. He was very pleased with this discovery and he concealed it; and he used it to find out secrets, and he put his knowledge to crooked and malicious uses. He became sharp-eyed and keen-eared for all that was hurtful.
[. . .]
He caught fish in deep pools with invisible fingers and ate them raw.[9]

Sméagol's uses for the Ring are personal and physical: he uses it to obtain knowledge within his community for personal gain, and also uses it for material sustenance. For his part, Bilbo almost immediately finds a practical and life-saving use for the Ring when he accidentally puts it on, while Sméagol is chasing him through dark tunnels beneath the mountains:

His head was in a whirl of hope and wonder. It seemed that the ring he had was a magic ring: it made you invisible! He had heard of such things, of course, in old old tales; but it was hard to believe that he really had found one, by accident.[10]

Throughout his adventure, Bilbo uses the invisibility granted by the Ring to elude goblins, save his dwarvish companions from giant spiders, organize an escape from the dungeons of an elven king, and spy on a dragon. Later, he finds more prosaic uses for it, such as avoiding unwelcome encounters with relatives. For his part, Frodo recognizes the Ring's utility nearly as quickly as Bilbo does when he comes into possession of it, though initially under less personally hazardous circumstances:

"You'll find [Bilbo's] will and all the other documents in there, I think," said [Gandalf]. "You are the master of Bag End now. And also, I fancy, you'll find a golden ring."

"The ring!" exclaimed Frodo. "Has he left me that? I wonder why. Still, it may be useful."

"It may, and it may not," said Gandalf. "I should not make use of it, if I were you. But keep it secret, and keep it safe!"[11]

The very next day, Frodo relates to Gandalf that he desired, as Bilbo had done, to use the Ring to avoid uncomfortable confrontations with his relatives. These examples show that Sméagol, Bilbo, and Frodo alike recognize the practical and useful nature of the Ring, similar to what we saw in hymns of the Subduing subcategory in the previous chapter. For these three hobbits, the Ring has value in promoting personal advantage in familial circumstances, as well as providing for physical needs. These users attempt to subjugate the Ring for their own personal wishes, for the presumed benefit of their own *musica humana*,[12] with little concern for the direct effects of its use on others.[13]

Alone among all the ringbearers in Tolkien's world, only Samwise comes into possession of the Ring with anything approaching a mindset of stewardship. Thinking that Frodo has been killed, after being poisoned by the spider Shelob, Samwise takes the Ring in order to continue the quest to destroy it:

> Already the Ring tempted him, gnawing at his will and reason. Wild fantasies arose in his mind; and he saw Samwise the Strong, Hero of the Age, striding with a flaming sword across the darkened land, and armies flocking to his call as he marched to the overthrow of Barad-dûr. And then all the clouds rolled away, and the white sun shone, and at his command the vale of Gorgoroth became a garden of flowers and trees and brought forth fruit. He had only to put on the Ring and claim it for his own, and all this could be.[14]

Samwise is tempted in two ways. First, he sees the possibility of overthrowing *evil* power through the agency of the Ring, with a concomitant preservation or advancement of *good* sources of power. This is also the temptation of Boromir, prince of Gondor, when he tries to convince Frodo to "lend" him the power of the Ring in defense of his city and country:

> We do not desire the power of wizard-lords, only strength to defend ourselves, strength in a just cause. And behold! in our need chance brings to light the Ring of Power. It is a gift, I say; a gift to the foes of Mordor. It is mad not to use it, to use the power of the Enemy against him.[15]

The wizard Saruman is tempted similarly, but over a much longer period of time, and with an initial view much broader in scope than the preservation of a single country or realm. But the end result is the same—a desire to meet power with power, and destroy evil so that good may remain:

> But none of these chances were impossible to be; for, strange indeed though this may seem, the [wizards], being clad in bodies of Middle-earth, might even as Men and Elves fall away from their purposes, and do evil, forgetting the good in the search for power to effect it.
> [. . .]
> Indeed, of all the [wizards], one only remained faithful [. . .]. And Curinír 'Lân, Saruman the White, fell from his high errand, and becoming proud and impatient and enamoured of power sought to have his own will by force, and to oust Sauron; but he was ensnared by that dark spirit, mightier than he.[16]

Samwise, Boromir, and Saruman alike are tempted to use the power of the Ring to overthrow Sauron, but if given the opportunity, they would be doomed to "[forget] the good in the search for power to effect it."

Samwise's second temptation to use the Ring is one closer to his heart, as he is a gardener by trade, and the stewardship of growing things is his particular concern. He desires to transform the barren volcanic plain of Gorgoroth into a vast garden full of living things, which appears to be a rather positive aspiration in a land that has been subjugated and denuded of natural life by Sauron. Here, using the Ring would (seemingly) allow Samwise to place the *musica mundana* of the created world in a privileged position—a strong temptation for a hobbit of his values and temperament. However, he is saved in the end by his own common sense, and the recognition that such power would eventually corrupt him, however noble his intentions:

> Deep down in him lived still unconquered his plain hobbit-sense: he knew in the core of his heart that he was not large enough to bear such a burden, even if such visions were not a mere cheat to betray him. The one small garden of a free gardener was all his need and due, not a garden swollen to a realm; his own hands to use, not the hands of others to command.[17]

The temptation to subdue and hold dominion over the natural world, using the power of the Ring, is ultimately defeated by Samwise's realization that such dominion is not his by right, and that he should rather aspire to exercise stewardship over only enough of creation sufficient for his own minor needs.

A curious character when considering the ethic of Subjugation is Isildur, who originally seizes the Ring from Sauron. While he clearly notes the aesthetic value of the Ring, as we saw above, it is not clear whether or not it tempts him with its potential for exercising power over people and things. We do not know exactly what Isildur thinks or attempts between the taking of the Ring from Sauron and his own death, but can make inferences from the following passage, part of a conversation between Isildur and his eldest son Elendur, which takes place as they are being attacked by orcs, just before both are killed:

> "*Atarinya*," [Elendur] said, "what of the power that would cow these foul creatures and command them to obey you? Is it then of no avail?"
> "Alas, it is not, *senya*. I cannot use it. I dread the pain of touching it. And I have not yet found the strength to bend it to my will. It needs one greater than I now know myself to be. My pride has fallen."[18]

It is clear from the passage that Isildur has not *yet* found the strength to subdue the Ring to his will, and that he must already have made some, ultimately unsuccessful, attempts to do so. These attempts must have made it clear to him that he did not have the innate strength to wield the power of the Ring, much as Samwise realized that "he was not large enough to bear such a burden." Even the powerful wizard Gandalf, though never himself possessing the Ring, recognizes his own limitations, as the following conversation with Frodo illustrates:

> [Frodo said] "You are wise and powerful. Will you not take the Ring?"
> "No!" cried Gandalf, springing to his feet. "With that power I should have power too great and terrible. And over me the Ring would gain a power still greater and more deadly."[19]

Isildur learns through experience, Gandalf perceives through wisdom and study, and Samwise grasps through simple common sense, the same notion: the Ring cannot be subjugated to any will but that of Sauron, its maker. This is true regardless of the innate power of the possessor, even that of formidable wizards such as Gandalf and Saruman, who are angelic creatures equal in celestial "rank" to Sauron. The Ring cannot be used by anyone, other than Sauron, as a tool for the domination of other wills; rather, one may only *become* a tool of the Ring. The Ring can only subdue—it cannot *be* subdued.

This brings us to the ethic of Conservation. Because the Ring is ultimately evil, and its power may only be used for corruption and domination, the sole method of "conserving" the power of the Ring is for it to remain unused, and ultimately to be destroyed. This is a true act of conservation, but one in which the effects remain ambiguous. The unmaking of the Ring only provides the peoples of Middle-earth the opportunity to pursue their *own* acts of conservation in the created world, which, given their new-found freedom from Sauron's domination, they may ultimately refuse to do.

The destruction of the Ring brings about a number of unintended consequences. Because the primary purpose of the Ring was to dominate the minds and wills of those possessing the other rings, which were created with the aid of Sauron's secret knowledge, the destruction of the Ring also ends the power of these rings. At least one of the three rings given to elves had been used to preserve a part of the created world, excluding it from the processes of death and decay. This is the living "time capsule" of Lórien, ruled by Galadriel, as discussed in chapter 3.5. The failing power of her ring represents the *opposite* of conservation, at least from the perspective of the residents of Lórien, as death and change can now enter their land, though they accept it as a fair price to pay for achieving the destruction of the Ring, and the permanent diminishment of Sauron. This represents the embrace of a lesser destruction, so that a greater potential conservation may occur.

In the final analysis, the Ring has true value only so far as it serves its original purpose—that of subjugating the minds and wills of others. To use it for any other purpose, no matter how noble, is to doom that purpose to failure. Just as with hymns and texts in the previous chapter, the Ring helps us to understand different modes of valuing sources of power and creative potential. Another important perspective is the observation of what happens to *musica humana*, when it is confronted and influenced by an object as dissonant as the Ring clearly is. In every case, the Ring serves to "de-tune" its possessors, so that they are no longer attuned to the *musica mundana* as they know it. If examined in this light, the Ring has no *value* whatsoever.

NOTES

1. Tolkien, *The Fellowship of the Ring*, xii.
2. Ibid., 253.
3. Isildur loses the Ring when it slips off his finger, as he is attempting to escape pursuing orcs by swimming across a river. Losing the invisibility granted by the Ring, he is killed by the orcs, and the Ring is lost for more than two thousand years.
4. Tolkien, *The Fellowship of the Ring*, 53.
5. So, assumedly, is Déagol, though he has precious little time to enjoy it.
6. Tolkien, *The Fellowship of the Ring*, 60.
7. Tolkien, *The Hobbit*, 65.
8. Samwise Gamgee's thoughts on this aspect of the Ring are not recorded. Neither are the thoughts of those "merely" tempted by the Ring, namely Boromir, Saruman, and perhaps Galadriel, all of whom are attracted by the power it offers, rather than by its physical beauty.
9. Tolkien, *The Fellowship of the Ring*, 53.
10. Tolkien, *The Hobbit*, 81.
11. Tolkien, *The Fellowship of the Ring*, 36.
12. Of course, selfishness is antithetical to *musica humana*, and as the negative experiences of the various possessors of the Ring illustrate, ultimately self-defeating.

13. Bilbo uses the Ring a number of times to rescue his companions, though he likely would have attempted to do so in any case, with or without the Ring.
14. Tolkien, *The Return of the King*, 911.
15. Tolkien, *The Fellowship of the Ring*, 401.
16. Tolkien, *Unfinished Tales*, 407–8.
17. Tolkien, *The Return of the King*, 911.
18. Tolkien, *Unfinished Tales*, 286.
19. Tolkien, *The Fellowship of the Ring*, 60.

Chapter 6

Bent Roads and *Bent* People

Noblest minds are easiest bent.[1]

Never has a man who has bent himself been able to make others straight.[2]

Throughout the book we have been exploring the uses and manifestations of various kinds of *musica* in works of theory, music, and literature. An important aspect of these forms of *musica* is how they "go out of tune," failing to exercise their full potential or influence. In chapter 3, we explored people and concepts that were *dissonant*, but a relatively novel, and potentially useful, approach to understanding mistuned *musica* is the idea of *bentness*. To be *bent* conveys the impression that a path of goodness, an ideal state of being, or a proper way of living exists, but is not followed.[3] Even when the term *bent* is not itself used, the idea of *bentness* nonetheless weaves its way through many of the texts we have examined thus far, together with several additional works of literature we will examine in this chapter. In general, *bentness*, along with the related concepts of *straightness* and *brokenness*, can be understood to be commentary on *musica*—most often *musica humana*, but sometimes *musica mundana* as well.[4]

Bentness may be found in a variety of mediums including individuals, objects, concepts, and physical locations. Among individuals, *bentness* may occur through conscious choice, the vagaries of one's genetic or physical condition at birth, or a combination of both. If good *musica humana* is defined as the proper balance of elements within an individual, as well as harmonious relationships within human societies, *bentness* expresses itself in negative qualities, both in the individual and in society. While one may actively choose to *bend* themselves, the cause of *bentness* may rather relate to a flaw in the *musica mundana*—a fault in the harmonious balance of the universe. In such a case, an individual may be *bent*, but the cause of the *bentness* lies in the imperfection of the created world itself, external to the individual.

Physical objects are another thing that may be *bent*, literally or conceptually. These include objects deliberately created or imbued with negative power and influence, as well as "neutral" objects that are loci of desire or conflict.[5] One expressly *bent* object is the Ring of Sauron, which instantly asserts negative influence on its possessor and those around them, regardless of their own innate virtue or positive intentions, as we saw in the previous chapter.

Likewise, there are *bent* concepts—systems of thinking and behaving that stray from received (or perceived) positive divine and human models. One such concept is found in Joseph Conrad's 1899 short novel *Heart of Darkness*, in which the purpose and mission of the company is to extract natural resources from the Congo, in spite of the horrendous human and social costs incurred. In *The Space Trilogy*, Dr. Edward Weston's motivation for achieving interplanetary travel is not exploration, or even resource extraction, but rather an obsessive desire to endlessly propagate the human species, while enslaving or exterminating all other forms of sentient life. In *The Invisible Man* of H. G. Wells, Griffin's wish to achieve invisibility is not simply the desire to make an important scientific breakthrough, but also to initiate a violent reign of terror. These ideas, concepts, and motivations are *bent*.

Finally, physical locations may also experience *bentness*. In Milton's *Paradise Lost*, sin enters Eden when Satan, in disguise as a serpent, convinces Eve to eat the forbidden fruit. As a result of this fall, the nature of the earth is changed, death and decay are introduced, the physical disposition of the earth is altered, and animals become enemies that attack one another. In Lewis' *The Great Divorce*, the gray town is a place where true matter does not exist, and where no one can stop quarreling and fighting with their neighbors.

In the sections that follow, we will explore *bentness* on each of these levels using examples from several sources, primarily nineteenth- and twentieth-century fiction.

BENT ROADS AND *BENT* LINES

We begin with *bent* roads in a literal sense, where the manner of moving from one place to another, or even the physical nature of the universe itself, is transformed from the ideal into something twisted or unnatural. In Tolkien's legendarium, the earth is initially conceived of as flat, or as we might say in the context of this chapter, *straight*. The innate *straightness* of the world becomes *bent* in the following way. When the evil Melkor escapes to Middle-earth after destroying the two trees and stealing the Silmarils, many elves living in Valinor depart in order to pursue him. These elves create powerful kingdoms in Middle-earth, and ally themselves with the new races of men they encounter there. After many battles against Melkor, the Ainur and the elves still remaining in Valinor march to Middle-earth and, together with the remaining elves and good men,[6] finally defeat him. The Ainur take Melkor and thrust him out into the dissonant void, where he must remain until the end of the world. The good men, as a reward for their help, are provided with instruction and wisdom from the Ainur, and a special island, named Númenor, is prepared and placed near Valinor. There, the men are safe from most of the evils that beset Middle-earth, and are able to live near their elven friends. However, while they are granted a lifespan much longer than that of other men, they are not exempt from death.

Over the course of centuries, the men of Númenor increase in power, wealth, and happiness, though the fear of death begins to grow on them. They become skillful mariners, exploring all the known world, with the exception of Valinor, which they are forbidden to approach or set foot on. The Númenorians eventually subjugate and colonize large portions of Middle-earth, where they encounter Sauron—Melkor's chief lieutenant—who has survived and escaped from earlier battles, setting himself up as the next dark lord. The men of Númenor defeat Sauron and bring him to their island as a prisoner, but in a few short years he corrupts nearly the entire kingdom, and advises the king to assault and conquer Valinor. Sauron deceives the king into believing that by doing so, the Númenorians will no longer be subject to death.[7] When the king comes ashore on the forbidden land, Eru finally unleashes his power. The invading army is buried under falling hills, and the land of Númenor sinks into the ocean. Eru changes the shape of the flat world, *bending* it into a sphere, so that the Númenorian survivors perceive that by sailing in one direction, they eventually return to their original point of departure. The land of Valinor is removed from the round earth, becoming entirely inaccessible without special permission or power. Men know that a "Straight Road" must still exist between Middle-earth and Valinor, for elves in Middle-earth are permitted to return when they become weary of the mortal lands. In these cases, the elven ships find the *straight* way, and rise above the curved (*bent*) surface of the earth and atmosphere, passing through a portion of space before arriving in Valinor.[8] The removal of Valinor from the physical world, or at least the physically *accessible* world, is likewise a kind of *bending*. Valinor is the dwelling place of the Ainur, and a place of physical perfection where nothing fades or withers.[9] While it exists within the confines of the world, it reminds the inhabitants of Middle-earth that a place without death and evil still endures, and serves as a beacon of hope.[10] However, after its removal, there is no longer any place within the physical world that does not retain memories of evil and decay. The world is further *bent*, because even the *potential* of the *straight* is lost to view for most of its inhabitants.

Further examples of literal, physical *bending* are found in other works of literature. In Milton's *Paradise Lost*, the release and passage of Sin and Death through the physical universe acts to blight the heavenly bodies—dimming, diffusing, and eclipsing their light.[11] This diminishes the capacity of light to perform its intended function, that of illuminating the earth. The curse of sin on the earth itself results in an even more disastrous *bending*. After the fall of Adam and Eve, God instructs the angels to wrench the earth off its perfect axis, causing the sun to shine unevenly during the different seasons of the year. The earth, which had until then enjoyed a perpetual spring, with equal amounts of light and darkness, now experiences excessive light and dark, and extremes of temperature, wind, and weather.[12] Like the *bending* of the "Straight Road" from Middle-earth to Valinor, the turning of the earth's axis in *Paradise Lost* unravels the world out of its intended design, destabilizing the perfect balance of elements, and spoiling the tuning of its *musica mundana*.

Authors also use images of practical music—*musica instrumentalis*—to illustrate the *bending* of the created universe. John Donne compares the created universe to a perfectly tuned string instrument, and also to a choir of perfectly tuned voices singing in harmony. The evil that causes the heavenly harmony to become discordant begins with the highest voices: the treble voices in the choir, or the highest strings on the instrument. These "highest voices" are equivalent to the highest created intellects—those possessing the greatest faculty of mind—among men and angels.[13] When these voices become mistuned through sin, they spoil the harmony of the entire system. This concept is easy to illustrate in practical music. If one physically *bends* the body or the playing mechanism of a musical instrument, the tuning system of that instrument may be thrown out of balance, and playing in tune, or playing at all, may become impossible.

Continuing to consider *bentness* as a physical phenomenon, it does not necessarily imply a specific line or shape; rather it indicates the artificial molding or shaping of an object, line, or shape, out of its natural or most efficient form. In three-dimensional geometry, the shortest distance between two points is a straight line, and any bending of that line represents a detour from the most efficient way of moving from one point to another. Likewise, a soap bubble is round because that is its most efficient form on the terrestrial surface. However, for our purposes, the *circle* is a shape that allows for a number of useful interpretations and readings. On the one hand, the circle is a perfect shape as well as a powerful one—it is commonly used as an image of the infinite or the divine in religious ritual, symbolism, and iconography. On the other hand, the circle can be considered perfect in its *imperfection*.[14] It is a line (specifically a simple closed curve) that can never travel in space outside the limits of its own circumference. There is no beginning or end to its bending, and while it so often represents the infinite, it is also singularly limited. In this sense, it is a perfectly *bent* shape. In two dimensions, a circle completely encloses the space within itself, while completely excluding the space without.

The particular manifestation of the circle as a *ring* is important, given the relative weight given to Tolkien's works in the book. Like a circle, the Ring is a perfectly *bent* object: nothing can escape its draw toward evil, its sole purpose of domination and exclusion. The exclusive nature of the Ring is made clear by Gandalf. When tempted to use the power of the Ring in league with his fellow wizard Saruman, who has fallen into evil, Gandalf says: "Only one hand at a time can wield the One, and you know that well, so do not trouble to say *we!*"[15] While shutting others out, the Ring also encloses, or traps, those who possess it. Sméagol, the first hobbit bearer of the Ring, is completely consumed by his desire for the Ring during his lifetime. The next possessors, Bilbo and Frodo, are also permanently physically and psychologically captured by the Ring, which necessitates their escape from Middle-earth, along the "Straight Road," to seek healing in Valinor. Just as Sauron's eye, as discussed in chapter 3, is an empty pit opening into the void, the Ring is a circle that likewise encompasses and encloses the void, entrapping the bearer within its emptiness. Ultimately, there is no escape from the *bentness* of the Ring, no tangent that can extend beyond its orbit, and no way to maintain a *straight* line.

BENT PEOPLE

If roads and shapes can be conceived of as *bent* out of their natural and most efficient forms, we also find many examples of people who are subject to the same forces. In Lewis' *The Space Trilogy*, various characters—from immortal, angelic beings, down to mortal, human-equivalent creatures—who stray from the correct path and do evil, are described as *bent*. However, this concept does not originate with Lewis. Medieval scholars referred to mankind in its unfallen state as *homo erectus*, or "straight man."[16] This image of humanity standing perfectly straight and pointing, as it were, toward God, is contrasted with what mankind becomes after its fall into sin—*homo incurvatus*, "curved (or *bent*) man." Here, fallen humanity crouches in an animal-like manner, pointing toward the earth and away from God, closing in upon itself in self-centeredness.[17] Tolkien likewise draws upon ancient etymologies of *bentness*. In *The Lord of the Rings*, the men enslaved by the rings Sauron gives them, who become something like living ghosts, are called "Ringwraiths." The Old English root of the word "wraith" means "to twist" or "bend."[18]

Though the examples from works of literature that I share below nearly never use the precise term *bent* to describe negative states of being,[19] nonetheless each of them is clear that a straying from the prescribed path, something missing in the mental or physical makeup, or the influence of a negative external force, indeed *bends* an individual out of tune with good *musica humana*. In some cases, the *bending* is so extreme or prolonged that a return to *straightness* is unforeseeable or impossible. Such characters may be described as *broken*.

THE *BENDING* OF SMÉAGOL, BILBO, AND FRODO

In previous chapters, we spent time with the three primary hobbit possessors of the Ring—Sméagol, Bilbo, and Frodo—and observed the negative physical and mental effects caused by that evil object. In general, those who possess the Ring longest feel and display its *bending* effects most severely. Sméagol, keeper of the Ring for hundreds of years, becomes a twisted and shriveled ghost-like creature, unrecognizable as a hobbit even to other hobbits. Though he has lived the equivalent of several natural lifespans, and possesses impressive physical strength and endurance, neither strength nor longevity leads to an increase in happiness or satisfaction—rather the opposite. Bilbo also experiences increased longevity. Friends and neighbors note, on the eve of his 111th birthday, that he looks very much the same as when he was fifty, and they think it quite strange. Being "well-preserved," as his acquaintances put it, likewise fails to provide Bilbo with a sense of contentment. He expresses this in a conversation with Gandalf:

> 'I am old, Gandalf. I don't look it, but I am beginning to feel it in my heart of hearts. *Well-preserved* indeed! [. . .] Why, I feel all thin, sort of *stretched* [. . .]: like butter that has been scraped over too much bread. That can't be right. I need a change, or something.'[20]

We could easily replace "stretched" in this passage with *bent*. There is no doubt that the influence of the Ring, which causes extension of physical life, without a simultaneous extension of *quality* of life, affects Bilbo just as it does Sméagol. This straying from the natural order of life (for hobbits, at least), is an example of an external *bending* force.

The *bending* effect of the Ring also includes a powerful mental and psychic component. Sméagol's mind is almost completely enslaved by the Ring, which allows him to achieve incredible feats of deprivation and fortitude. He also compulsively talks to the Ring, referring to it as "my precious." Bilbo also begins to feel the mental pull of the Ring, noting "it has been so growing on my mind lately," and becoming uncharacteristically angry and defensive when questioned about it.[21] Frodo's own inevitable mental breakdown is treated in close detail by Tolkien, and in some ways the *bending* force of the Ring is far worse for him, than that experienced by either Sméagol or Bilbo. One reason is the particular nature of Frodo's relationship with the Ring. He is the first keeper to understand its perfectly evil nature, and despite its enchanting aesthetic beauty, he knows he must destroy it. Another reason is that Frodo is actively pursued by servants of Sauron, who are themselves enslaved through the power of the Ring. When these servants are near, the Ring becomes more "active," placing more intense mental pressure on Frodo. Finally, as Frodo nears the volcanic Mount Doom where the Ring was made—the only place it can be destroyed—it exerts more explicit power, in some cases controlling Frodo's body and mind. In such situations, it is reasonable to say that the Ring is inexorably *bending* Frodo to its own will. This is actually successfully done, as Frodo fails at his task at the moment of decision, and claims the Ring for himself, being saved only when Sméagol bites the Ring from his finger, and falls with it into the fiery abyss.

THE *UNBENDING* AND *BENDING* OF DR. ELWIN RANSOM

The experiences of Ransom in Lewis' *The Space Trilogy* parallel those of Frodo in a number of respects. In the second book of the trilogy, *Perelandra*, Ransom is sent by angelic beings to the planet Venus, where the first pair of humans have recently been created. There, he assists the first woman, the Venusian Eve, in resisting a temptation to disobey God, which would have brought sin and death into that perfect world. The tempter is in possession of the body of Dr. Edward Weston, who will be treated in his own section below. Ransom eventually comes to the realization that he will have to physically fight and kill the body of Weston, in order to expel the tempter from Venus. In a running battle that occupies a number of days, Ransom finally succeeds in killing Weston by crushing his head with a stone, but not before Ransom receives many wounds, among them a deep bite on his heel. This recalls the Genesis account of the fall of mankind. After Adam and Eve sin, God appears and curses the tempting serpent, prophesying the future relationship between humanity and the devil: "And I will put enmity between you and the woman, and between your offspring and hers; he will crush your head, and you will strike his heel."[22] Ransom and Weston fulfill this prophecy, but in a different "garden," on a different planet. In the end, these actions of crushing and wounding set off the process of Ransom's own *bending* and *unbending*.

The course of *unbending* continues throughout Ransom's time on Venus. While there, he breathes the air, tastes the waters, and eats the food of this young and vital world, and its essential youth and vitality influences his body. On his arrival on Venus, he is a relatively sedentary, middle-aged scholar, with an old wound received during service in World War I. However, in the planet's vibrant atmosphere, Ransom becomes stronger and tougher, able to perform feats of physicality he would never have attempted back on Earth. In short, his own physical limitations—his *bentness*—cease to limit him on Venus—rather the environment reverses his *bentness*, causing him to *unbend*. The process accelerates when Ransom visits a holy mountain, where he speaks with angelic creatures who put him to sleep for an entire year. When he is awakened he returns to Earth, where he appears a very fit young man— his friends think he looks about twenty years old—who never seems to age. The invigorating environment of Venus is treated in much the same way as Narnia, when it is visited by people from our world. In Narnia, children seem to become older and stronger, and elderly people become younger and more physically capable. In both cases, human physical limits—restrictions on physical ability or potential, which are signs of an imperfect, or *bent musica humana*—are reduced or removed, resulting in *unbending*.

Ransom's subsequent *bending* process is similar to that experienced by Frodo. Like Frodo, Ransom receives a deep wound[23]—the deep bite in his heel made by Weston—and like Frodo, his wound cannot be healed in the present world. While Ransom's body is otherwise in excellent condition, and he appears to enjoy perpetual youth after his return from Venus, the wound on his heel causes him constant pain, from which there is no relief or hope of healing. In a sense, we can visualize Ransom as a being whose *musica humana* is almost perfectly in tune, with the exception of a single, and powerful, mistuned pitch. In the third book of the trilogy, *That Hideous Strength*, Ransom escapes his burden of pain by being translated out of the world—in a sense dying and moving on to another phase of existence.[24] This is similar to how Frodo and the other surviving bearers of the Ring only find rest and peace in Valinor, a world separated from Middle-earth. In both cases, the only cure for physical and mental *bending*, and the only chance at becoming *unbent*, is by leaving the world forever.[25]

BENT BY DESIGN—VICTOR FRANKENSTEIN'S MONSTER

Of all the fictional characters treated in this chapter, Frankenstein's monster is probably the most familiar and entrenched within Western culture. However, the 1818 novel by Mary Shelley is not a story about an unworthy creation—as is often the case in modern adaptations for film and television—but rather a story about an unworthy *creator*, and it serves as a warning against hubris and ambition untempered by moral reasoning. The young Victor Frankenstein, brought up on books of alchemy and magic, undertakes a university education in the sciences, where he discovers a method for bringing dead tissues back to life. Deciding what kind of creature to assemble and reanimate, he chooses something resembling humankind. His stated motivations are as follows:

> A new species would bless me as its creator and source; many happy and excellent natures would owe their being to me. No father could claim the gratitude of his child so completely as I should deserve theirs.[26]

While somewhat grandiose, these are noble sentiments, and the gratitude he expects would perhaps have been realized, if only Frankenstein had claimed his responsibilities as creator, source, and father. Those responsibilities should have included, at the very least, unconditional love for his creation, provision for its physical and material needs, some education of and introduction into the world it would inhabit, and a sense of place and purpose within the larger community. Like the humans in whose image he is created, the monster has a desire for love and companionship, and a keen sense of intellectual curiosity and ability, in addition to his purely physical needs. Such desires and abilities are raw materials, required for any creature to begin to reach its potential of personal growth and happiness in a human society—to achieve a high level of *musica humana*.

However, Frankenstein impedes—*bends*—his monster's potential through two acts: one is accidental, though negligent, and the other is intentional. First, Frankenstein constructs the creature in human form, but of hideous dimensions—about eight feet tall and proportionally large. This giant stature, together with a generally unattractive appearance, evinces reactions of horror and disgust in the humans he encounters. The size and general appearance of the monster are the result of Frankenstein's own technical limitations. Because the human body is so complex, and contains so many minute systems, he is forced to increase the scale of his creation, in order to achieve human-equivalent functions—a negligence born of impatience and hubris. The second act—the intentional one—that serves to inhibit the monster's potential, is related to the first. Frankenstein, having fashioned his creation himself, and thus intimately familiar with its form, is nevertheless utterly repulsed when he brings it to life. The monster seems to recognize him as his creator, and appears to show some affection, but Frankenstein abandons him, leaving him to his fate, alone, in the wide world. It is a miracle that the monster survives his initial encounters with the outside elements, and is able to learn enough to survive. That he then goes on to attempt a full and *unbent* life is another miracle.

The results of Frankenstein's actions—the creation of a being repulsive to humankind, and his own rejection and abandonment of that creature—are predictable. The monster sets out to find the human companionship and fellowship he seeks, and through observation and study learns to speak and to read. However, whenever he reveals himself to others, he is rejected, driven away, and hunted like an animal. Under this treatment, he becomes *bent*, and seeking revenge against Frankenstein, kills a member of his family and frames a close friend as the murderer. Soon creator and creation meet again, and the monster eloquently describes the *bentness* of Frankenstein's arrogance, which is the cause of his own *bentness*:

> How dare you sport thus with life? Do your duty towards me, and I will do mine towards you and the rest of mankind.
> [. . .]
> I am thy creature, and I will be even mild and docile to my natural lord and king, if thou wilt also perform thy part, the which thou owest me. Oh, Frankenstein, be not equitable to every other and trample upon me alone, to whom thy justice, and even thy clemency and affection, is most due. Remember, that I am thy creature; I ought to be thy Adam, but I am rather the fallen angel, whom thou drivest from joy for no misdeed. Everywhere I see bliss, from which I alone am irrevocably excluded. I was benevolent and good; misery made me a fiend. Make me happy, and I shall again be virtuous.[27]

The monster describes the nature of his *bentness* as a natural result of rejection, and consequent lack of fellowship and friendship.[28] Knowing through experience that acceptance in human society is impossible, the monster demands that Frankenstein create a second being to serve as his companion. That this will cure the *bentness* to which the monster has been driven is made clear in the following passage: "My vices are the children of a forced solitude that I abhor; and my virtues will necessarily arise when I live in communion with an equal."[29] Frankenstein agrees, but when faced with the prospect of having created two monsters, he destroys the second before bringing it to life. The result of this action is also predictable, as the monster goes on to destroy all that Frankenstein holds dear. This story is a case study of the results of creating life with all the potential for a well-tuned *musica humana*—balance within the self, and harmonious relationships with others—and the subsequent neglect of that potential. *Bentness* is the inevitable result of such negligence.

WHEN *BENT* AND *UNBENT* MEET—THE CASE OF BILLY BUDD AND JOHN CLAGGART

Our character studies thus far provide a fair sampling of *bentness*, as manifested in the physical and mental experiences of specific individuals. It is also helpful to juxtapose *bent* characters with *unbent*, or *straight*, ones. By holding them up for comparison, both the *bent* and the *unbent* elements can be thrown into sharper focus. Such is the case with the characters of Billy Budd and John Claggart, in Herman Melville's short novel *Billy Budd*, written between 1888 and 1891.

The novel is set at the end of the eighteenth century, aboard an English warship during a time of hostility with revolutionary France, and just after a number of high-profile mutinies on English vessels. During this era, British naval ships could forcibly impress men into service, in order to make up deficiencies in their own crew complements. Billy Budd, a crewman aboard a private merchant vessel, is forced into service in the Royal Navy in this way. John Claggart is a senior petty officer, and serves as master-at-arms, which at that time was roughly equivalent to the chief of security on a warship. The difference in rank between the two characters, and the social and political circumstances of the setting, are integral to the events of the novel. Given the recent mutinies aboard warships, and the fact that England is fighting against a France still in its revolutionary period, there is tremendous fear of radical and mutinous sentiments circulating among the crews. When Claggart falsely accuses Billy of sedition, this culture of fear, and the difference in rank between the two men, guarantees that Claggart's accusation is taken seriously. When Billy then strikes and kills Claggart, in front of the ship's captain no less, Billy's lower rank increases the severity of his offense, leading to his swift execution. However, the most significant difference between the two characters is not their relative rank and position, but rather their physical and moral characteristics. In short, Claggart is *bent* and Billy is not.

Billy Budd is a perfect physical specimen, nicknamed the "Handsome Sailor" by his shipmates. He is, at various times, compared with Apollo, Hercules, Achilles, Hyperion, a young Adam before the Fall, and an angel of God—all models of great physical beauty. Billy is described as an example of proto-English Saxon racial purity, undiluted by Norman and other racial influences, similar to what the Romans would have encountered in Britain during the first century. His voice is highly musical, and Melville describes this musical voice as suggestive of the harmony within,[30] a clear sign of a well-tuned *musica humana* natural to Billy. He has only a single physical defect: a stutter that manifests itself during times of stress or excitement. This defect illustrates that, even in the relative physical perfection enjoyed by Billy, his humanity still exists within an imperfect world, and is subject to its negative influences. But Billy is as perfect as a mortal man *can* be.

Billy Budd's physical perfection is mirrored in his character and personality. Though he is a sailor, and surrounded by the rough and violent personalities one expects in such an environment, Billy is not touched by their coarseness. Rather, Billy's natural purity and harmlessness invariably make a good impression on his shipmates, and his very presence promotes peace and order among the groups of battle-hardened sailors. If he has one character defect—if defect it may be called—Billy is simple, innocent, and inexperienced. Like the pre-fall Adam in the Garden of Eden, he has gained as yet no "apple of knowledge" of evil.[31] Thus, Billy has no concept of the indirect, the devious, or the sinister, and so satire, double meanings, and subtexts are generally lost on him. Melville notes that men as unsophisticated as Billy retain at least *some* intuitive knowledge of depravity or evil. Billy, however, has none of this intuition, or things may have turned out very differently for him. His nearly perfect *straightness*—the excellent tuning of his *musica humana*—shines as a beacon (or a target) for those who are *bent* and mistuned, and such a person is John Claggart.

John Claggart's *bentness* is not characterized by any gross physical malformations, like those that mark Sméagol or Frankenstein's monster, nor by any obvious signs of mental oppression, as with Bilbo or Frodo. Melville's characterization of Claggart is noteworthy due to the lack of any overt, external signs of *bentness*. Indeed, Claggart also possesses attractive physical features, enjoys an above-average intelligence and education, and even has a musical voice. However, his facial features are not *quite* perfect. Though his face is as cleanly cut as a Greek medallion, his chin has a "strange protuberant heaviness," that mars the effect.[32] Claggart's voice, though musical, has a slight accent that causes the observer to believe that he may have immigrated at an early age. Therefore, he is an Englishman, but with a touch of the foreign and alien about him, certainly not of the pureblooded, unadulterated English stock like Billy Budd. Claggart's physical form and manner subtly hints at "something defective or abnormal in the constitution and blood."[33] This subtle *bentness* in Claggart, observed in his *slightly* imperfect physique and pedigree, is amplified by the reactions he evinces among the members of the crew. Where Billy Budd promotes a universally positive influence on all who see him, Claggart's moral influence is entirely negative. Even the captain of the ship, whom we would expect to be familiar, and comfortable, with the range of natures and personalities among the sailors under his command, perceives that Claggart provokes a "vaguely repellent distaste."[34] This further deepens the sense of mistuned *musica humana*.

Melville gives the reader a much clearer view of Claggart's *bentness* from the inside, as it were, when he enters into the mind and internal motivations of the senior petty officer. At first sight, Claggart feels immediate antipathy toward Billy Budd, though he masks this hatred in smiles and seemingly kind words. Claggart recognizes the innate harmlessness and purity of Billy, but having *himself* no power to share in that goodness, he rejects and despises it. Claggart's own depravity is not a result of brutishness caused by poverty, a lack of opportunity or education, or any other negative influence in his life, but is a "depravity according to nature," inborn and innate.[35] Melville tells us that such men are not prone to vices, and are not the sort seen populating the jails and the gallows. Claggart is intellectual and rational, but uses his intellect and rationality for ultimately *irrational* ends—in this sense, Claggart is among the ranks of "true madmen."[36] Billy is described as a living saint, and Claggart the "direct reverse of a saint."[37] It is reasonable to ask why such a corrupted nature does not qualify Claggart as a *broken* character, rather than a *bent* one. One passage in the novel points to a small—perhaps vanishingly so—piece of lingering humanity within him. Just as Sméagol, who on the very edge of a terrible betrayal, nearly repents at the sight of the sleeping Samwise and Frodo, Claggart experiences a measure of tender yearning and melancholy at the sight of the laughing and joking Billy Budd. This points to a *bent* nature, one that could potentially repent, and turn away from evil. However, as with Sméagol, the moment is fleeting, and Claggart suppresses his tender feelings, before fatally denouncing Billy to the ship's captain.

After accusing Billy of having revolutionary tendencies, Claggart, Billy, and the captain meet in a private room to discuss the allegations. This is the point in the novel where *bent* and *unbent* meet. Billy, who until now has been largely unaware of Claggart's animosity and subterfuge, is utterly baffled, and due to his speech impediment, is unable to answer the charges against him. As if to accentuate the depths of Claggart's malice, Melville describes the eyes of the officer during this confrontation, emphasizing their inhumanity. At first they appear as those of a serpent, and then bulging and alien, like the eyes of some uncatalogued monster species of the ocean depths.[38] Unable to speak, Billy gives the only response he can—a single blow of his fist, which instantly kills Claggart. Given the charged atmosphere of wartime, the recent mutinies, and Claggart's position as a senior petty officer, the captain feels he has no choice but to have Billy hung at dawn. This encounter is illustrative of the inevitable outcome when *unbent* and *bent* meet—mutual annihilation. Melville demonstrates that the two cannot exist in close proximity, even for a short period of time, without each destroying the other.

WHEN *BENT* AND *UNBENT* MEET— THE CASE OF ST. JOHN RIVERS

If the case of Billy Budd and John Claggart illustrates the harmful consequences of close proximity between *bent* and *unbent* individuals, a further step brings us to the existence of the *bent* and the *unbent* within a *single* individual. To a certain extent this is not remarkable, as the internal struggle between good and evil is a major feature of Western Christianity, and thus of Western philosophy and culture. However, this case and others like it are remarkable, due to many novel delineations between the two conditions, as provided by literary authors. We saw a version of this phenomenon in the case of Elwin Ransom above, but there are important qualifications. In Ransom's case, the process of *bending* and *unbending* were both the result of external forces, namely the permanent wound he received from Weston on the one hand, and the invigorating physical and spiritual environment of the planet Venus on the other. The case of St. John Rivers, a character in Charlotte Brontë's 1847 novel *Jane Eyre*, is very different. While much critical analysis of the novel naturally focuses on differences between Jane's two major love interests—the wealthy, impulsive, and hypermasculine Edward Rochester, versus the self-denying, cerebral, and loveless St. John—these polar opposites exist also *within* the character of St. John himself. The conflict between *bent* and *unbent* takes place within St. John's own mind, and are the result of his own internal, conscious choices.

Jane Eyre is an orphan who grows up among relatives who dislike and mistreat her. She is sent to an austere and abusive boarding school, where she nonetheless excels in her studies, eventually becoming a teacher, and later taking a position as governess at the Rochester manor. Over a period of time, Edward Rochester and Jane fall in love and decide to marry. However, on the morning of the wedding it is revealed that Rochester is already married, and his wife still living, though imprisoned as a lunatic in an upper room of the house. Jane leaves the manor secretly, traveling as far as her scant resources will allow, eventually wandering hungry and faint among the hills and moors. She collapses from exhaustion, and is taken in by St. John Rivers and his sisters, who nurse her back to health and allow her to live with them. St. John is a parish curate and, seeing evidence of Jane's good manners and education, asks her to teach the girls' school he has founded in the local village. During this time he watches Jane meticulously, measuring her abilities and aptitude, and decides she will be a perfect wife to assist him in his ultimate plan of becoming a missionary to India.[39] It is in this context that we see the conflict between the *bent* and the *unbent* in St. John's mind.

In the world of *Jane Eyre*, to be *unbent* may be described as a willingness to follow one's natural impulses toward love and companionship, while remaining within the bounds of propriety and decency. Jane initially overcomes her own *bentness* by allowing herself to fall in love with Rochester, who is her intellectual equal, though her social superior, as well as her elder by two decades. She leaves him—agreeing to resume and retain her *bentness*—because pursuing love would violate the Victorian religious and societal dictates against living with a married man. The conflict between *bentness* and *unbentness* in the character of St. John Rivers manifests itself differently, but is still rooted in the same realities of Victorian society. St. John actually loves the daughter of the local lord of the manor, and is passionately loved by her in return. However, since he has decided that his lifelong calling is missionary service, he rejects the girl as a potential wife, seeing her as an ineffective partner in this physically demanding vocation. In his religious zeal he determines that the only one who will serve is Jane, whom he sees as both physically and mentally capable. St. John does not offer love in any measure, and his *bentness* is revealed by his willingness to enter into a marriage without love, demanding that Jane accept it for what he sees as a higher purpose.

Although St. John affects a calm and severe outward appearance, the observant Jane is able to detect traces of the conflict beneath. She draws a portrait of St. John's true love, leaves it where he will find it, and measures his reaction. We are able to see, for a short time, his *unbent* sentiments as he gazes fondly at the picture, allowing Jane to speak of his love's regard for him. St. John even admits his true feelings: "I love [her] so wildly, with all the intensity, indeed, of a first passion, the object of which is exquisitely beautiful, graceful, and fascinating."[40] However, the time he allows for pleasure in true and honest reflection is short, as he takes out his watch and allots exactly fifteen minutes before resuming his cold, hard exterior, *bending* himself back out of shape. The method that St. John uses for this *bending* is sheer willpower, fueled by religious fervor: "It is hard work to control the workings of inclination, and to turn the bent of nature; but that it may be done, I know from experience."[41] Jane sees this attitude as both unnatural and harmful, and though she is willing to accompany St. John in his missionary endeavors as a *sister*, she will never consent to do so as his wife, with no love experienced because none is offered. She sees the fundamental *bentness*—a mistuning of *musica humana*—in his offer, feeling it entirely unnatural "to be chained for life to a man who [regards] one but as a useful tool."[42] By forcibly disregarding his own natural human sentiments, St. John also denies the needs of those around him, and it is easy to predict that this *bent* missionary will undertake a *bent* mission.[43] While this is not the mutual, physical destruction of Billy Budd and John Claggart, it does result in a kind of self-annihilation, though "self-denial" is undoubtedly how St. John would describe it.

FROM *BENT* TO *BROKEN*—DR. EDWARD WESTON: THE "UN-MAN"

The characters treated above are *bent* for several reasons. Some are born *bent*, some make themselves *bent*, and others become so through external means or circumstances. To be *bent*, failing to follow a prescribed path, or not living up to an expected potential, assumes at least the theoretical possibility of becoming *unbent*, and turning to follow the proper path. However, there are cases in which a character—by circumstance or by choice—becomes *broken*. Brokenness may be thought of as a *bentness* so extreme, that no return to a *straight* way is conceivable or possible. This concept is proposed and explored in Lewis' *The Space Trilogy*, and the differences between *bent* and *broken* are explained there. A scene from the first book of the trilogy, *Out of the Silent Planet* (briefly related in chapter 3.5) depicts an episode in which Ransom is brought before the angelic ruler of Mars. The two humans who have kidnapped Ransom and taken him to the red planet—Dr. Edward Weston and a man ironically named Dick Devine—are also brought to the ruler, who questions them. After this interrogation, the ruler discovers the intentions of the two men: Weston desires the endless propagation of the human species, and Devine simply wants to extract material wealth from the planet. The ruler determines that Devine is *broken*, as his sole motivations are simple selfishness and greed, divorced from any other consideration. Weston, however, is merely *bent*. Though Weston's view of the future of humanity is warped and twisted—he is willing to commit multiple genocides to achieve his goal—at the very least he has a purpose outside of himself, that might conceptually benefit others.[44] However, when we next meet Weston on the planet Venus in *Perelandra*, his motivations have evolved, and we see a *broken* version of this individual.

In the universe created by Lewis in *The Space Trilogy*, various angelic beings are assigned to the different planets of the solar system. These beings are not native to any of the terrestrial surfaces—their own natural environment is interplanetary space—and they appear on the planets only at certain times when needed. The one exception is Earth, where the sinful, fallen angels are confined, and not permitted to leave. Thus the fallen angels and their leader, called the Bent One (equivalent to Satan), have no independent method of traveling to other planets to tempt or corrupt beings there. However, because humans have now discovered the principles of space travel—Weston, a physicist, invents and constructs the spaceships used to travel to Mars and Venus[45]—*they* are permitted to visit other worlds. Though the precise mechanism is not explained, it is clear that Weston has invited a *bent* spirit, presumably Satan himself, into his body and mind. This spirit travels within Weston's body, and is the means by which evil finds its way onto Venus.[46] When Ransom encounters Weston there, he is at first surprised that the physicist appears to be completely fluent in the interplanetary language (known as "Old Solar"), since on Mars Weston knew very little of it. When Ransom asks about this, Weston replies: "Guidance, you know, guidance [. . .]. Things coming into my head. I'm being prepared all the time.

Being made a fit receptacle."[47] While it is not immediately clear to Ransom who Weston is speaking for, or with *whose* voice he is speaking, he removes all doubt with declarations like the following:

> Do you see, you timid, scruple-mongering fool? I *am* the Universe. I, Weston, am your God and your Devil.[48]

> I am older than [Ransom] [. . .], and he dare not deny it. Before the mothers of the mothers of his mother were conceived, I was already older than he could reckon. I have been with [God] in Deep Heaven where he never came and heard the eternal councils. And in the order of creation I am greater than he, and before me he is of no account.[49]

> It is for this that I came here, that you may have Death in abundance.[50]

Weston has plainly been possessed by the devil. Weston's previous *bentness* had been based on an overriding selfishness, but at least on behalf of the human race. Now he has been fully *broken*, as even this motivation has been taken away, and replaced by the selfishness of his demonic possessor. It is not only the shocking statements above that demonstrate Weston's *brokenness*, but also his actions and body language, that cause Ransom to consider him no longer Weston at all, but a being he refers to as the Un-Man. To use an example of a musical instrument, to be mistuned involves at least the *possibility* of becoming re-tuned at some point in the future. Even Ransom acknowledges the metaphor, when he realizes that the improvement of his own physique, due to the positive influence of the Venusian environment, is like an "instrument [being] tuned up to concert pitch."[51] For Weston, however, nothing that can be tuned remains, so rather than speaking of him as a character with a mistuned *musica humana*, we must speak of him as having nothing at all to do *with* music, or with *humana* either. Ransom notices this almost immediately. Weston's face is "subtly unfamiliar,"[52] he is "curiously unlike himself," his smile is "a fixed and even slightly twisted grin," and his laughter is "almost an infantile or senile laughter."[53] All of this causes Ransom to think that "something which was and was not Weston was talking."[54]

Even more appalling to Ransom is Weston's response to pain. At one point, Weston has a convulsion, and Ransom attempts to revive him with a sip from a bottle of brandy. Weston bites through the neck of the bottle, chewing and swallowing the broken glass, and yet the next day he is entirely unaffected. His attitude toward *inflicting* pain is likewise heedless. Weston destroys vegetation, and maims and kills living creatures, for no particular reason. When Ransom observes this, he notes that Weston does not "look like a sick man: but he [looks] very like a dead one." Ransom notes his "expressionless mouth, the unwinking stare of the eyes, something heavy and inorganic in the very folds of the cheek,"[55] which convinces him that Weston is no longer human. Rather he is anti-human, an Un-Man. What Ransom sees in Weston makes him realize that all the evil he has ever observed on Earth has been only half-hearted.[56] The pure, whole-hearted evil he sees in Weston's face causes him to faint, and wonder whether he will survive the sight. Weston's final *brokenness*, and the cessation of any form of *musica humana*, is illustrated in Ransom's thought: "[he] did not defy goodness, [he] ignored it to the point of annihilation."[57]

THE PROCESS OF *BREAKING*—
THE OBJECTIVITY ROOM

The means and processes by which Weston becomes *broken* are not explained in *Perelandra*, though we are given a number of clues. Occasionally, the demon allows Weston's mind and personality to resurface for a few moments. During these brief periods of relative lucidity, Weston tells Ransom things like the following: "They've taken off my head and put someone else's on me," and "he does all my thinking for me."[58] In *That Hideous Strength*, the third book of *The Space Trilogy*, the reader is given much more information about the *breaking* process, which sheds light on what is earlier revealed in *Perelandra*.

Back in Britain after the events of *Perelandra*, former associates of Weston, including Dick Devine—already identified as *broken* by the ruler of Mars—create an organization called the National Institute for Co-ordinated Experiments, paradoxically known as the N.I.C.E. This institute slowly begins to exert political and police control over much of British society, with the goals of eliminating undesirable and recalcitrant sectors of society, and improving overall national "efficiency." Many of the scientists who work for the N.I.C.E. speak openly about the elimination of organic life on Earth, and the transplantation of human consciousness into an entirely inorganic medium. However, this is merely a front for the true purpose of the organization: contact and cooperation with the fallen angels on Earth, who are referred to as the Macrobes.

Near the beginning of *That Hideous Strength*, a young wife and doctoral student, Jane Studdock, experiences a dream, in which a condemned criminal's head is removed for some unknown purpose. At about the same time, her husband Mark, a research fellow at a local college, begins working for the N.I.C.E.[59] There, Mark is "introduced" to the disembodied head from Jane's dream, which the institute's scientists have seemingly been able to keep alive and semi-conscious. This is not true, however, as the head is merely a device through which the evil angels, the Macrobes, communicate with members of the institute. Only two senior members of the organization know the full truth, and they have allowed themselves to become possessed, as Weston had in *Perelandra*. The nature of their possession is rather fascinating. They undergo "training," a process that makes them scarcely human, even when they retain nominal control of their own minds. Unlike Weston, who more or less reverts to his own personality when given control of his consciousness, the training has allowed the two N.I.C.E. men to permanently eliminate all natural human reactions, thus removing any sense of motive or purpose. Unsurprisingly, by destroying their own sense of purpose, they provide free and untrammeled space for the evil purposes of the Macrobes.[60] At times when the Macrobes assert full control, the effects are terrifying—the two men appear entirely inhuman, and behave like animals, full of malice. The means by which they achieve this state, and which they use to attempt to draw in others, is the Objectivity Room.

Lewis notes that the twentieth century's despair of finding objective truth through the sciences, together with the experiences of the dissecting room and the pathology lab, have pushed back or eliminated human notions of repugnance and obscenity. Scientists at the N.I.C.E. likewise reject these notions, and the concept of morality in general, as simple human subjective by-products that must be suppressed or eliminated.[61] The purpose of the Objectivity Room is to train the mind to reject subjective moral principles, thus achieving a "true objectivity," where all ethical, aesthetic, or logical motives are eliminated, in what is compared to destroying a nerve so that it no longer functions.[62] Mark Studdock is brought into this room, which is not initially terrifying in any way—just slightly off-putting. It is a simple, oblong space with a large table in the middle, like a conference room, with a number of paintings hung along the walls. Mark begins to notice a number of subtle oddities as he looks around: the general shape of the room is not well-proportioned, the arch above the door is slightly off-center, there are spots painted on the ceiling and on the table that seem to be in regular patterns, but which ultimately frustrate one's expectations, producing a general sense of distaste. The paintings add to this effect. At first, they are relative absurdities: surrealist images of a woman growing hair from her mouth, or of a man swimming with corkscrew arms. However, many of the paintings are of familiar biblical scenes, such as Jesus raising Lazarus from the dead, and the Last Supper. However, the paintings include added elements, like angles and proportions that the eye rejects, or additional characters placed into the scenes, or strange elements such as a large number of beetles on the floor near Jesus' and His disciples' feet. Mark's experience of these scenes is akin to observing ordinary and expected images through the lens of delirium or a nightmare, giving them a highly menacing quality.[63]

Mark correctly deduces that the purpose of the Objectivity Room is to gradually eliminate visceral human reactions. He supposes that he will eventually move on to eating repulsive food, handling blood and dirt, and engaging in various indecencies, and this is indeed what begins to happen. At first, he is asked to perform petty and meaningless obscenities, things that a child would laugh at, but Mark soon realizes that he is being trained to reverse his natural inclinations, separating himself from what makes humans truly human.[64] In short, he is being trained to silence his own *musica humana*, to *bend* himself until he *breaks*. Fortunately for Mark, he has already internally rejected the N.I.C.E. and their agenda, and is determined to resist them. During his sessions in the Objectivity Room, the effects on Mark are different from what the possessed men training him expect. Rather than falling into a more "objective," and therefore less humane, frame of mind, Mark finds that the obscenities he is asked to perform move him into a state of desiring the "Normal," or the *straight*. For his final task, he is ordered to trample on the face of a life-sized crucifix. Though Mark is not religious, he balks at committing this blasphemy, and ultimately refuses. At this point, and despite the danger of not complying, he finds that he is truly happy for the first time in his life.[65] His internal rejection of the N.I.C.E. represents an arresting and stopping of the *bending* process, while his outright refusal to obey allows him to start to *unbend*.

BORN *BROKEN*—CATHY AMES

Until now, our exploration of *bent* and *broken* characters has focused on those who have worked to *bend* or *break* themselves, or who have been *bent* or *broken* through external pressures and circumstances. Now we turn to a character who is born *broken*, an intriguing concept because society cannot logically—though it often does in practice—blame a naturally *broken* person for being so. Such a person is Cathy Ames,[66] a major character in John Steinbeck's 1952 novel *East of Eden*. Steinbeck notes that, just as humans may be born with physical deformities, they may also be born without empathy or a conscience, and just as those with physical disabilities can achieve success, so also can a "mental or psychic monster" make a mark in the world.[67] Steinbeck describes Cathy in the following way:

> Some balance wheel was mis-weighted, some gear out of ratio. She was not like other people, never was from birth.
> [. . .]
> There was a time when a girl like Cathy would have been called possessed by the devil. She would have been exorcised to cast out the evil spirit, and if after many trials that did not work, she would have been burned as a witch for the good of the community.[68]

Cathy's *broken* nature does not express itself in any obviously external manner. Indeed, we learn that she is quite pretty and attractive, with a very delicate build and striking facial features. However, even in childhood, Cathy had a quality about her that made people uneasy, as if in the presence of something vaguely foreign. This was not an uneasiness that repulsed, but one that caused others to watch her closely, in order to determine the source of the disturbance they felt. There was something odd about Cathy's eyes, and if the proverb is true that eyes are windows into the soul, it may be that people detected something animal and inhuman there. In this chapter, we have already experienced this particular impression of inhumanity. The officials of the N.I.C.E. possessed by the Macrobes are described as having occasional "animal looks," and the eyes of John Claggart in *Billy Budd* are compared to serpents and unnamed creatures of the deep ocean. Elsewhere in *East of Eden*, another character becomes unsettled by Cathy's eyes. He remembers an execution he witnessed as a child in which a ruthless criminal was hanged. The condemned man looked directly at him, and he felt that the eyes were not human, but like those of a goat.[69]

Cathy Ames utilizes two primary tools to achieve her goals in *East of Eden*: deceit and sexuality. As for the latter, Cathy realizes at a very early age that sexuality "is the most disturbing impulse humans have,"[70] particularly in the repressive environment of New England at the turn of the twentieth century. She recognizes the sexual impulse—being *broken*, she likely does not experience it as others do—and begins to experiment with its power over others. At age ten, Cathy frames two teenage boys for molestation, and they are publicly whipped and sent to a penal institution. In her early teens she becomes adept at creating chance encounters with boys as she takes long walks, and is particularly skillful at "finding" things such as money and jewelry. While the sources of these found objects are never specified—they are never claimed, even when advertised in the local newspaper—it is strongly suggested that they are gifts given in exchange for sexual favors. Later, Cathy seduces her high school Latin teacher, who commits suicide over the relationship.[71] As an adult, she becomes a prostitute, and then a madam and brothel owner, whose house specializes in particularly gross or taboo acts. Cathy keeps her prostitutes, employees, and customers in line through a combination of blackmail and drug dependency.

As for deceit, Cathy has a tremendous amount of patience and self-control. At sixteen, she manufactures an adolescent rebellion against her parents by refusing to attend school, making a show of running away from home. After she is brought back and whipped by her father, Cathy presents a complete change of heart. Always a good student, she begins to excel at school. She becomes sweet, cheerful, obedient, and helpful around the house, taking the initiative to oil the squeaky hinges and locks on the doors. She keeps all the lamps filled and their chimneys clean, keeping a big can of kerosene in the basement for that purpose. Cathy also begins visiting her father at his tanning business, asking questions about loans, payments, billing, and payroll. Her father, impressed by her interest and ability to absorb information quickly, teaches her all about his business, and shows her how to use the safe. All of this aligns on a day when her mother is busy at church, and she asks Cathy to pick up the payroll money from the bank, and place it in her father's safe. That night, exiting through and locking doors that no longer squeak, and leaving behind perfectly clean and filled lamps with plenty of spare kerosene in the basement, she sets the house on fire. Cathy also stages a kidnapping scene in the family carriage house, and a burglary at her father's business. With her parents dead, herself assumed kidnapped or murdered, and a large amount of money in her possession, Cathy is now free and independent, ready to make her own way in the world.[72] Unfortunately for all who cross her path, her lack of any discernible *musica humana*—her *brokenness*—leaves little but pain and wreckage in her wake.

WHEN *BROKEN* AND *BENT* MEET—THE STRANGE CASE OF DR. JEKYLL AND MR. HYDE

We have already seen the juxtaposition of *bent* and *unbent* characters, and even the existence of the *bent* and the *unbent* within a single individual. In this example, we will compare the *broken* and the *bent*. As the title of the story by Robert Louis Stevenson suggests, it is a very "strange case," as we encounter these two conditions within the same individual, but in separate characters. The premise of the story is the internal moral struggle of Dr. Henry Jekyll, a respected London doctor and philanthropist. Dr. Jekyll feels oppressed by his personal experience of the primitive duality of mankind: one side of him strives toward the good, the spiritual, and the uplifting, while the other pulls him down toward earthy, sensual pleasures. Noting that *other* men may simply accept, or even embrace, this duality, Dr. Jekyll feels that his own high calling and aspirations make this impossible, and thus the division between good and evil is more sharply defined in him than in others.[73] In short, he sees his own particular *bentness* as unique.

Dr. Jekyll conceives of a novel idea for dealing with his dueling natures. By separating them entirely, the good side of himself can rejoice in its unalloyed goodness, and the evil side can revel in its essential badness. The doctor accomplishes this through the use of a concoction that, when consumed, achieves a "switching" between the two personalities. However, Dr. Jekyll discovers that, while the evil nature produced by the potion is indeed purely evil, and ready to engage in all kinds of debauchery, the "good" side is simply his own original, conflicted personality that existed before. When he drinks the potion, the doctor's physical form changes, becoming the small and shriveled, yet muscular and powerful, Mr. Edward Hyde. Because the original Dr. Jekyll contains a greater proportion of good than of evil, the evil personality is smaller in size and stature, so that Mr. Hyde is sometimes identified as a dwarf. Though Dr. Jekyll intends to create two characters more or less "equally weighted" between good and evil—thereby maintaining his original balance—the result is the creation of a mixed character and an evil one, which tilts the balance inevitably toward evil.[74]

Stevenson's characterization of Mr. Hyde is worth noting, as it contains certain echoes of *broken* characters we have encountered above. Mr. Hyde's actions are not limited to a simple wallowing in vice, but also a display of vicarious depravity, that delights in inflicting suffering on others. At different times, he knocks over and tramples a little girl in the street, and punches in the face a woman offering to sell him a box of matches. His very face and physical presence is disturbing—like those of Edward Weston, Cathy Ames, and John Claggart—so disturbing that people break into sweats, developing feelings of disgust, loathing, fear, nausea, and general distaste for life.[75] Just *what* causes these reactions is difficult for observers to define. Mr. Hyde *seems* deformed, but not through any observable external deformation. The feelings of revulsion and hatred that people display in his presence are ultimately due to a natural reaction of human nature, when it is in the presence of something foreign and hostile.[76] Mr. Hyde is not only evil and hellish, but *inorganic*—someone who is dead but who usurps the outward functions of life.[77] Those who come into contact with him subconsciously recognize that Mr. Hyde is not merely a man with a very mistuned *musica humana*, but one that has no *musica* at all.

Unfortunately for Dr. Jekyll, the efficacy of his potion begins to deteriorate, and he is sometimes forced to double or triple the dosage in order to achieve the change, particularly the transformation from Mr. Hyde back into the doctor. At times, when in the body of Dr. Jekyll, he changes into Mr. Hyde without the use of the concoction. At other times, the consciousness of Mr. Hyde is able to intrude even when the body of Dr. Jekyll is present, forcing the doctor to scrawl shocking blasphemies in the margins of a favorite religious work, and to destroy treasured pictures and letters from his father.[78] In the end, he is unable to revert to the form of Dr. Jekyll at all, and as he is about to be discovered in his now-permanent form as Mr. Hyde, he commits suicide. The characters of Dr. Jekyll and Mr. Hyde illustrate, in ways similar to those of Billy Budd and John Claggart—and even St. John Rivers—the inability of such strongly opposed natures to coexist, whether they are the *straight* and the *bent*, or the *bent* and the *broken*. In both cases, the result is mutual destruction.

Chapter 6

BROKEN ACROSS UNIVERSES—
JADIS, THE WHITE WITCH

We first encountered Jadis in chapter 3, when she was present at the musical creation of the world of Narnia. Not much was said there about her background and character, other than her identity as a witch queen from the universe of Charn. In the two books in which Jadis appears—*The Magician's Nephew* and *The Lion, the Witch and the Wardrobe*—we are not told how she becomes *broken*—whether she was born *broken*, or later becomes so by her own will or that of others. That she is indeed *broken* is clear, and she has the dubious distinction of exercising that *brokenness* in three separate universes.

In *The Magician's Nephew*, the children Polly and Digory are tricked into traveling to the world of Charn by Digory's uncle—a scheming and unscrupulous dilettante magician. The children arrive in a large and empty palace, which they explore. They eventually stumble upon a great hall filled with chairs, and occupying many of them are hundreds of images of kings and queens, wearing regal robes and crowns. This is clearly a visual, chronological record of the rulers of Charn, and as Polly and Digory proceed down the aisle of the hall, they observe gradual changes in the character of these rulers. The first few rows of kings and queens look "kind and wise," but within a few steps they start to appear more solemn and stern. Later, the faces are "strong and proud and happy, but [. . .] cruel," and then crueler still, and eventually cruel and *unhappy*. Finally, they come to faces filled with despair, "as if the people they belonged to had done dreadful things and also suffered dreadful things." The last image is of a queen, "with a look of such fierceness and pride that it took your breath away."[79] These images represent the gradual moral decline of the rulers of Charn, down to the final queen, Jadis. Jadis wakes up and leads the children through the crumbling palace, all the while reciting litanies of torture and murder performed by herself and her immediate ancestors. Outside, the children see a great city, but completely empty and devoid of life. Jadis explains that she and her sister had fought a war over the possession of the throne of Charn. When she was finally defeated, Jadis resorted to her final weapon, the Deplorable Word, which destroyed all living things, except the one speaking the spell. No *brokenness* we have yet encountered in works of fiction, no mistuning or lack of *musica humana* compares to this: the intentional, instantaneous destruction of all life. Jadis explains herself when Polly and Digory express shock and horror at her use of the Deplorable Word:

> You must learn, child, that what would be wrong for you or for any of the common people is not wrong in a great Queen such as I. The weight of the world

is on our shoulders. We must be freed from all rules. Ours is a high and lonely destiny.[80]

This statement is quite as shocking a rejection of *musica* as was the use of the Deplorable Word. Here, Jadis exempts herself from all connection with, and responsibility to, *humana* and *mundana* alike, placing herself in a god-like position above both.

Fortunately for the inhabitants of Earth and Narnia, Jadis does not wield nearly the same amount of power in those universes as she does in Charn. She follows the children back to England, where she spends several hours, but her magic is of no use there, and her only weapons are her great physical strength and her fierceness. The children attempt to force her back into Charn, but accidentally take her into the as-yet uncreated world of Narnia. In Narnia, Jadis, known there as the White Witch, gains considerable power, such as the ability to turn creatures to stone with her wand, and control of the weather. Indeed, when the events of *The Lion, the Witch and the Wardrobe* take place, Narnia has been locked in winter for more than a century. This ability to personally effect the *musica mundana* of Narnia illustrates her power, but also her complete lack of concern for the created world.[81]

Like Cathy Ames, Jadis is able to read the desires and motivations of others, as a means of tempting and entrapping them. She seduces Edmund to betray his siblings through his greedy appetite—she feeds him a box of enchanted Turkish delight—and also his desire to extricate himself from the shadow of his older brother Peter. For this latter desire, Jadis offers to make Edmund a prince, and later a king, with his siblings relegated to the status of social inferiors.[82] In *The Magician's Nephew*, Jadis tries to convince Digory to steal a forbidden magic apple by telling him that it will cure his mother, who is terminally ill back in England.[83] However, Jadis ultimately miscalculates, as many *broken* characters do: having no truly altruistic motives of her own, she cannot imagine such motives existing in others. She suggests that Digory take the apple, and leave Polly behind in Narnia. Digory, who is loyal to his mother *and* to Polly, is shocked by the meanness and faithlessness of this suggestion, and rejects it.[84]

Jadis also does not take into consideration the natural reaction that humans, and other sentient beings, have in the presence of someone *broken*. Just as in the cases of Mr. Hyde and Cathy Ames, Jadis' lack of any discernible *musica humana* fills others with dread and loathing. Edmund's siblings shudder at the sight of her, the atmosphere becomes strangely cold in her presence, and Narnian creatures bristle and growl at her approach.[85] Even Edmund, already enchanted by the witch, knows deep down that she is "bad and cruel."[86] In the case of Jadis and the other *broken* characters we have examined in this chapter, they may attempt with greater or lesser success to mask their *brokenness*, but it cannot ultimately be hidden.

BREAKING AND REPAIRING CIRCLES—THE *UNBENDING* OF MARK AND JANE STUDDOCK

We last saw the Studdocks above, in the context of Mark's rejection of the evil and authoritarian N.I.C.E., in *That Hideous Strength*. Mark and Jane provide important insights into the notion of *musica humana*, as they undergo a process of *unbending* both in their individual lives, and in their relationship as a married couple. Their example has much to do with the idea of rings or circles. The reader will remember the concept, explored at the beginning of the chapter, of the ring as a "perfectly bent" shape—one that completely encloses the area within itself, while entirely excluding the area without. Mark and Jane Studdock represent either side of this conceptual circle.

Mark Studdock's primary motivation in life is to gain status as a member of the "inner circle." Whether fitting in with a popular group of boys at school to the exclusion of his true friends, spying on his sister and her companions as they whisper secrets, or being a part of the "progressive element" of research fellows at his college, inclusion within the inner circle is worth any cost to Mark, and being cast out is the greatest evil.[87] This constant drive to fit in makes Mark rather selfish and superficial. So when he is invited to join the N.I.C.E., Mark is flattered at being considered for admission into this secretive and exclusive organization. The N.I.C.E., as noted above, is rather dubious where legal and moral issues are concerned, and though Mark does maintain personal misgivings about his association, they are nothing in comparison to the allure of the inner circle. Lewis speaks of this phenomenon elsewhere: "Of all the passions, the passion for the Inner Ring is most skillful in making a man who is not yet a very bad man do very bad things."[88] Mark indeed begins to do some rather bad things, such as pre-writing newspaper articles about a manufactured riot in order to influence public opinion, and creating other false reports.[89] Even though he is horrified to learn that the goal of the N.I.C.E is the destruction of most of humanity, and the elimination of human emotions and motivations in cooperation with the super-human Macrobes, the lure of being admitted to the innermost circle is still extremely powerful.[90] Mark's saving grace is when the N.I.C.E. orders him to bring his wife Jane to the institute. While his initial motives for being reticent to bring her are rather self-serving, as he feels she will scorn the petty politics, and criticize his now-habitual excessive drinking, he eventually acts out of genuine concern for her safety and well-being, demonstrating a strong measure of empathy, perhaps for the first time in his life. This is the moment at which he abandons his mission to break into the inner circle. Mark's change of heart—the beginning of his *unbending*—occurs when he changes his priorities, with Jane acting as the catalyst. Instead of an overbearing desire for inclusion in the inner ring of the N.I.C.E., Mark slowly realizes that he truly wants to be included in *Jane's* inner circle—the circle of her thoughts, desires, ideas, and dreams.

Jane Studdock's situation is somewhat different. Unlike Mark, Jane is already on the inside of a conceptual circle, but is trying to *prevent* others from entering. This circle is not a secret academic society, but rather a ring of defense that she has built around her sense of value and self-respect. Jane strongly avoids entanglements and interferences in her life, and she hates the idea that her own self, whether body or mind, could be invaded and controlled by someone else. She balks at the idea of having children, as this would entrap her within the status and duties of motherhood, diminishing her own desires and objectives. For these reasons, and for others, Jane resents Mark for marrying her, and any time she shows vulnerability in his presence, she becomes angry at herself and him. If Mark's fear is being left out of the inner circle, Jane fears that her circle will be broken *into*, resulting in her being treated as a mere object for others to barter and possess. Though physically attractive, she doesn't want to be thought of as fresh and sweet, but rather interesting and important.[91] Jane rejects the loud, boorish, earthy masculinity she experienced with the men in her family from an early age—a rejection only intensified by the sexual objectification she was subjected to as a teenager. This causes her to take refuge in the "intense seriousness" of school debating societies, and the cerebral world of academics.[92] She is fearful of "being taken in." However, when she begins having lucid dreams—actually visions—she is informed that she *has* been "taken in," whether she wants it or not, and the only question is which side will benefit from her gift of second sight.[93] Like Mark, she is not religious, but her experiences in *That Hideous Strength* do not allow her to maintain her unbelief. The start of her *unbending*, or as Lewis puts it, the smashing of "the old ring-fence" of her view of the world, begins when she realizes that religion and the supernatural are undoubtedly real.[94]

These above accounts represent the *beginning* of *unbending* for both Mark and Jane, as individuals, but the final *unbending* is the repairing of the broken circle of their marriage. They are unhappy in their life together, and each assumes that the other takes no note of what they say, or appreciates who they truly are.[95] For Mark, as he *unbends*, he sees that his love for Jane is based on the deepness and freshness she brings into the "dry and dusty" world his mind inhabits—due to his preoccupation with inner circles—and he feels that he must appear truly "dull, inconspicuous, frightened, calculating, [and] cold" in comparison. He also realizes that he has no right to exercise power or ownership over Jane, and by doing so he is treating with a bumbling, violent disregard something that should be treated with delicacy and respect.[96] For Jane's part, when she finally accepts the spiritual reality of the universe, she assumes that it will be a kind of democratic system, without femininity and masculinity, and without sense and sex. She hopes that her own distaste and rejection of sex will be confirmed, and sex excluded as the vestige of animalistic instinct, or of outmoded patriarchy. However, she learns that things like gender and sex exist, even on higher planes of existence,[97] and they are an integral part of humanity, together with bearing and raising children. Mark and Jane each come to realize that mutual obedience and humility is the only way to tune their individual and collective *musica humana*. This tuning—or *unbending*—ends up drawing a new circle, not one to be broken into, and not one that excludes others, but that includes both of them, and their future family. The final act of "harmony" in their marriage comes at the very end of the book, where it is suggested that Mark and Jane are about to conceive a child together.[98]

HUBRIS, NEMESIS, AND RETUNING THE *MUSICA MUNDANA*

We have seen that the consequences of *bending* or *breaking*, especially when done with intent, can be quite severe. In countless stories and accounts, such mistuning of *musica humana* also effects the tuning of the *musica mundana*, which is forced to react in an attempt to reestablish equilibrium—to re-tune. This echoes the ancient Greek concept of hubris and nemesis. Hubris occurred when a human, often a powerful ruler, felt they were above or exempt from natural laws governing human behavior. This upset the balance of human society—an integral part of *musica humana*—while at the same time contesting mankind's subservient position in the universal order vis-à-vis the gods, a disruption of the *musica mundana*. Such hubris caused the gods to send Nemesis, the goddess of divine retribution, to destroy the offending humans and all their works, and restore proper order in the universe.[99]

Many of the characters we have analyzed in this chapter, as well as in chapter 3, are subject to this hubris-nemesis effect through their own intentions and actions. Melkor makes his own music, disregarding other divine musicians during creation, and desires to usurp the creative abilities of Eru. As a result of his actions, Melkor is cast into darkness.[100] Similarly, Sauron creates the Ring to dominate the minds and wills of others, the Ring is taken from him and at length destroyed, and he is forever diminished. Likewise, Jadis aspires to godlike status by destroying the world of Charn, and locking the land of Narnia in a hundred-year winter. This prompts the creator himself, in the form of Aslan, to appear and kill her. In *Paradise Lost*, when Adam and Eve accept Satan's offer of divine power, God excludes them from the Garden of Eden and changes the nature of the Earth, tilting its axis and allowing predation and death among the created animals. In *The Silmarillion*, the Númenorians fight against the death that is part of their created destiny, attack the forbidden land of the gods, and prompt the destruction of their own land. Furthermore, Dr. Edward Weston allows himself to be influenced by an evil spirit in his mission to endlessly propagate the human race across the universe, and he is possessed and destroyed. Victor Frankenstein aspires to a kind of divinity by creating a new human species, but his abandonment of his creation brings Nemesis in the form of the spurned monster, who returns to kill his family and friends. Lastly, Dr. Henry Jekyll's hubristic view of himself causes him to attempt the division of his intrinsically dualistic nature into independent parts, which results in the loss of his *entire* self. In each of these cases, an individual or a society seeks to *bend* or *break* the established hierarchy through hubris, but Nemesis arrives and reestablishes order in a universe striving to re-tune itself.

There are various ways of being *bent*, whether we are speaking of objects, concepts, or people. *Bentness* can be thought to lie along a continuum, from slight to extreme, until such an extreme and unrecoverable state is reached, that it becomes *broken*. When used to describe people, it becomes another way of looking at the fundamental tuning of the inner self, of the *musica humana*. To be *straight* is to be in tune, to be *bent* is to be out of tune, and to be *broken* is to have no music at all. In the next chapter, we will examine the various ways that *musica humana*—or at least *perceptions* of *musica humana*—effect the actual creation of audible music, *musica instrumentalis*.

NOTES

1. Homer and Edward Earl of Derby, tr., *The Iliad of Homer*, vol. 2 (New York: Charles Scribner & Co., 1865), 88–9.
2. James Legge, tr., *The Chinese Classics, Vol. 2: Containing the Works of Mencius* (Hong Kong and London: Trübner & Co., 1861), 140.
3. I initially encountered this use of the term in *The Space Trilogy*, where the concept is explored in some depth.
4. I am aware that the terms "straight" and "bent" have strong social connotations, and are an integral part of popular and academic discourse on sexuality and representation. However, these particular uses of the terms were not widespread when Lewis was writing *The Space Trilogy*, and it is unlikely that he intended his work to be read in that sense. While there is some danger of it being perceived as outdated, a

misstep, or uninventive, I will use "straight" and "bent" as analogues to "consonant" and "dissonant," while freely admitting that other (and better) readings are possible.

5. Gold, jewels, water, land, etc. are often desired and fought over, but do not possess within themselves a moral component, unless of course they are "cursed" or "possessed" in some way.

6. Just as when elves awoke at their creation, men were quickly discovered and corrupted by the servants of Melkor. In the battles in Middle-earth, the men friendly with elves fight on their behalf, but most of the race of men fight on the side of Melkor.

7. Sauron knows this to be false, but encourages this act to sow discord between elves and men, to alienate men from the Ainur, and to exact revenge on the Númenorians for having played a role in the earlier defeat of Melkor.

8. Tolkien, *The Silmarillion*, 259–82.

9. Ibid., 37–8.

10. Ibid., 262. I am aware that death and evil does indeed come to Valinor, through the agency of Melkor and Ungoliant. However, this evil comes from outside, and is not *endemic* to Valinor. It remains a place in which death and evil are not natural.

11. Milton, *Paradise Lost*, 248.

12. Ibid., 255–7.

13. Bertolgio, "Polyphony, Collective Improvisation, and the Gift of Creation," 12.

14. This brings to mind the discussion of intervals from chapter 1, in which Johannes de Garlandia's interval classifications include *perfect discords*—intervals that are perfectly imperfect.

15. Tolkien, *The Fellowship of the Ring*, 261.

16. This use of the Latin term predates its later use in anthropology by several centuries.

17. John R. Holmes, "'Inside a Song': Tolkien's Phonaesthetics," in Bradford Lee Eden, ed., *Middle-earth Minstrel: Essays on Music in Tolkien* (Jefferson, NC and London: McFarland & Company, Inc., Publishers, 2010), 39.

18. Ibid.

19. Some authors use synonymous terms like "twisted" and "crooked."

20. Tolkien, *The Fellowship of the Ring*, 32.

21. Ibid., 34. Fortunately for Bilbo, he feels instantly better after voluntarily giving up the Ring, though it still burdens his mind for decades afterward.

22. Genesis 3:15 (NIV).

23. Frodo actually receives several serious physical wounds, to say nothing of severe emotional and psychological damage.

24. Though Ransom does not "need" to die—indeed, he has become effectively immortal—he knows that he must leave Earth in order to be healed. As he tells his companions, "the wound will only be healed in the world where it was got," that is, on Venus. Lewis, *That Hideous Strength*, 366.

25. In Aslan's Country, which is the heaven of Narnia and all of the other universes (including ours), any *bending* caused by injury and age is instantly reversed. Edmund notices that a recent rugby injury has disappeared, and Digory notes that

he and Polly—by now quite elderly—have become "unstiffened." Lewis, *The Last Battle*, 158. In fact, it seems that in Aslan's country, the concept of age is largely erased, as are its effects. Jill realizes this when she notes that no one seems to have any particular ages there. Lewis, *The Silver Chair*, 238.

26. Mary Shelley, *Frankenstein* (New York: Dover Publications, Inc., 1994), 32.

27. Ibid., 68–9.

28. These themes are briefly explored in another novel by Mary Shelley, *The Last Man*, published in 1826. Two orphaned children, Lionel and Perdita, must survive on general charity, and are therefore spurned by society. This results in an early life of solitude and isolation in Perdita's case, and a life of antisocial behavior and crime in Lionel's. However, both eventually find acceptance and human companionship, and so their fate is not that of Frankenstein's monster.

29. Shelley, *Frankenstein*, 106.

30. Herman Melville, *Billy Budd* (New York: Washington Square Press, 1962), 16.

31. Ibid., 14–15.

32. Ibid., 27.

33. Ibid.

34. Ibid., 55.

35. Ibid., 39.

36. Ibid., 37.

37. Ibid.

38. Ibid., 61.

39. Jane eventually refuses St. John's proposal and returns to Edward Rochester, whose wife has died in a fire that destroyed the manor house, blinding and maiming him, but also making him legally (and morally) eligible to remarry.

40. Charlotte Brontë, *Jane Eyre* (New York: Barnes & Noble Classics, 2003), 434.

41. Ibid., 419.

42. Ibid., 484.

43. A similar study in contrasts between "natural" humanity, and Victorian-era society and religiosity, can be found in Thomas Hardy's 1891 novel *Tess of the d'Urbervilles*. Hardy consistently contrasts the lives of simple country folk with those of the educated, urbane elites in the church and the landowning/aristocratic classes. The countryside is characterized as a semi-Edenic paradise, bursting with life and growth (a perfect, or at least a positive, *musica mundana*), and those who live in close harmony with it are likewise full of pure, natural life—having good *musica humana*. This is in direct opposition to the cold formalism, unnatural denial of the physical, and exploitative nature of the church and ruling classes who, in Hardy's novel, are clearly "out of tune."

44. Lewis, *Out of the Silent Planet*, 134–6.

45. Weston, Devine, and Ransom travel aboard a spaceship for their trip to Mars, while Weston travels alone to Venus. Ransom arrives on Venus, and returns to Earth, aboard a device created by the ruler of Mars.

46. Lewis, *Perelandra*, 124.

47. Ibid., 81.
48. Ibid., 82.
49. Ibid., 102.
50. Ibid., 98. This statement is a blasphemous retelling of the words of Jesus: "I am come that they might have life, and that they might have it more abundantly." John 10:10b (KJV)
51. Lewis, *Perelandra*, 128.
52. Ibid., 73.
53. Ibid., 81.
54. Ibid., 91.
55. Ibid., 95.
56. This statement is even more potent when one considers that Ransom fought in some of the bloodiest battles of World War I.
57. Lewis, *Perelandra*, 95.
58. Ibid., 111.
59. Mark and Jane Studdock's marital relationship will receive its own treatment below.
60. Lewis, *That Hideous Strength*, 354.
61. Ibid., 200.
62. Ibid., 293–4.
63. Ibid., 294–6.
64. Ibid., 307.
65. Ibid., 331–3.
66. Cathy Ames later marries and becomes Cathy Trask, but as most of the discussion in this section focuses on her early life, I will use her maiden name.
67. John Steinbeck, *East of Eden* (New York and London: Penguin Books, 1986), 95–6.
68. Ibid., 96.
69. Ibid., 235.
70. Ibid., 99.
71. Ibid., 101–7. No one suspects Cathy's involvement with her teacher, or in any of these other events and coincidences. Cathy has a particular skill in reading the desires of others, satisfying them, and keeping them quiet afterward.
72. Ibid., 111–16.
73. Robert Louis Stevenson, *The Strange Case of Dr. Jekyll and Mr. Hyde and Other Stories* (New York: Barnes and Noble Classics, 2003), 67–8. It is impossible not to detect a note of pride and arrogance in this attitude, as Dr. Jekyll seems to say that, because his calling and capacity for excellence and good is greater than that of other men, so too are his follies less acceptable.
74. Ibid., 71–2.
75. Ibid., 8–21.
76. Ibid., 62.
77. Ibid., 84. This is very similar to Ransom's description of the possessed and *broken* Weston in *Perelandra*.
78. Ibid, 56.

79. Lewis, *The Magician's Nephew*, 52–3.
80. Ibid., 68.
81. Assumedly, not all animals and plant life would have been able to survive this perpetual winter, so Jadis is likely responsible for at least the localized extinction of any number of species. Given her previous actions in Charn, this behavior is not surprising.
82. Lewis, *The Lion, the Witch and the Wardrobe*, 35–9.
83. Jadis is not necessarily lying here, as the apple she has herself stolen and eaten makes her immortal in Narnia. In the end, Digory *is* given a magic apple to take to his mother, who is cured by it, though not made immortal.
84. Lewis, *The Magician's Nephew*, 177–8.
85. Lewis, *The Lion, the Witch and the Wardrobe*, 140–1.
86. Ibid., 89.
87. Lewis, *That Hideous Strength*, 107.
88. C. S. Lewis, "The Inner Ring," *Memorial Lecture*, 1944. King's College, University of London.
89. Lewis, *That Hideous Strength*, 132.
90. Ibid., 107.
91. Ibid., 315–16.
92. Ibid., 299–300.
93. Ibid., 113.
94. Ibid., 231.
95. Ibid., 143.
96. Ibid., 358.
97. Ibid., 312–13. Indeed, there are *seven* genders among the angelic beings.
98. Ward, *Planet Narnia*, 87.
99. Unfortunately, the results of the actions of hubristic humans, together with the subsequent vengeance of Nemesis, were often quite destructive to humanity and the local environment.
100. Only after countless ages have passed. The interval of time between hubris and nemesis is often very slow.

Chapter Vignette 6.5

Musica Humana and the Limits of Musical Genius

Since the man can never be separated from the artist, general, moral, and intellectual culture must be the foundation of . . . art.[1]

The concept of a divine model of music—*musica mundana*—has been fairly well established in the course of the book, though the precise contours of the model have undergone significant fluctuations over time. The specifications of audible, practical music—*musica instrumentalis*—which may be thought to be a faithful representation or application of the divine model, have also been variable, and subject to the caprices of style and taste, as we have already observed, particularly in chapter 4. However, music does not write itself, and the conduit *through* which music is transferred from the rarefied and inaudible reaches of the cosmos, down to the earthbound concert hall and opera stage, is the human composer, whose own *musica humana* will naturally be of interest to others. The quality of the *human* conduit, in the opinion of many connoisseurs and critics, will determine the quality of the *musical* output. To borrow imagery from the previous chapter, a *bent* composer will compose *bent* music, and a *straight* composer will compose *straight* music. That the terms "bent" and "straight" have multiple usages is both evident and relevant, as we will see below.

IMPERFECT COMPOSERS AND IMPERFECT MUSIC—CHOOSING OUR HEROES

Choosing musical heroes is a process fraught with difficulty and potential pitfalls. Any issue may be a source of contention, and what is considered acceptable is in a constant state of flux, from the philosophical and practical models used to identify "good" music, to the characteristics and personality traits indicative of "good" composers. Often, partisan forces are at play, and the acceptance or rejection of composers and music is made on political, national, religious, ethnic, sexual, and socioeconomic grounds. There may also be strong preferences for either the new or the old. In the late medieval era, music more than twenty years old was termed "ancient," and unworthy of performance alongside newer, more innovative styles. Conversely, from the early- to mid-nineteenth century, musical culture became more and more "classical," in the sense that the concert and stage repertoire included many older works, alongside newly composed ones. This latter process accelerated throughout the nineteenth century and into the twentieth, and today I would venture to guess that more than 99 percent of the current performance repertoire is music by dead composers—most of them dead for centuries.

The composers who live on in the concert hall long after death include many of the cultural heroes of the Western world: Bach, Handel, Haydn, Mozart, Beethoven, Brahms, Wagner, and Verdi. The influences of literary romanticism in the late eighteenth and nineteenth centuries inspired the cult of the artist as a semi-divine personage, who bridges the gulf between the human and the celestial. In the realm of music, no single composer personifies this image more than Beethoven, who is universally placed at the pinnacle of the musical pantheon and who, though cursed with the loss of his physical hearing, is nevertheless held up as a perfectly *straight* and pure spiritual conduit for the *musica mundana*. However, even if we agree that Beethoven's (or any other composer's) *musica instrumentalis* accomplishes this, there is no avoiding the fact that the Western world has permitted a staggering degree of mistuned *musica humana* in its musical heroes. While the range of acceptable "mistunings" has evolved over time, and been subjected to various local prejudices, "great" composers have been allowed to be, among other things, substance abusers, swindlers, philanderers, racists, and bigots.

Beethoven was a difficult and suspicious person—character traits no doubt exacerbated by his early-onset deafness—and at times he was rather vulgar, and even visited prostitutes. Richard Wagner was both a brilliant composer and a talented charlatan, a German nationalist and racist of the first water, who inspired Adolf Hitler and the Nazi party. In these cases the musical world has been willing to excuse or ignore such imperfections, carefully gardening biographies and narratives, to pare away potentially undesirable elements. Interestingly, in cases where composers did *not* achieve a level of success and popularity expected by the public, *post hoc* analyses of the composer's music and lifestyle could be undertaken, in order to identify elements that would explain this failure to reach their potential. One such example is that of the nineteenth-century Russian composer Modest Mussorgsky.

David Tame, in his 1984 book, *The Secret Power of Music*, uses Mussorgsky as an example of how perceived flaws in a composer's *musica humana* infects their musical output, making it less "great" than it could have been, contributing to critical and commercial failure. Like many of his contemporaries, Mussorgsky abused alcohol,[2] and his heavy drinking and related illnesses ended his life prematurely at the age of 42. Tame argues that Mussorgsky's weaknesses and moral failures are indelibly imprinted on his music:

> Other composers, too, had encountered difficulties during their careers, yet had persevered in faith until their success finally arrived. Mussorgsky, however, having become an alcoholic, died poverty-stricken and alone. It is difficult not to perceive the reflection of his life and circumstances within his music.[3]

For Tame, Mussorgsky's personal circumstances of poverty and alcoholism are, and *must be*, mirrored in his music. While the usefulness of such a reading may be the subject of debate, it is not itself unreasonable to look for an artist's personal perspective within their art. However, what is highly questionable are the moral judgments made—because Mussorgsky had (assumedly) personal moral failings, his music was of necessity destined to fail. Tame notes that other composers also encountered difficulties, but they—presumably *greater* composers—persisted and had faith, which ultimately ensured critical and financial success. While the application of this kind of logic, in which composers are successful because they achieve success (and *vice versa*), is problematic to say the least, even more problematic is the implicit notion that success is directly linked to morality. As noted above, many composers deemed great, and thus considered to have well-tuned *musica humana*, exhibited any number of questionable behaviors and moral failings during their lives. These have largely been overlooked, either because the behaviors were not generally known to the public, or because they were not the "wrong" kinds of behaviors.

FROM GENIUS TO ABOMINATION AND BACK—
THE CASE OF PYOTR ILYICH TCHAIKOVSKY

The life and creative work of the Russian composer Pyotr Ilyich Tchaikovsky is an excellent illustration of the perceived limits of genius, and how critical opinion can shift in order to cast a composer out of the musical pantheon. Tchaikovsky is probably best known for his ballet scores for *Swan Lake*, *The Sleeping Beauty*, and *The Nutcracker*, the *1812 Overture*, and his six symphonies. The composer died in 1893 at the age of 53, possibly of cholera, and his reputation at the time of his death, and over the subsequent two decades, was almost universally positive. Near the end of his life, Tchaikovsky was declared by some to be the greatest composer living, and within a few years of his death he was widely ranked among the greatest classical composers of the past. His music was often described as essentially emotional and melancholic, but this was attributed to Tchaikovsky's Russian and Slavic identity, and not to any undue or inappropriate indulgence of sentimentality. The emotional nature of his music signaled a frank, sincere, and true commentary on the universal human condition.[4] Tchaikovsky's own personality and character was described as reserved, painstaking, and fastidious, but not overly self-absorbed or misanthropic, and at times even warm, kind, and good-natured—he was a man of good *musica humana*. However, this perception began to change, at least among professional music critics, around 1910.

Speculation and rumors about Tchaikovsky's sexuality were widespread during his lifetime and immediately after his death. The composer did marry, but the marriage was a disaster, and he and his wife lived together for less than three months. Tchaikovsky's attraction to men was not a secret to those who knew him, and while the degree to which the composer himself accepted his sexuality is a subject of debate among scholars, the fact that he was gay is not a point of dispute (with one important exception, treated below). The reality of Tchaikovsky's sexuality began to invade the world of musical criticism in the second decade of the twentieth century, and the identification of the composer as *great* simultaneously underwent a drastic reexamination. From being described as somewhat of a tortured genius—but tortured in ways that illustrated his essential humanity—Tchaikovsky was transformed into a man possessed of "psychopathic temperament," suffering from "nervous diseases," and "psychasthenia." These perceived mental deficiencies were both implicitly and explicitly tied to his homosexuality, couched in terms of "morbid perversities," and "idiosyncrasies of a sexual nature."[5] In short, he was now considered very out of tune.

At this point, the musical intelligentsia was quick to take issue with Tchaikovsky's musical output itself. Music that at one time celebrated the struggles of a universal humanity, now became the ravings of a sick man's "chronic hysteria," and "helpless, dreadful [. . .] hypochondria," that was "tortuously self-absorbed," leading to music that was "truly pathological."[6] There are at least two reasons why critical opinion soured on Tchaikovsky in the early part of the twentieth century. One was the gradual critical rejection of romanticism in music and the arts, with its interest in the inner emotional life of the composer, in favor of a more cool, dry, and "objective" modernist aesthetic.[7] The second reason, and one far weightier with many of the critics, was the need for Tchaikovsky's sexuality to pervade his music.[8] If the composer was gay, then the music must be identifiably gay as well. As homosexuality was not one of the accepted "weakness and moral failures" allowed to artists (in the opinion of many critics), it followed that Tchaikovsky's *musica humana* was not a proper conduit between the *musica mundana* and the audible *musica instrumentalis*. To put it another way, his music was now found to be *bent*. The task of *bending* his music, from a critical point of view, was accomplished through some rather deft logical and analytical maneuvering, illustrated in the following paragraph.

The final three of Tchaikovsky's six symphonies were held up in musical criticism as examples of what was imperfect in the composer's music, being as they were a "musical revelation" of his "temperamental sickness." For example, the Fourth Symphony could not be "great" because it was not *really* a message of suffering and agony from the inner soul of the composer, but rather a mere physical-sexual communication, and thus superficial and incapable of speaking universal truths. Rather, the symphony reeked of "distaste," and thus could not be truly appealing. Some critics saw the Fifth and Sixth Symphonies as indicators of conscious duplicity on the part of Tchaikovsky, in terms reminiscent of Dr. Jekyll and Mr. Hyde from the previous chapter. These critics described a composer who falsely and insincerely maintained an urbane, benign, and gentlemanly façade, while concealing and nurturing a "neurotic, depraved" inner life, which society rejects as "shameful, if not absolutely criminal." Thus, the Fifth Symphony, with its bright and triumphant final movement—entirely conventional in traditional symphonic form—reveals Tchaikovsky's deliberately false exterior. Since Tchaikovsky's music *must* highlight his sexuality, and that sexuality *must* represent a negative value, the Fifth Symphony and its optimistic finale becomes "contrived and histrionic," insincere, unconvincing, and "mawkishly theatrical."[9] The Sixth Symphony, in contrast, ends with a slow, sorrowful finale (the symphony is nicknamed the *Pathetique*), and critics felt it was a true, and final,[10] expression of Tchaikovsky's inner personality: a gloomy, grief-stricken recognition of his fundamental and intractable moral failure. Tame exemplifies this attitude toward the three final symphonies:

> Many earlier composers had displayed imperfect traits of one kind of another, yet they had nevertheless striven ceaselessly to perfect themselves. In their music they had portrayed only that which is divine and beautiful in life; only that which the consciousness of man should always endeavour to move towards. In Tchaikovsky's last three symphonies, however, we are called to move in another, and less enlightened, direction. What can, at least, be said of them is that they offer a most instructive lesson: that rarely, if ever, can the work of an artist rise above the main direction of his own consciousness. It is doubtful that a masterful music can ever result where the heart and mind of the musician are not themselves, for the main part, so mastered.[11]

Tame issues an additional warning to the careless listener, which echoes those of Tchaikovsky's earlier critical detractors: "By attuning ourselves to the tones of such music, even without consciously knowing the programme, we automatically absorb its philosophy of submission and despair."[12] Thus, we are left with only two possible conclusions. First, though many other composers strove to perfect themselves, so that only the "divine and beautiful" was present in their music, Tchaikovsky was either unable or unwilling to do so. Second, that homosexuality is an "imperfect trait" of an entirely different kind and degree than other "faults" that have afflicted composers, which not only cannot be "mastered," but is insidiously and subliminally contagious as well.

Apart from reading into Tchaikovsky's works a vaguely generalized sexuality, critics also found specific compositional techniques that indicated the composer's pathology. The structure of many of Tchaikovsky's melodies, especially those in the style of Russian folk music, do not always allow for the kind of harmonic development typical in much of the other traditional symphonic literature. Instead, he often uses repetition as an organizing structural principle. In early criticism, this was considered a great achievement, an innovation that illustrated the composer's great skill and expressiveness. However, later commentators perceived the very same technique as "hysterically excessive" and "obsessive."[13] Of course, the shift in opinion did not relate to any evolution in Tchaikovsky's actual compositional technique, as the criticism—both positive and negative—was made well after the composer's death. The only difference was in public and critical awareness of his sexuality, which served to transform a musical strength into a musical weakness.

The last few decades of the twentieth century saw a reevaluation and subsequent critical reacceptance of Tchaikovsky's music, with one important exception. In the composer's homeland of Russia during the Soviet era, authorities quickly censored and suppressed published references to his sexuality. Even in the decades since the fall of the Soviet Union, Tchaikovsky's homosexuality has been widely denied by Russian cultural officials. After the passing of a controversial "gay propaganda" law in 2013, a number of planned biographical films about the composer (some of them funded by the Russian ministry of culture), edited references to his sexuality out of screenplays and scripts. At least one film portrays Tchaikovsky as a man who suffers emotionally because he is *falsely* rumored to be gay.[14]

It is clear that bigotry and homophobia are the proximate causes for the historical, and even current, rejection of Tchaikovsky's music. In contrast, a male composer who is a known philanderer and womanizer may be fully accepted, wherever patriarchal systems embrace such toxic forms of masculinity. As with all criticism and public reception, this serves to illustrate our own societal biases and prejudices, as well as what we value and approve. Our musical heroes are those who we identify as having a proper connection to divine sources of musical inspiration, and who are fit to transmit that music to the rest of us.

NOTES

1. Adoph Bernhard Marx and August Heinrich Wehrhad, tr. *The Music of the Nineteenth Century and its Culture* (London: Robert Cocks and Co., 1855), 279.
2. In the creative and bohemian circles in which Mussorgsky moved, excessive drinking was expected and widely practiced as a particular marker of anti-establishment sentiment.
3. Tame, *The Secret Power of Music*, 82.
4. Smith, "Perceptions of Homosexuality in Tchaikovsky Criticism," 4.
5. Ibid., 5.
6. Ibid.
7. It should be noted, however, that Tchaikovsky's music *never* went out of style with the general concert-going public, regardless of the utterances of music critics.
8. As it stands to reason that Tchaikovsky was not the first gay composer, or even the first suspected as such, why did musical and social critics of the early twentieth century care so much? Prior to the turn of the century, homosexuality was generally considered a category of sexual *acts*—which may or may not have been regulated by society—rather than a distinct *identity*. With the rise of the new medical specializations of psychology and psychiatry, sexuality and sexual identity were folded into the vocabularies of disease pathology and treatment.
9. Smith, "Perceptions of Homosexuality in Tchaikovsky Criticism," 7.
10. Tchaikovsky died nine days after conducting the premiere of this work.
11. Tame, *The Secret Power of Music*, 86–7.
12. Ibid., 84.
13. Smith, "Perceptions of Homosexuality in Tchaikovsky Criticism," 8.
14. Alec Luhn, "Tchaikovsky's Sexuality 'Downplayed' in Biopic under Russia's Anti-Gay Law." *The Guardian*, August 25, 2013, online edition. Accessed July 11, 2021. https://www.theguardian.com/world/2013/aug/25/russia-anti-gay-law-tchaikovsky-sexuality

Chapter 7

The Music of the Spheres and the Modern Worship Wars[1]

Our fathers' heir-loom of time-honoured faith,
No reasoning shall cast down,
Not though the lore Hath been the invention of the keenest wit.[2]

In this final major chapter we will complete the path we began in chapter 1, with the consideration of ancient and medieval music theory and practice, and continued in chapter 4, with reexaminations of those theories and practices at the turn of the seventeenth and twentieth centuries. Here, we will see how concepts of *musica mundana*, *musica humana*, and *musica instrumentalis* have been utilized and applied in Christian worship over the past century or so.[3] This period, sometimes called the "worship wars," has seen the perceived influx of secular musical styles, forms, and instrumentation into the liturgical, devotional, and praise music of many Christian congregations and denominations. This influx is often considered a relatively recent phenomenon, with previous centuries enjoying relative conservatism and stability. In fact, music for worship in the Western church has undergone nearly constant fluctuation and change, since at least the medieval era. Unlike in previous chapters, here I will include examples from my own personal experience. Having grown up in religious communities in the 1980s and 1990s in the United States, I have observed at first hand some of the social, cultural, and religious issues at play within the worship debates. Furthermore, having been an active church musician in my own Seventh-day Adventist denomination, as well as serving as a minister of music in Lutheran congregations, I have perforce been a participant—though not a *partisan*—in the "worship wars." Moreover, I am a music historian specializing in the history of theory and liturgical music, and this added training and perspective may help provide a measure of context to these modern discussions and disputes. However, my own experiences should be taken as strictly illustrative, and not widely representative or exhaustive.

GOOD OLD MUSIC

While serving as music minister for a local Lutheran congregation, one of my responsibilities was to help plan weekly worship services, together with the organist and the parish pastor. We chose the music to be sung by the parish choir, pieces for the organist to play at different points in the worship service, and hymns for choir and congregation. These selections were made with various elements in mind, such as difficulty and comprehensibility, length, and the extent to which the music was appropriate to the liturgical season, the scripture readings, and the subject of the pastor's homily. In this particular congregation, parishioners could fill out anonymous cards, used to request prayers and to make suggestions. On a number of occasions, members of the congregation would comment on our choice of congregational hymns, saying in essence: "why are you choosing hymns we don't know; we want to sing the *good old hymns.*" Sometimes the card would include examples of such hymns, which were nearly always ones that had been written between 1890 and 1920, and thus were popular, "standard" hymns for those who grew up in the first half of the twentieth century. In contrast, the hymns I helped select were often traditional Lutheran chorales from the sixteenth and seventeenth centuries—undoubtedly "old," and unquestionably "good."[4] The parishioners' comments pointed rather to another, important concern: real or perceived generational divides existing within congregations and within society at large. I perceived that the underlying desire was not for what was *actually* "good and old," but for a return to the comfort and familiarity of tradition, in the context of an ever-changing world that seemed not to value it.

While the worship wars are often seen as a part of wider social upheavals in the United States during the 1950s and 1960s—the rise of rock and roll, the Civil Rights movement, the mainstreaming of drug culture, and the rejection of traditional sexual mores, among others—they are actually only the latest in a series of musical debates going back many centuries. We have already examined a few of these in previous chapters, such as the medieval use of dissonance, and the Artusi-Monteverdi controversy at the turn of the seventeenth century. At their core, these perennial debates are disputes over *musica mundana*, and how *musica instrumentalis* and *musica humana* validate the celestial music. Ultimately, they are generational disputes. Before I give specific examples, I will share some humorous commentary on technology from Douglas Adams, which is happily appropriate to this discussion:

1. Anything that is in the world when you're born is normal and ordinary and is just a natural part of the way the world works.
2. Anything that's invented between when you're fifteen and thirty-five is new and exciting and revolutionary and you can probably get a career in it.
3. Anything invented after you're thirty-five is against the natural order of things.[5]

We have already seen this very attitude manifested during several points in Western music history, but we will focus on theoretical arguments and practical changes with strictly religious connotations, such as those encountered in chapter 1. Among the greatest tectonic shifts experienced in Western Christianity was the Protestant Reformation of the early sixteenth century. In Germany, it gained currency when an Augustinian priest, Martin Luther, openly disputed certain aspects of Roman Catholic religious doctrine and practice. This eventually led to the fragmentation of the Western church, and the rise of numerous denominations and religious communities identifying themselves as "Protestant." It should be made clear that Luther did not initially intend to create a *new* church and hierarchy, but rather desired to reform the existing ones. However, official rejection of his dissent and his suggested reforms served to force the issue, and he and other reformers set about creating new church organizations.

Martin Luther was an avid amateur musician, a composer of some ability, and a great lover of the refined Latin polyphonic music of the late fifteenth and early sixteenth centuries. He felt that music, next to scripture, was the gift from God most highly to be praised, and he considered music his greatest ally in winning souls. Luther knew and acknowledged the concept of *musica mundana*, noting that "nothing is without sound or harmony."[6] He also recognized music's power in the realm of *musica humana*, asserting that it could move the affections and emotions, and help the Christian avoid shameful desires and evil company.[7] Though Martin Luther is widely recognized for his promotion of music, worship, and scripture in vernacular languages—German, in his case—he was not antagonistic to the use of Latin. He advocated for the composition of simple songs in German, so that local congregations could participate in worship, and if the congregation was not highly educated, the entire Mass could be said in German. Conversely, if a church included many students and scholars, a Mass in Latin would be appropriate. Likewise with music, when a church had sufficient musical and financial resources, they could perform polyphonic Latin Masses and motets, but if it could not provide the requisite talent and funding, worship music could be in a simpler style, and sung in German.[8] These communal songs were designed to be pleasurable and easy to sing, and their melodies were often based on familiar liturgical, devotional, and even secular tunes (or tunes in popular or secular styles). This promoted participation by congregations, and also helped aid parishioners in memorizing and internalizing the religious messages of the texts.[9] Luther and his colleagues also created four-part German devotional songs for youth, so they would have something to replace their "love ditties and wanton songs."[10] Those who criticized these musical innovations pressed Luther to prove his positions from the scriptures, the writings of the Church Fathers, and respected music theorists—essentially, to connect his new practices to established notions of *musica mundana*. Luther's reply was that "liberty must prevail in these matters and Christian consciences not be bound by laws and ordinances."[11] While accepting the existence of the *musica mundana*, Luther allowed for celestial music to speak with much more universal voice, one that could be understood by all.

Not all Protestant reformers were on the same page regarding music. Jean Calvin agreed with Luther that music has the power to move the affections, and is one of the most important tools given by God to the church. However, because music is *so* powerful, Calvin mistrusted it, and demanded that it be tightly regulated in order to avoid abuses.[12] For Calvin, music in worship should not be light or frivolous, but must have weight and majesty, in order to reflect the seriousness and gravity of heavenly principles. Thus, polyphonic and multi-part choral music was eliminated, no instruments were permitted in worship, and only simple, unaccompanied unison melodies could be sung by the congregation.[13] The contents of sung texts were also restricted, with only the words of the Psalms and a few other biblical and liturgical texts allowed.[14] Like Luther, Calvin was attempting to provide a divine model for music. Unlike Luther, his concept of *musica mundana* argued that the "full strength" of divine music is too powerful and too easily abused, and must therefore be tempered, before it can become a safe tool for the use of *musica humana*.

The Catholic hierarchy did not turn a deaf ear, so to speak, to the complaints and criticisms of the reformers. The church formulated its official responses to the Reformation during the Council of Trent, which met intermittently between 1545 and 1563, spurring a large number of reforms of its own. Among the complaints made from at least the late fifteenth century, was that polyphonic liturgical music had reached such a level of refinement, especially in its use of imitative counterpoint, that it was impossible to hear or understand the words.[15] If music was intended to adorn the text, enhancing and strengthening its meaning, then the high level of complexity in polyphonic church music was seen by many to defeat that intent. The desire of Calvin to restore the primacy of the text is what caused him to place such severe restrictions on music, and he argued that it was mockery to say that a congregation was listening to liturgical music, when nothing could be understood. Only when the message of the text was clearly comprehended, could the Holy Spirit touch the heart and mind of the listener.[16] The Council of Trent agreed in part, decreeing that liturgical music should reach the ears and hearts of the listeners "tranquilly," not giving mere "empty pleasure to the ear," but being of a character to draw the congregation to higher ideals, including the "heavenly harmonies."[17]

While the desire of many musicians in the sixteenth century was a return to the intent and spirit of earlier music—music that heightened the sense and meaning of the text—few or none at that time were suggesting an *actual* return to the musical styles and forms of former centuries. Later, however, there were indeed movements that advocated a return to the "good old music" of the distant past. In the nineteenth century, choral societies—active in Catholic and Protestant areas alike—sponsored large choral festivals dedicated to the performance of music of past masters, such as Johann Sebastian Bach, George Frideric Handel, and Joseph Haydn. The Cecilian Movement, which began in Germany and spread to other Catholic areas of Europe during the second half of the nineteenth century, promoted the restoration of medieval forms of Gregorian chant, and the revival of the polyphonic choral style that flourished around the turn of the seventeenth century.[18] This desire to return to the musical styles of the past was, in part, a reaction against the liberalizing Enlightenment ideals of the eighteenth century, and in part a desire to return to the perceived simplicity of the past, in the context of rapidly increasing European urban industrialization.[19] The restoration of Gregorian chant was aided by the academic work of the French monks of the Benedictine abbey of Solesmes. These monks collected, studied, and edited collections of medieval chant from all over Europe, and created practical reconstructions that could be easily performed by religious communities and congregations. The ultimate imprimatur for these movements of musical restoration came in 1903, after the elevation of Pius X to the papacy. A strong supporter of the Cecilian Movement and the work of the Solesmes monks, Pius' first major promulgation was the *Tra le sollecitudini*, which treated the subject of music in the Mass. He felt that too many secular influences had entered into liturgical music, especially forms and styles associated with nineteenth-century Italian opera. Pius felt that this profaned the sacredness of the rites and ceremonies, even when the intentions of the musicians were pure:

> Nothing should have place, therefore, in the temple calculated to disturb or even merely to diminish the piety and devotion of the faithful, nothing that may

give reasonable cause for disgust or scandal, nothing, above all, which directly offends the decorum and sanctity of the sacred functions and is thus unworthy of the House of Prayer and of the Majesty of God.

[...]

Such is the abuse affecting sacred chant and music. And indeed, whether it is owing to the very nature of this art, fluctuating and variable as it is in itself, or to the succeeding changes in tastes and habits with the course of time, or to the fatal influence exercised on sacred art by profane and theatrical art, or to the pleasure that music directly produces, and that is not always easily contained within the right limits, or finally to the many prejudices on the matter, so lightly introduced and so tenaciously maintained even among responsible and pious persons, the fact remains that there is a general tendency to deviate from the right rule.[20]

In order to prevent such deviations from "the right rule," Pius argued for the elimination of practices at odds with *musica mundana*—as he perceived it—and the return of practices in agreement with it:

We consider it Our first duty, without further delay, to raise Our voice at once in reproof and condemnation of all that is seen to be out of harmony with the right rule [...] in the functions of public worship and in the performance of the ecclesiastical offices.[21]

The primary method for restoring this harmony was a return to the purity of medieval Gregorian chant and "Classic Polyphony"—the strict polyphonic style following the rules of Zarlino—which would stand as the measurement by which all other music would be judged:

Gregorian Chant has always been regarded as the supreme model for sacred music, so that it is fully legitimate to lay down the following rule: the more closely a composition for church approaches in its movement, inspiration and savor the Gregorian form, the more sacred and liturgical it becomes; and the more out of harmony it is with that supreme model, the less worthy it is of the temple.

[...]

The above-mentioned qualities are also possessed in an excellent degree by Classic Polyphony, especially of the Roman School, which reached its greatest perfection in the sixteenth century ... and continued subsequently to produce compositions of excellent quality from a liturgical and musical standpoint. Classic Polyphony agrees admirably with Gregorian Chant, the supreme model of all sacred music, and hence it has been found worthy of a place side by side with Gregorian Chant.[22]

We see that Pius provides a framework for judging sacred music, reminiscent of that provided by Boethius and his followers, with its intention to draw from and imitate perceived divine and celestial models. There are a number of other instructions given in the *Tra le sollecitudini*, some of which echo the sixteenth-century Council of Trent, such as an ordinance that liturgical music must be performed "always in a manner intelligible to the faithful who listen."[23] Also, Pius notes that secularly derived styles, and certain instruments, could not foster a sense of reverence and seriousness among the members of the congregation, and so they were banned. The portion of Pius' promulgation that had perhaps the greatest effect on church musicians and worshipers, was one having to do with the membership of parish and cathedral choirs. Because musicians were considered to possess a true liturgical office, and women could not by definition hold any such office, they were henceforth excluded from participation in choirs, and their parts given to boys, as per the ancient custom of the church.[24] What is alarming about this pronouncement, from the standpoint of *musica humana*, is the claim that women, by their very presence and participation in liturgical celebrations, will automatically *decrease* the gravity and solemnity of that worship.[25]

MUSICA MUNDANA AND WORSHIP IN THE TWENTIETH CENTURY

The *Tra le sollecitudini* of Pius X was, in many ways, an attempt to shore up the church against the onslaught of modernity, which was gaining momentum at the turn of the twentieth century. However, this new century, with its many social, political, moral, and technological changes, could not ultimately be held back. By mid-century, the Catholic church came to realize that its forms and practices—including the use of Latin as the language of much of the liturgy, and its very conservative styles of music—threatened to make the institution irrelevant in a rapidly transforming world. In response, the church called the Second Vatican Council (generally known as "Vatican II"), which met between 1962 and 1965. Among the documents released during the council were some having significant consequences on liturgical music. The *Sacrosanctum Concilium* was published in 1963, and addressed the use of vernacular languages in the liturgy:

> But since the use of the mother tongue, whether in the Mass, the administration of the sacraments, or other parts of the liturgy, frequently may be of great advantage to the people, the limits of its employment may be extended.[26]

The document also allowed for styles of liturgical music to conform to local usages and customs, so long as they did not partake of any egregious "superstition and error":

> Even in the liturgy, the Church has no wish to impose a rigid uniformity in matters which do not implicate the faith or the good of the whole community; rather does she respect and foster the genius and talents of the various races and peoples.
> [. . .]
> In certain parts of the world, especially mission lands, there are peoples who have their own musical traditions, and these play a great part in their religious and social life. For this reason due importance is to be attached to their music, and a suitable place is to be given to it, not only in forming their attitude toward religion, but also in adapting worship to their native genius.[27]

A later document, *Musicam Sacram*, was released in 1967 to provide more specialized guidance on music, than the more general *Sacrosanctum Concilium*. Importantly, this document effectively reversed the prohibition of Pius X on women participating in musical portions of the liturgy:

> The choir can consist, according to the customs of each country and other circumstances, of either men and boys, or men and boys only, or men and women, or even, where there is a genuine case for it, of women only.[28]

Such allowances for the use of local languages and locally relevant musical traditions, the participation of women in the liturgy, and the acceptance of a much wider range of musical instruments for use in worship,[29] served to spur an explosion of creativity in liturgical composition across the world. In the Western church, the post-Vatican II period witnessed the performance of Mass settings in contemporary styles, sometimes known collectively as "guitar masses," which included liturgical music in folk, gospel, rock, jazz, and hybrid idioms.

This new openness to modern styles and forms of music in Catholic worship had a strong influence on Protestant worship music.[30] The Jesus Movement of the late 1960s and early 1970s included a number of musicians, many of them coming from well-known secular folk and rock groups, who brought modern popular music styles into Christian worship. "Maranatha! Music," a record label founded in 1971, distributed this music to national and international audiences, together with collections of sheet music and chord charts, for use by local churches and youth groups. In my own experience, such music was tolerated as long as it was confined to the youth chapel, and did not enter into the main "adult" service, except on very special occasions, such as when the youth took a leading role in worship. My own recollection of the music was that it was rather tame,[31] accompanied by a pianist or perhaps an acoustic guitarist if one was available. Nonetheless, the music was upbeat and rhythmic, and thus a source of controversy in certain parts of the religious community. This controversy only intensified as the instrumentation was updated to include electric guitars and bass, synthesized keyboards, and drum sets.

THE PROBLEM OF ASSOCIATION

One of the primary complaints against contemporary Christian music is that of association. The argument often goes, because the instruments and musical forms resemble, to a greater or lesser degree, those of secular music, they are thus inappropriate for use in worship. In the 1963 *Sacrosanctum Concilium* document, the Catholic church allows for use of native musical traditions, while noting that in the West, the pipe organ is such a traditional instrument, and thus may take pride of place in worship. The relevant passage is reminiscent of the *musica mundana* language we have encountered throughout the book: "[the pipe organ] . . . adds a wonderful splendor to the Church's ceremonies and powerfully lifts up man's mind to God and to higher things."[32] This language is important, as it connects the particular instrument and its sound—*musica instrumentalis*—to divine patterns and associations. Given that this description of the pipe organ is subject to the flexibility already expressed in the *Sacrosanctum Concilium*, where various instruments may be used where they are culturally appropriate, it stands to reason that other culturally relevant musical instruments may *also* share in the divine patterns of the *musica mundana*. However, in the context of the (generally) Protestant discomfort with instruments and secular association, even the pipe organ has had a problematic history, and was similarly resisted when introduced into worship in the medieval church.[33] Dan Lucarini makes the following point in the context of his opposition to the use of popular music styles:

> A clever Contemporary may remind you that the organ was considered an evil instrument of the devil when it was first introduced to the church. Apparently some Christians strongly objected to its use in worship. Contemporaries look upon those Christians in the same way they treat Traditionals today. But do not be so quick to judge! We have the unfair advantage of looking back on them from a time and culture where the organ is very acceptable in church. Any objections of the past are long forgotten.[34]

Lucarini accuses "Contemporaries" of using the historical example of the pipe organ to excuse their own adoption of modern instruments and rock-infused styles, forcing "Traditionals" to accept them against their will. He argues that the corrective of time renders any objection to the religious use of the pipe organ moot. However, Lucarini also makes the following statement that seems to contradict this principle:

> I argue that [rock style] is clearly and unequivocally associated with immorality, especially promiscuous and adulterous sex, glorification of drugs, and rebellion against authority [. . .]. Decades of rock music in our culture have permanently stamped that music style with the dimension of immorality. Changing the lyrics and substituting Christian musicians cannot remove that stigma.[35]

The key term that Lucarini uses in this passage is *permanent*—the rock genre is forever unrecoverable due to its current associations. This is rather a difficult position to maintain, unless he is arguing that the pipe organ's historical associations are less problematic than those of rock music, or that an *instrument* can lose its negative associations, while a *style* cannot. While this may be Lucarini's intention, he does not make the distinction. Other authors, however, do make such arguments regarding instruments associated with jazz and rock music, particularly drums. Karl Tsatalbasidis, a former jazz and rock drummer, asks the following rhetorical question: "Can acts and instruments associated with rebellion, sexual perversity, and the occult be considered Christian . . . by saying we're thinking of the Lord?"[36] He answers his question by affirming the drum set's unrecoverable status: "If rock and jazz are unsuitable forms of music for worship, then the trap set is automatically implicated because it was designed solely to be the fundamental driving force of that music!"[37] Finally, Tsatalbasidis argues that, "it's clear that rock music (and by implication the drum set) is designed to refute the biblical understanding of truth."[38] In short, the drums are an instrument that, due to the particular aspects of its history and construction, can have no connection with the divine pattern. Unfortunately, many arguments of this kind have their historical roots in some rather virulent racist discourse, which I will treat in its own section below.[39]

Here I will take a brief moment to reflect on the irrevocable and permanent "stamp of immorality" that Dan Lucarini ascribes to rock music, and that Karl Tsatalbasidis connects to certain musical instruments. These viewpoints are, in my opinion, opposed by the experience of the last few generations of children who have grown up around contemporary Christian music. I will use my own daughters as an example. Throughout their lives, they have seen drum sets and solid-body electric guitars in church.[40] Given that we do not generally frequent rock concerts or other venues where secular music is played,[41] my children are much more likely to identify such instruments as belonging in *church*, rather than places that promote "promiscuous and adulterous sex," "drugs," or "rebellion against authority," though I suppose that might depend on the church one attends.

Arguments over association are common in Western music history. One illustrative, and amusing, anecdote comes from an eighteenth-century Moravian church in Bethlehem, Pennsylvania. According to a popular account, a newly returned missionary thought it was inappropriate that some of the younger members of the congregation were playing their musical instruments in a secular venue. He asked them, "Do you mean to worship the Lord on Sunday with those same instruments?" The young people answered: "Yes, and will you use the same mouth for preaching with which you have just been eating sausages?"[42] The argument that music in Christian worship should be noticeably *different* than that used in secular settings, persists to the present. Paul S. Jones asserts this point of view:

> God's ways are timeless, unchanging, and true. We must meaningfully interact with people immersed in popular culture, yes; but we do not have to take on its character or speak with its trendy musical accents. So often when this is attempted (when we try to sound fashionable), the result is an inferior version at which the world scoffs. In fact, the more *different* worship music is from popular culture, the clearer the alternative it offers to those seeking depth, peace, truth, and hope in a dark, pagan, and pluralistic consumer age.[43]

Jones' argument about maintaining distinct differences between sacred and popular music is noteworthy, when examined in an historical context. Returning to the Protestant Reformation, questions regarding the sources of Luther's chorale melodies have frequently been topics of discussion and contention. Often, those supporting the use of modern or contemporary musical styles will point to the fact that Luther used all kinds of secular music, even "tavern melodies." A widely quoted statement attributed to Luther is, "Why should the devil have all the good tunes?," which inspired the title of a 1979 book on the subject by Paul Baker.[44] While Luther did not seem to have made this statement,[45] and only one tune used by him can be directly attributed to a secular source,[46] he did indeed imitate the melodic textual style of the secular narrative ballads popular during his time.[47] This ballad style would have been familiar to his listeners—much as the textual and rhythmic style of a limerick is obvious to English speakers today. Moreover, many of Luther's contemporaries widely adapted secular tunes and forms, even if he did not do so himself.[48] One such contemporary was the Nuremburg poet Hans Sachs, who wrote a number of *contrafacta*—parodies of secular songs, with newly written texts. The melodies of these *contrafacta* were fully intended to be associated with the secular songs they were parodying,[49] and they had titles such as "Das lied Rosina [. . .] Christlich verendert, von der erkenntnis Christi"

[The song *Rosina* . . . Christianly altered according to the understanding of Christ].[50] Another secular song parodied by Sachs is a dialogue between the narrator and the god Jupiter, subsequently Christianized to become a dialogue between the sinner and Christ.[51]

The use of *contrafacta* was not limited to the earliest generation of reformers. A favorite example of mine comes not from Luther or his immediate contemporaries, but from a composer active almost a century later.[52] Such later composers had the benefit of a hoard of sacred melodies composed over many decades, and so their use of secular tunes could not be attributed to a lack of available musical material. My example comes from a 1601 collection of secular songs, by the composer Hans Leo Hassler. Included in the collection is a love song entitled *Mein G'müt ist mir verwirret von einer Jungfrau zart*—loosely translated as "my heart is all confused by a tender maiden." Within the space of only ten years, the tune had already been wedded to a religious text, and by the early eighteenth century, it was most commonly used in text settings of the crucifixion. Today, the melody is best known through J. S. Bach's harmonization, and sung today under the title *O Sacred Head Now Wounded*. There is palpable irony that a song we now associate with the most somber and grave of subjects—the mortal sufferings of Christ—began as a sentimental love ballad.

Despite these historical examples, it is no surprise that the use of modern musical forms and styles in worship, has touched off firestorms of controversy and resistance within Protestant Christianity. Part of this is certainly generational, as folk and rock music was associated with countercultural and anti-establishment movements of the 1960s, which were themselves a threat to polite, religious Western society. There are also distinctly racial components threading their way through the debate, and these deserve a closer look, as they have significant nuances related to *musica humana* and *musica mundana*, strange though that may seem.

THE DARK SIDE OF THE WORSHIP WARS— *MUSICA HUMANA* AND THE "AFRICAN"

The Catholic church during and after Vatican II maintained quite an enlightened position regarding indigenous music traditions. While the Catholic hierarchy allows for "due importance to be attached to [indigenous] music," so it can "[adapt] worship to their native genius," many Protestant churches have remained highly suspicious and resistant to such "native" music. Much of this discomfort has roots in European colonialism, manifested in the massive British, French, Belgian, Dutch, German, and American expansionist colonial adventures of the nineteenth and early twentieth centuries.[53] Apart from a purely avaricious desire to extract resources, and compete with other Western powers for prestige on the world stage, these colonial projects gained *moral* cover for their actions through the work of early social scientists, such as the anthropologist Lewis H. Morgan, the anthropologist and sociologist Herbert Spencer, and the sociologist and eugenicist Francis Galton. Though these scholars worked in different fields, much of their output established models of human development and society, in which various "classes" were assigned to categories along a continuum, from "Savagery" through to "Civilization." Thus, diverse cultures around the world could be easily placed within this evolutionary model, based on metrics such as technological discoveries, familial structures, agricultural techniques, and systems of literacy.[54]

It is not surprising that European powers, with their large economies and militaries, were able to subjugate large portions of the rest of the world that did not enjoy such advantages. It is also not surprising that Europeans were eager to buy into the new sociological and anthropological models, which allowed them to recast their colonizing projects as "civilizing missions." In addition to providing moral justification to begin and maintain colonial adventures, it allowed them to advertise the positive effects of these civilizing projects back home. Among the most effective means for showcasing such projects were the large international World's Fairs, which served to highlight the home country's power, enlightenment, and benevolence, by exhibiting the range and diversity of their colonial possessions. Large collections of native peoples from the colonies were imported and displayed, often living in ersatz villages, producing native handicrafts, and engaging in religious and musical ceremonies. Such performances were influential on a number of Western composers, who took these "exotic" sounds as raw material for new compositions. For the paying public, however, the primary purpose of the international exhibition was the observation of the evolutionary continuum—of peoples from around the world fitting into various categories of civilization, as defined by the host country. This categorization was often accomplished through the physical layout of the fair itself. For instance, at the Chicago World's Fair in 1893, native villages "were arranged according to a Darwinian scheme that located the most primitive examples . . . farthest from the White City."[55] Such a schema allowed fairgoers to "look down a foreshortened evolutionary tunnel boring deep into the prehistoric past."[56] Even more importantly, it provided visitors—who were overwhelmingly comprised of members of the society materially benefiting from the displays—"a certain degree of reassurance about [their] place in the hierarchical structure of the universe."[57] It is clear that this "place" was one of distinct privilege in the overall hierarchy of the *musica humana*, with the added honor of being the means of properly "tuning" the lower grades of humanity, though the benefit of colonial tutelage.

While such exotic and fascinating peoples, and their cultural commodities, were perfectly "wholesome" for public viewing while enjoying a day out at the fair, they also presented potential dangers. During the Chicago Fair, the Japanese teahouse was one of the most popular attractions. Seemingly concerned over its popularity, commentators warned fairgoers against close contact with non-Western peoples and practices, cautioning them about what might happen, if the tea "goes to the head of the visitor . . . and finally his ideas get perverted, and everything seems perfectly natural and worthy of imitation."[58] Returning to the topic of worship music, similar warnings about the hazards of imitation are also present there, but largely in the context of the history of slavery in the United States, and America's simultaneous fascination with, and loathing of, African American culture.[59]

Many arguments against rock music in general, and the inclusion of rock or hybrid forms in Christian worship in particular, include warnings against "voodoo" rhythms, and their perceived spiritual characteristics—often categorized as "demonic" or "satanic." The rock music of the 1950s, and even the jazz styles of the first half of the century, were widely castigated by detractors as "jungle music." Wilberforce Whiteman, Sr., an American music educator, and father of noted jazz band leader Paul Whiteman, had this to say:

> They say swing started with the savages back in the wilds of darkest Africa. As far as I am concerned, they can have it right back. I am not a jungle chieftain, and I don't see why I should have to listen to jungle music any more than I have to eat jungle food.[60]

At the very least, we cannot accuse Whiteman of concealing his opinions about the perceived African roots of jazz.[61] Modern commentators on the rock era are similarly clear in their views. Blanchard and Lucarini include accounts of listeners being disturbed by African and Afro-Cuban rhythms,[62] and though they provide a nuanced history of the multiple music streams that came together to create rock music,[63] they nevertheless focus on voodoo as the driving spiritual force of rock, which makes it unacceptable for use in *any* context, not just in worship.[64] Tsatalbasidis notes that the basic unit of rock rhythm, the backbeat, "grew out of African rhythms and African sensibility."[65] In a passage that has not aged well since it was written in 1971, Bob Larson makes the following statement about changes in European dancing in the Americas:

> The innovations that were to come were derived from the Negro, who has had a greater creative inleuence [sic] on music and dancing than any other ethnic group. The origin of this Negro influence was, of course, Africa. These innovations were connected with heathen tribal and voodoo rites.[66]

Elsewhere, Larson notes that, "the stress rock places on the repetitious beat and syncopation undeniably labels it as African in origin."[67] He also asserts that "Negro music" is becoming "more African in its essentials."[68] It is clear that the reader is intended to read "African" as an entirely negative value, from a Western and Christian point of view. Continuing along the same lines, Kimberly Smith states that, "the African influence on music came out of a culture of pagan beliefs and practices."[69] She finds it ironic that Western culture subsequently adapted them:

> African-Americans, after conversion to Christianity, took their pagan musical heritage and turned it into beautiful and uplifting spirituals. Conversely, white men, whose musical foundations are "Christian," have rebelliously taken the pagan rhythms of the African culture and "married" them to Western civilization's music—forming "rock" music.[70]

There are many further examples of this sort of awkward generalization and problematic racial discourse. However, even authors who do not specifically attack the rhythmic aspects of rock music, continue to decry it as satanic in nature.[71] If we are to be completely honest, it is no stretch of logic to replace "satanic" with "black," and *vice versa*.

Ultimately, discomfort caused by "African" and African American music styles and forms, springs from a Christian cosmology that can have difficulty including non-white and non-European elements within its framework. If a *musica instrumentalis* is derived from racial or ethnic groups considered to have defective or under-evolved *musica humana*, it cannot therefore exist as an image or model of the *musica mundana*. While very few Christian denominations and communities would say such things openly, the sentiment is not always very deeply buried, as the above examples illustrate.[72] Because the Bible has little to say about music—other than specific descriptions of its use in ancient liturgical settings—Christian anti-rock literature seeks to define a set of general biblical *principles* to guide one's choice and selection of music styles. These principles are generally broad and vague, allowing an author to easily build an argument to suit themselves. Essentially, each commentator has the flexibility to create their own cosmological model—their own system of *musica mundana*, *musica humana*, and *musica instrumentalis*. While the lengths to which some will go to carve out a set of standards strains all credulity, I can understand the satisfaction of having one's own musical preferences confirmed by divine approbation. It does, however, illustrate the most pertinent issue raised in this book. Since ancient times, commentators and theorists have sought to define a universal, celestial musical system, built upon what was most respected and valued in their society. Modern Western Christianity is simply among the latest to make the attempt.

Chapter 7

NOTES

1. By "modern," I am referring to the years after the Protestant Reformation of the early sixteenth century. In this chapter we will examine a number of examples, most of them topics current in the twentieth and twenty-first centuries. A decently full treatment of worship debates, even if limited to the second half of the twentieth century, would occupy a rather large book of its own.

2. John Edwin Sandys, *The Bacchae of Euripides* (Cambridge: Cambridge University Press, 1880), 128.

3. A proper treatment of the last hundred years will take some extensive setting up, so I will spend a portion of the chapter examining the foundations laid between the sixteenth and twentieth centuries.

4. It would be difficult to find a Lutheran who grew up in the first half of the twentieth century describing the chorale settings of Johann Crüger, Melchior Vulpius, or Johann Sebastian Bach as anything but "good."

5. Douglas Adams, *The Salmon of Doubt* (New York: Harmony Books, 2002), 95. I have eagerly awaited an appropriate opportunity to quote Douglas Adams my entire academic career. I made a few largely unconscious attempts at writing in his style during college and graduate school, which usually resulted in professors asking why I was being so sarcastic and edgy (I never said the attempts were *successful*). Adams was the first author I had ever read, beginning in middle school, that showed me that one could write extremely well with humor. His work eventually directed me toward such masters of the form as P. G. Wodehouse and Dorothy Sayers, to say nothing of Charles Dickens and his generation. If it were up to me—and it isn't—academic writing would be just as enjoyable to read.

6. Weiss and Taruskin, *Music in the Western World*, 100–1.

7. Ibid., 101.

8. Treitler, *Source Readings in Music History – Vol. 3: The Renaissance*, 83.

9. Weiss and Taruskin, *Music in the Western World*, 105. In the early years, the Reformers did not have many good tunes and texts (Luther called upon German poets and composers to provide them), and so they were obliged—in a way—to use popular tunes. Luther felt their use was positive, as it made church more attractive to the population, while detractors felt that they demeaned the sacred services. This will not be the last time we hear that complaint!

10. Treitler, *Source Readings in Music History – Vol. 3: The Renaissance*, 84. Luther felt that great use could be made of music in the teaching of youth which, in his opinion, had been generally neglected.

11. Weiss and Taruskin, *Music in the Western World*, 104.

12. Ibid., 107–8.

13. This restriction was specifically for corporate worship. Simple multi-part polyphonic songs were permitted for home devotional use.

14. Treitler, *Source Readings in Music History – Vol. 3: The Renaissance*, 88. Luther was well aware of these restrictions on music in worship, and he is likely talking about Calvin, Zwingli, and other Reformers with similar views when he says there are some who feel that all the arts should be "crushed to the earth and perish." Ibid., 84.

15. Weiss and Taruskin, *Music in the Western World*, 136.

16. Treitler, *Source Readings in Music History – Vol. 3: The Renaissance*. Introductions and dedications in sets of composed masses by Catholic composers show the influence of the Council of Trent. After the close of the council in 1563, these dedications generally include statements by the composer to the effect that they are doing their best to make the texts clearly understandable. Weiss and Taruskin, *Music in the Western World*, 138.

17. Ibid., 137.

18. As discussed in chapter 4, this is music that followed "the rules," valued the intelligibility of the liturgical texts, and frowned upon unneeded dissonances—music that would be approved of by Giovanni Maria Artusi.

19. Siegfried Gmeinwieser, "Cecilian movement," *Grove Music Online*, 2001. https://www.oxfordmusiconline.com/grovemusic/view/10.1093/gmo/9781561592630.001.0001/omo-9781561592630-e-0000005245. Accessed August 19, 2021.

20. Pius X, *Tra le sollecitudini*, https://adoremus.org/1903/11/tra-le-sollecitudini/. Accessed on August 19, 2021.

21. Ibid.

22. Ibid.

23. Ibid.

24. Ibid.

25. This was not a unique attitude in general, even at the dawn of the twentieth century. There is a long history of exclusion of women from participation and leadership in sacred ritual. Many of the reasons come from certain interpretations of *musica humana*, as they relate to the *musica mundana*—women are created lower in the earthly hierarchy than men, and so cannot access the divine, except through male agency.

26. https://www.vatican.va/archive/hist_councils/ii_vatican_council/documents/vat-ii_const_19631204_sacrosanctum-concilium_en.html. Accessed on August 19, 2021.

27. Ibid.

28. Ibid.

29. The *Sacrosanctum Concilium* allowed for almost any instrument to be used, so long as it was appropriate for sacred use, or could be adapted to be appropriate.

30. I only recently came to realize that many of the worship songs sung in my Seventh-day Adventist parochial school in the 1980s were taken from Catholic folk masses of the late 1960s and early 1970s. This knowledge would likely have terrified many members of my religious community, given the traditionally antagonistic position the denomination has taken toward Catholicism.

31. This is, of course, coming from the perspective of a child growing up in the 1980s and 1990s, for whom the sight of an acoustic guitar, or the sound of folk-inspired contemporary music, did not inspire any particular discomfort.

32. https://www.vatican.va/archive/hist_councils/ii_vatican_council/documents/vat-ii_const_19631204_sacrosanctum-concilium_en.html.

33. There is a long history of banning *all* musical instruments in worship, from the earliest centuries of the Christian church. Many of the Church Fathers spoke against instruments in general, because of their association with pagan rituals in the Mediterranean world. Unable to deny the many biblical references to musical instruments, commentators spiritualized them, so that mentions of actual instruments were transformed into metaphors for spiritual concepts.

34. Dan Lucarini, *Why I Left the Contemporary Christian Movement* (Webster, NY: Evangelical Press, 2002), 109–10.

35. Ibid., 90–1.

36. Karl Tsatalbasidis, *Drums, Rock, and Worship: Modern Music in Today's Church* (Roseville, CA: Amazing Facts, Inc., 2003), 24.

37. Ibid.

38. Ibid., 41.

39. I want to be clear that I am not accusing any of these commentators of knowingly harboring racist sentiments. There are countless aspects of Western culture that depend on racist, sexist, colonialist, and other tropes. Very many of us have unknowingly adopted such problematic ways of seeing the world.

40. They see pipe organs and other "traditional" instruments there as well.

41. I do, however, occasionally appear in such venues as a performer.

42. M. A. DeWolfe Howe, "'Venite in Bethlehem'—The Major Chord," *The Musical Journal* 28, no. 2 (April 1942): 179.

43. Paul S. Jones, *What is Worship Music?* (Phillipsburg, NJ: P&R Publishing Co., 2010), 25–6. Jones' point on the *quality* of worship music is well-taken. However, I am willing to give church musicians the benefit of the doubt that they are performing to the best of their ability, and not merely posturing in order to appear "trendy" and "fashionable." Not every church, whether traditional or contemporary, has the resources to provide professional-quality music.

44. Paul Baker, *Why Should the Devil Have All the Good Music?* (Waco, TX: Word Books, 1979)

45. According to Joseph Herl (*Worship Wars in Early Lutheranism*, 21 and ff. 61 and 62), the wording of this statement is attributable to the English preacher Rowland Hill, who was active in the later eighteenth and early nineteenth centuries. Hill seemed to have approved of the use of secular tunes, such as *Hail, Britannia*, in services at his church. By 1931, Friedrich Blume attributed a similarly worded quote to Luther, but without citation. Given that there is now a searchable database of all of Luther's published works, and scholars have long searched in vain for this quotation, it is likely that it does not exist in his writings. This does not mean that he never uttered the words—we just do not have any evidence that he did.

46. Ibid., 21. Luther used the popular tune *Ich komm auf fremden landen her* for the hymn *Vom Himmel hoch, da komm ich her*. He later wrote a new melody for the hymn, which is still in use today.

47. Ibid., 13.

48. Robin Leaver, *Luther's Liturgical Music: Principles and Implications* (Grand Rapids, MI: William B. Eerdmans Publishing Co., 2007), 17–18.

49. The main purpose of a parody is that the melody *be* recognizable, making the message of the modified text more powerful through its placement in a familiar setting.

50. Leaver, *Luther's Liturgical Music*, 15.

51. Ibid., 17.

52. This section is inspired by a conversation I had some years ago with Dr. Warren Trenchard, a colleague at La Sierra University. This was his favorite example of a *contrafactum*, and has become mine as well.

53. There were other European powers involved in such colonial projects, particularly Spain and Portugal. However, their colonial empires had undergone significant contraction and decline by the nineteenth century.

54. Lewis H. Morgan, *Ancient Society: or Researches in the Lines of Human Progress from Savagery through Barbarism to Civilization* (Chicago: Charles H. Kerr & Company, 1877), 9–29. It goes without saying that each Western colonial power placed *itself* at the top of the continuum.

55. Charles Kennedy, "When Cairo met Main Street: Little Egypt, Salome Dancers, and the World's Fairs of 1893 and 1904," in Michael Saffle, ed., *Music and Culture in America, 1861–1918* (New York and London: Garland Publishing, Inc., 1998), 272. The "White City" was the central area of the fair and displayed the achievements of the United States. The identification of the city as "White" is both coincidental *and* singularly appropriate, given the ultimate purpose of the fair.

56. Paul Kramer, "Making concessions: Race and empire revisited at the Philippine exposition. St. Louis, 1901–1905," *Radical History Review* 73 (New York: MARHO, 1999): 99.

57. Eric Breitbart, *A World on Display: Photographs from the St. Louis World's Fair 1904* (Albuquerque: University of New Mexico Press, 1997), 13.

58. Benjamin Truman, *History of the World's Fair* (New York: Arno Press, 1976), 435–6.

59. World's Fairs in the United States sometimes featured African American themes in exhibits from the southern states. These were often presented in a bucolic manner, as part of the nostalgic legend of the antebellum south.

60. Quoted in Eddy Determeyer, *Rhythm is Our Business: Jimmie Lunceford and the Harlem Express* (Ann Arbor: University of Michigan Press, 2010), 8.

61. It is standard practice for commentators of this sort to use Africa as a general catch-all term—a kind of monolithic indicator of a "certain" kind of culture and people. It is nearly always used to indicate something foreign, highly sexualized, and "black." The lack of even the most elementary nuance is, sadly, revealing.

62. John Blanchard and Dan Lucarini, *Can We Rock the Gospel?* (Webster, NY: Evangelical Press, 2006), 22.

63. Ibid., 40–2.

64. Ibid., 89–90. Voodoo was not the only non-Western practice or tradition that caused discomfort among rock critics. Fear of "eastern" and "oriental" philosophies and religions likewise created a high level of concern, particularly after the late 1960s. Bob Larson, *Rock: Practical Help for Those Who Listen to the Words and Don't Like What They Hear* (Wheaton, IL: Tyndale House Publishers, Inc., 1980), 33–38.

65. Tsatalbasidis, *Drums, Rock, and Worship*, 31. Just what such a sensibility entails is not clear, but it seems intended to sound scary.

66. Bob Larson, *Rock and The Church* (Carol Stream, IL: Creation House, Inc. 1971), 63.

67. Bob Larson, *The Day Music Died* (Carol Stream, IL: Creation House, Inc., 1972), 87. Larson also claims that "musicologists have found evidences of rock melodic and rhythmic styles in Africa centuries before classical music appeared in Europe." Ibid. This statement is absurd.

68. Ibid., 88.

69. Kimberly Smith with Lee Smith, *Oh Be Careful Little Ears* (Enumclaw, WA: Winepress Publishing, 1997), 22.

70. Ibid.

71. Jimmy Swaggart and Robert Paul Lamb, *Religious Rock 'n' Roll: A Wolf in Sheep's Clothing* (Baton Rouge, LA: Jimmy Swaggart Ministries, 1987), vi. Swaggart's book includes a few truly bizarre passages, such as a claim that the Psalms chanted in ancient Israel were in the minor mode, and after Jesus' resurrection they gradually shifted into the major mode, and thus "was [their] full potential realized." He also asserts that the music of the ancient world, in addition to being "demonic in origin," also had "little or no melodic flow." Ibid., 24. We know little about the melodic contour of the music of antiquity, and absolutely nothing about the modes used by worshippers in ancient Israel.

72. There are many, many more such examples found in Christian literature, some more blatant and some less.

Conclusion
Da Capo

> Music is the language of the soul's deepest emotions, and,
> in our objective word-language, is indescribable.[1]

Music's ability to speak to its listeners, influencing their emotions and actions, is a concept with a very long history. These perceived influences were so important that prominent philosophers suggested various methods to control and regulate the use of music in society. In the Greek world, it was strongly recommended that aristocratic young men be properly educated in the art of music, as part of their preparation for taking leading roles in society. Plato argued, "education in music is most sovereign, because more than anything else rhythm and harmonia find their way to the inmost soul and take strongest hold upon it."[2] This was not to say that future leaders should be trained as *professional* musicians, as Aristotle notes: "Professional musicians we speak of as vulgar people, and indeed we think it not manly to perform music, except when drunk or for fun."[3] As noted earlier in the book, the youth should be trained in music at a sufficient level to judge its quality and, as future political leaders, to properly regulate its use. All this education, judgment, and regulation is concerned with practical, performed music—*musica instrumentalis*.

It was also held that music had the ability to influence the minds, morals, and souls of the listeners. This was not only true of the educated upper classes, but of all humanity, as Aristotle again tells us:

> It is proper [. . .] to participate in the common pleasure that springs from it, which is perceptible to everybody (for the pleasure contained in music is of a natural kind, owing to which the use of it is dear to those of all ages and ethoses), [and] to see if its influence reaches also in a manner to the ethos and to the soul.[4]

This universality of music and its influence is another reason for its strict control, and Plato suggests that societies "employ that simple music which [. . .] [engenders] sobriety." This would then help the youth "guard themselves against falling into the need of the justice of the courtroom."[5] Such concern for music and its role in the growth of the individual and of society is the province of *musica humana*.

The strength of practical, performed music to positively affect the human psyche, is built upon the resemblance of music to divine patterns and models. The rational human soul is prepared to receive and recognize this likeness through the process of "divine suffusion," as Aristotle says many times in his *Politics*.[6] Likewise, in the *Timaeus*, Plato notes that the pattern of the universe is imprinted on the very construction of mankind.[7] In chapter 1, we saw that Plato "paired" the sciences of astronomy and music, one allowing humanity to perceive the nature of the universe through its eyes, and the other through its ears. This concern with the revealed secrets of the created world—the divine models of musical harmony—is *musica mundana*.

That these three kinds of *musica* are closely related, is confirmed in another passage from Plato, where he touches on each of them in the context of a good education in music:

> Omissions and the failure of beauty in things badly made or grown would be most quickly perceived by one who was properly educated in music, and so, feeling distaste rightly, he would praise beautiful things and take delight in them and receive them into his soul to foster its growth and become himself beautiful and good.[8]

Plato argues what many ancient music theorists, and many more theorists of the Christian era, would also argue about music. These arguments can be summarized in the following way:

- Proper education in *musica instrumentalis* allows the observer to detect what is good or bad in the physical universe—the *musica mundana*;
- This perception, evidenced by praising the beautiful, and "feeling distaste" for the "badly made," occurs within the observer's *musica humana*;
- The *musica humana* receives these "beautiful things" into its soul, in order to be further "tuned";
- This well-tuned *musica humana*—strengthened by communion with the patterns revealed in the *musica mundana*—allows an observer to detect and judge proper patterns in *musica instrumentalis*.

This training in, and tuning of, different kinds of *musica* is a continuous and mutually supporting process. The more one is educated in music, the more one's mind and soul is attuned to the divine patterns that exist in the cosmos. This awareness of cosmic attunement reinforces the proper balance of internal and societal human systems, which in turn improves the performance of practical, audible music—and the process repeats.

Whether we are looking at the societal realities of Plato and Aristotle's time, the perspectives of Boethius and his followers, the musical practices of the sixteenth-century reformers, the reevaluation of dissonance by the Second Viennese School, or the debates of the modern worship wars, we have always been talking about *musica*, and in the same ways. The questions we ask about music point to the same concerns. What are the divine patterns? How can our music conform to these patterns? What are the effects of music on the mind, body, and soul? How can our music serve to improve humans and their societies? These questions, which we have addressed throughout the book, are universal ones, touching every aspect of spirituality, religion, culture, health, education, and artistic expression. These questions have also spurred authors across centuries to consider and explore these implications in works of fiction, including the creation of entire universes based on musical principles. This makes the first passage of this book especially relevant: "all nature sings, and around me"—and within me, and through me—"rings the music of the spheres."

NOTES

1. Chas Purdy, "Soul Music," *The Esoteric: A Magazine of Practical Esoteric Thought* 9 (July 1895–June 1896): 307.
2. Leo Treitler, gen. ed., *Source Readings in Music History – Volume 1: Greek Views of Music* (New York and London: W.W. Norton & Co., 1998), 14.
3. Ibid., 27.
4. Ibid., 28.
5. Ibid., 17.
6. Ibid., 24–34.
7. Ibid., 19–23.
8. Ibid., 14.

Bibliography

Adams, Douglas. *The Salmon of Doubt*. New York: Harmony Books, 2002.
Alexander, Cecil Frances. *Hymns for Little Children*. London: Joseph Masters, 1852.
Alighieri, Dante. *The Divine Comedy*. Translated by Allen Mandelbaum. New York and London: Everyman's Library, 1995.
Alighieri, Dante. *The Divine Comedy of Dante Alighieri: I Inferno*. Translated by John D. Sinclair. New York and Oxford: Oxford University Press, 1961.
Alighieri, Dante. *The Divine Comedy of Dante Alighieri: II Purgatorio*. Translated by John D. Sinclair. New York and Oxford: Oxford University Press, 1961.
Alighieri, Dante. *The Divine Comedy of Dante Alighieri: III Paradiso*. Translated by John D. Sinclair. New York and Oxford: Oxford University Press, 1961.
Alighieri, Dante. *The Paradiso*. Translated by John Ciardi. New York: Signet Classics, 2009.
Alford, Henry. *The Poetical Works of Henry Alford*. Vol. 2. London: Francis & John Rivington, 1845.
Allanbrook, Wye Jamison. *Source Readings in Music History Volume 5: The Late Eighteenth Century*. Rev. ed. New York and London: W.W. Norton & Company, 1998.
Allen, Sydney. *The Electric Grass Company*. Nashville, TN: Southern Publishing Association, 1974.
American Student Hymnal. New York: Fleming H. Revell Co., 1928.
Anderson, Arvid C. *Masters of Music*. Washington, DC: Review and Herald, 1948.
Aniol, Scott. *Worship In Song: A Biblical Approach to Music and Worship*. Winona Lake, IN: BMH Books, 2009.
Aquinas, Thomas. *Selected Philosophical Writings*. Translated by Timothy McDermott. Oxford and New York: Oxford University Press, 1993.
Ars Cantus Mensurabilis Mensurata per Modos Iuris. Translated by C. Matthew Balensuela. Lincoln and London: University of Nebraska Press, 1994.
Aurelian of Réôme. *Musica Disciplina (The Discipline of Music)*. Translated by Joseph Ponte. Colorado Springs, CO: Colorado College Music Press, 1968.

Austen, Jane. *Persuasion.* 2nd ed. Edited by Patricia Meyer Spacks. New York and London: W.W. Norton & Company, 2013.
Bacchiocchi, Samuele, ed. *The Christian & Rock Music: A Study on Biblical Principles of Music.* Berrien Springs, MI: Biblical Perspectives, 2000.
Baker, Paul. *Why Should The Devil Have All The Good Music?* Waco, TX: Word Books, 1979.
Banchieri, Adriano. *Conclusions for Playing the Organ (1609).* Translated by Lee R. Garrett. Colorado Springs, CO: Colorado College Music Press, 1982.
Beldon, F. E., Compiler. *Christ In Song.* Revised and Enlarged. Washington, DC: Review and Herald Publishing Assn., 1908.
Beltz, Oliver S. *Te Decet Laus: To Thee Belongeth Praise.* Berrien Springs, MI: Andrews University Press, 1982.
Benson, Louis F. *The English Hymn: Its Development and Use In Worship.* Richmond, VA: John Knox Press, 1962.
Bertoglio, Chiara. "Polyphony, Collective Improvisation, and the Gift of Creation." In *Music in Tolkien's Work and Beyond.* Edited by Julian Eilmann and Friedhelm Schneidewind, 3–28. Zurich and Jena: Walking Tree Publishers, 2019.
Billings, William. *The Continental Harmony.* Edited by Hans Nathan. Cambridge, MA: The Belknap Press of Harvard University Press, 1961.
Blanchard, John and Dan Lucarini. *Can We Rock the Gospel?: Rock Music's Impact on Worship and Evangelism.* Webster, NY: Evangelical Press, 2006.
Boccaccio, Giovanni. *The Decameron.* Translated by G. H. McWilliam. 2nd ed. London: Penguin Books, 1995.
Bockmann, Melanie Scherencel. *UnRapped.* Hagerstown, MD: Review and Herald Publishing Association, 2007.
Boff, Leonardo. *Ecology and Liberation: A New Paradigm.* Translated by John Cumming. Maryknoll, NY: Orbis Books, 1995.
Boff, Leonardo. *Toward an Eco-Spirituality.* Translated by Robert H. Hopke. Pearl River, NY: The Crossroad Publishing Company, 2015.
Brehaut, Ernest. *An Encyclopedist of the Dark Ages: Isidore of Seville.* New York: Longmans, Green & Co., 1912.
Breitbart, Eric. *A World on Display: Photographs from the St. Louis World's Fair 1904.* Albuquerque: University of New Mexico Press, 1997.
Bridges, Robert S. and H. Ellis Woolridge, eds. *The Yattendon Hymnal.* Oxford: B. H. Blackwell, 1905.
Brontë, Charlotte. *Jane Eyre.* New York: Barnes & Noble Classics, 2003.
Brontë, Emily. *Wuthering Heights.* 4th ed. Edited by Richard J. Dunn. New York and London: W.W. Norton & Company, 2003.
Brown-Borthwick, Robert, ed. *Select Hymns for Church and Home.* Edinburgh: Edmonston and Douglas, 1871.
Catholic Hymns. London: Burns and Lambert, 1853.
Charles Kingsley: His Letters and Memories of His Life. Vol. 2. 11th ed. London: C. Kegan Paul & Co., 1878.
Chism, Christine. "Middle-earth, the Middle Ages, and the Aryan nation: Myth and history in World War II." In *Tolkien the Medievalist.* Edited by Jane Chance, 63–92. New York: Routledge, 2003.

Christian Science Hymnal. Revised and Enlarged. Boston, MA: The Christian Science Publishing Society, 1932.

Church and Sunday School Hymnal. Scottdale and Penna: Mennonite Publishing House, 1902.

Church Hymnal. Cleveland, TN: Tennessee Music and Printing Company, 1951.

Clark, Linda J. *Music in Churches: Nourishing Your Congregation's Musical Life*. New York: The Alban Institute, 1994.

Cohen, David E. "Metaphysics, Ideology, Discipline: Consonance, Dissonance, and the Foundations of Western Polyphony." *Theoria: Historical Aspects of Music Theory* 7 (1993): 1–85.

Conrad, Joseph. *Heart of Darkness and Selected Short Fiction*. New York: Barnes & Noble Classics, 2003.

Crocker, Richard L. *Studies in Medieval Music Theory and the Early Sequence*. Aldershot, Hampshire: Variorum, 1997.

Cunningham, Michael. "An Impenetrable Darkness: An Examination of the Influence of J. R. R. Tolkien on Black Metal Music." In *Music in Middle-earth*. Edited by Heidi Steimel and Friedhelm Schneidewind, 215–40. Zurich and Jena: Walking Tree Publishers, 2010.

Day, David. *Guide to Tolkien's World: A Bestiary*. New York: Metro Books, 1979.

da Brescia, Bonaventura. *Breviloquium Musicale (Rules of Plain Music)*. Translated by Albert Seay. Colorado Springs, CO: Colorado College Music Press, 1979.

de Garlandia, Johannes. *De Mensurabili Musica (Concerning Measured Music)*. Translated by Stanley H. Birnbaum. Colorado Springs, CO: Colorado College Music Press, 1978.

de Grocheo, Johannes. *De Musica (Concerning Music)*. Translated by Albert Seay. Colorado Springs, CO: Colorado College Music Press, 1973.

de Handlo, Robertus and Johannes Hanboys. *Regule (The Rules)* and *Summa (The Summa)*. Translated and Edited by Peter M. Lefferts. Lincoln: University of Nebraska Press, 1991.

Determeyer, Eddy. *Rhythm is Our Business: Jimmie Lunceford and the Harlem Express*. Ann Arbor: University of Michigan Press, 2010.

Dickinson, Clarence, ed. *The Hymnal*. Philadelphia: Presbyterian Board of Christian Education, 1933.

Eliade, Mircea. *The Sacred and the Profane: the Nature of Religion*. Translated by Willard R. Trask. New York and Evanston: Harper & Row, 1961.

Ellsworth, Oliver B., trans. and ed. *The Berkeley Manuscript*. Lincoln: University of Nebraska Press, 1984.

Euripides. *The Bacchae and Other Plays*. Translated by Philip Vellacott. London: Penguin Classics, 1986.

Field, David. *Free to Do Right*. Downers Grove, IL: InterVarsity Press, 1973.

Fisher, Tim. *The Battle For Christian Music*. Greenville, SC: Sacred Music Services, 1992.

Flieger, Verlyn. *Interrupted Music: The Making of Tolkien's Mythology*. Kent and London: The Kent State University Press, 2005.

Flieger, Verlyn. *Splintered Light: Logos and Language in Tolkien's World*. Rev. ed. Kent and London: The Kent State University Press, 2002.

Frame, John M. *Contemporary Worship Music: a Biblical Defense*. Phillipsburg, NJ: P&R Publishing, 1997.

Fuller, Sarah. "Theoretical Foundations of Early Organum Theory." *Acta Musicologica* 53 (1981): 52–84.

Fuller, Sarah. "Tendencies and Resolutions: The Directed Progression in *Ars Nova* Music." *Journal of Music Theory* 36 (Fall 1992): 229–57.

Fündling, Jörg. "An Imperialist Battle Cry behind the Lament for Boromir." In *Music in Tolkien's Work and Beyond*. Edited by Julian Eilmann and Friedhelm Schneidewind, 111–31. Zurich and Jena: Walking Tree Publishers, 2019.

Garlock, Frank and Kurt Woetzel. *Music in the Balance*. Greenville, SC: Majesty Music, Inc., 1992.

Geer, E. Harold, ed. *Hymnal for Colleges and Schools*. New Haven: Yale University Press, 1956.

Gills, James P. *The Dynamics of Worship*. Rev. ed. Tarpon Springs, FL: Love Press, 1992.

Goode, Helen Dill and Gertrude C. Drake, trs. *Cassiodorus - Institutiones*: Book II, Ch. V; *Isidore of Seville - Etymologies*: Book III, Ch. 15 - 23. Colorado Springs: Colorado College Music Press, 1980.

Griffith, Mark and Glenn W. Most. *Aeschylus II*. 3rd ed. Translated by Richard Lattimore and Mark Griffith. Chicago and London: University of Chicago Press, 2013.

Halter, Carl. *The Practice of Sacred Music*. St. Louis, MO: Concordia Publishing House, 1955.

Hamel, Paul. *The Christian and his Music*. Washington, DC: Review and Herald Publishing Association, 1973.

Hanegraaff, Hank. *Counterfeit Revival*. Rev. ed. Nashville, TN: W Publishing Group, 2001.

Hanslick, Eduard. *The Beautiful in Music*. 7th ed. Rev. Translated by Gustav Cohen. London: Novello and Company, 1891.

Hardy, Thomas. *Tess of the d'Urbervilles*. New York: Barnes & Noble Classics, 2005.

Hayden, Keavin. *Lifestyles of the Remnant*. Hagerstown, MD: Review and Herald Publishing Association, 2001.

Herl, Joseph. *Worship Wars in Early Lutheranism*. Oxford: Oxford University Press, 2004.

Herzel, Catherine. *Christians at Worship*. Philadelphia: Lutheran Church Press, 1964.

Holbrook, David and Elizabeth Poston, eds. *The Cambridge Hymnal*. Cambridge: Cambridge University Press, 1967.

Holmes, John R. "'Inside a Song': Tolkien's Phonaesthetics." In *Middle-earth Minstrel: Essays on Music in Tolkien*. Edited by Bradford Lee Eden, 26–46. Jefferson, NC and London: McFarland & Company, Inc., Publishers, 2010.

Howard, Jay R. and John M. Streck. *Apostles of Rock: The Splintered World of Contemporary Christian Music*. Lexington: The University Press of Kentucky, 1999.

Howe, M. A. DeWolfe. "'Venit in Bethlehem'—The Major Chord." *The Musical Journal* 28/2 (April, 1942).
Hustad, Donald P. *True Worship: Reclaiming the Wonder & Majesty*. Colorado Springs, CO: WaterBrook Press, 1998.
Hutchins, Charles L., ed. *The Church Hymnal*. Edition B, Rev. and Enlarged. Boston, MA: The Parish Choir, 1899.
Hymns Ancient and Modern. London: William Clowes and Sons, Ltd., 1904.
Hymns for the Family of God. Nashville, TN: Paragon Associates, Inc., 1976.
Hymns of the Church of Jesus Christ of Latter-Day Saints. 2nd ed. Rev. Salt Lake City, UT: The Church of Jesus Christ of Latter-Day Saints, 2002.
Innes, Mary M. *The Metamorphoses of Ovid*. New York: Viking Penguin, 1955.
Jensen, Keith W. "Dissonance in the Divine Theme: The Issue of Free Will in Tolkien's *Silmarillion*." In *Middle-earth Minstrel: Essays on Music in Tolkien*. Edited by Bradford Lee Eden, 102–13. Jefferson, NC and London: McFarland & Company, Inc., Publishers, 2010.
Jonas, Hans. *The Gnostic Religion: The Message of the Alien God and the Beginnings of Christianity*. 2nd rev ed. Boston: Beacon Press, 1963.
Jones, Paul S. *What is Worship Music?* Phillipsburg, NJ: P&R Publishing Company, 2010.
Joyful Meeting in Glory Song Book No. 1. Columbus, OH: [n.p.], 1919.
Julian, John. *A Dictionary of Hymnology*. New York: Charles Scribner's Sons, 1892.
Kennedy, Charles. "When Cairo met Main Street: Little Egypt, Salome Dances, and the World's Fairs of 1893 and 1904." In *Music and Culture in America, 1861–1918*. Edited by Michael Saffle. New York and London: Garland Publishing, Inc., 1998.
Kimball, Dan. *The Emerging Church: Vintage Christianity for New Generations*. Grand Rapids, MI: Zondervan, 2003.
Kramer, Paul. "Making concessions: Race and empire revisited at the Philippine exposition. St. Louis, 1901–1905." *Radical History Review* 73 (1999).
Kraut, Richard, ed. *The Cambridge Companion to Plato*. Cambridge and New York: Cambridge University Press, 1992.
Kromer, Marcin. *De Musica Figurata*. Edited and Translated by Albert Seay. Colorado Springs, CO: Colorado College Music Press 1980.
Larson, Bob. *The Day Music Died*. Carol Stream, IL: Creation House, Inc., 1972.
Larson, Bob. *Rock & The Church*. Carol Stream, IL: Creation House, 1971.
Larson, Bob. *Rock: Practical Help for Those Who Listen to the Words and Don't Like What They Hear*. Wheaton, IL: Tyndale House Publishers, Inc., 1980.
Leaver, Robin. *Luther's Liturgical Music: Principles and Implications*. Grand Rapids: MI: William B. Eerdmans Publishing Co., 2007.
Lewis, C. S. *The Great Divorce: a Dream*. New York: HarperOne, 2001.
Lewis, C. S. *The Last Battle*. New York: HarperCollins Publishers, 1994.
Lewis, C. S. *The Lion, the Witch and the Wardrobe*. New York: HarperCollins Publishers, 1994.
Lewis, C. S. *The Magician's Nephew*. New York: HarperCollins Publishers, 1994.
Lewis, C. S. *The Silver Chair*. New York: HarperCollins Publishers, 1994.

Lewis, C. S. *The Space Trilogy*. New York and London: Scribner, 2011.
Lindsay, Hal and C. C. Carlson. *Satan is Alive and Well on Planet Earth*. Grand Rapids, MI: Zondervan Publishing House, 1972.
Lippius, Johannes. *Synopsis Musicae Novae (Synopsis of New Music)*. Translated by Benito V. Rivera. Colorado Springs, CO: Colorado College Music Press, 1977.
Longfellow, Samuel and S. Johnson, eds. *Hymns of the Spirit*. Boston: Ticknor and Fields, 1864.
Lovelace, Austin C. and William C. Rice. *Music and Worship in the Church*. New York and Nashville: Abingdon Press, 1960.
Lucarini, Dan. *Why I Left the Contemporary Christian Movement*. Webster, NY: Evangelical Press, 2002.
Luhn, Alec. "Tchaikovsky's Sexuality 'Downplayed' in Biopic under Russia's Anti-Gay Law." *The Guardian*, August 25, 2013, online edition. Accessed July 11, 2021.
Lutheran Service Book. St. Louis, MO: Concordia Publishing House, 2006.
Martin, George C., ed. *The Book of Common Praise being The Hymn Book of The Church of England in Canada*. Toronto: Oxford University Press, 1910.
Mathiesen, Thomas J., ed. *Source Readings in Music History Volume 1: Greek Views of Music*. Rev. ed. New York and London: W.W. Norton & Company, 1998.
Matthews, W. S. *Memoirs and Select Remains of the Rev. Thomas Rawson Taylor*. London: Westley and Davis, 1836.
Maxwell, Lawrence. *What Stopped the Music and Other Stories*. Mountain View, CA: Pacific Press Publishing Association, 1966.
McBride, Sam. *Tolkien's Cosmology: Divine Beings and Middle-earth*. Kent, OH: The Kent State University Press, 2020. New York and London: W.W. Norton & Company, 1998.
McCutchan, Robert Guy. *Our Hymnody: a Manual of The Methodist Hymnal*. 2nd ed. New York and Nashville: Abingdon-Cokesbury Press, 1937.
McKinnon, James, ed. *Source Readings in Music History Volume 2: The Early Christian Period and the Latin Middle Ages*. Rev. ed.
Melville, Herman. *Billy Budd*. New York: Washington Square Press, Inc., 1962.
Menconi, Al and Dave Hart, *Today's Music: A Window to Your Child's Soul*. Elgin, IL and Weston, ONT: LifeJourney Books, 1990.
Mitchell, Robert H. *Ministry and Music*. Philadelphia: The Westminster Press, 1978.
More, Thomas. *Utopia*. Translated by Paul Turner. London: Penguin Books, 1965.
Morgan, Lewis H. *Ancient Society: or Researches in the Lines of Human Progress from Savagery through Barbarism to Civilization*. Chicago: Charles H. Kerr & Company, 1877.
Morgan, Robert P., ed. *Source Readings in Music History Volume 7: The Twentieth Century*. Rev. ed. New York and London: W.W. Norton & Company, 1998.
Milton, John. *Paradise Lost & Paradise Regained*. New York: Signet Classics, 2010.
Murata, Margaret, ed. *Source Readings in Music History Volume 4: The Baroque Era*. Rev ed. New York and London: W.W. Norton & Company, 1998.
Musica Enchiriadis (Music Handbook). Translated by Léonie Rosenstiel. Colorado Springs, CO: Colorado College Music Press, 1976.

Nash, Jr., Robert N. *An 8–Track Church in a CD World: the Modern Church in a Postmodern World.* Macon, GA: Smyth & Helwys Publishing, Inc., 2001.
Naveh, Reuven. "Tonality, Atonality and the Ainulindalë." In *Music in Middle-earth.* Edited by Heidi Steimel and Friedhelm Schneidewind, 29–51. Zurich and Jena: Walking Tree Publishers, 2010.
Ortlund, Anne. *Up With Worship: How to Quit Playing Church.* Rev. ed. Ventura, CA: Regal Books, 1982.
Palisca, Claude. "The Artusi-Monteverdi Controversy." In *The New Monteverdi Companion.* Edited by Denis Arnold and Nigel Fortune, 127–58. London: Faber and Faber, 1985.
Parks, Bob. *Music: Does It Make Any Difference?* Grand Rapids, MI: Grand Rapids School of the Bible and Music, 1970.
Paolucci, Henry, ed. *St. Augustine – The Enchiridion on Faith, Hope and Love.* Chicago: Henry Regnery Co., 1961.
Peters, Dan, Steve Peters, and Cher Merrill. *What About Christian Rock?* Minneapolis, MN: Bethany House Publishers, 1986.
Pilgrim Hymnal. Boston, MA: The Pilgrim Press, 1958.
Reynolds, William Jensen. *A Survey of Christian Hymnody.* New York and Chicago: Holt, Rinehart and Winston, Inc., 1963.
Rogal, Samuel J. *A General Introduction to Hymnody and Congregational Song.* Metuchen, NJ and London: The American Theological Library Association and The Scarecrow Press, Inc., 1991.
Roberts, Alexander and James Donaldson, eds. *Ante-Nicene Christian Library: Translations of the Writings of the Fathers, Vol. IX.* Edinburgh: T. & T. Clark, 1869.
Routley, Erik. *Music Leadership in the Church.* Nashville, TN: Abingdon, 1967.
Sachs, Curt. *Our Musical Heritage: A Short History of Music.* 2nd ed. Englewood Cliffs, NJ: Prentice-Hall, Inc., 1955.
Schachter, Carl. "Landini's Treatment of Consonance and Dissonance: A Study in Fourteenth-Century Counterpoint." *The Journal of Musicology* 7 (Summer 1989): 366–89.
Schakel, Peter J. *Imagination and the Arts in C.S. Lewis: Journeying to Narnia and Other Worlds.* Columbia and London: University of Missouri Press, 2002.
Scott, Cyril. *Music: Its Secret Influence Throughout the Ages.* Exp. ed. Wellingsborough, Northamptonshire: The Aquarian Press, 1958.
Segler, Franklin M. *Understanding, Preparing for, and Practicing Christian Worship.* Revised by Randall Bradley. 2nd ed. Nashville, TN: Broadman & Holman Publishers, 1996.
Service Book and Hymnal of the Lutheran Church in America. Minneapolis, MN: Augsburg Publishing House, 1958.
Shakespeare, William. *The Merchant of Venice.* Edited by David Bevington. New York and London: Bantam Books, 1988.
Shaw, Martin, Percy Dearmer, and Ralph Vaughan Williams, eds. *The Oxford Book of Carols.* Oxford: Oxford University Press, 1928.
Shelley, Mary. *Frankenstein.* New York: Dover Publications, Inc., 1994.

Shelley, Mary. *The Last Man.* London: Wordsworth Classics, 2004.
Sir Gawain and the Green Knight, Pearl, and Sir Orfeo. Translated by J. R. R. Tolkien. New York: Ballentine Books, 1975.
Smith, David B. *Rock-Solid Living in a Run-amok World.* Hagerstown, MD: Review and Herald Publishing Association, 1999.
Smith, Kimberly. *Music and Morals: Dispelling the Myth That Music Is Amoral.* Enumclaw, WA: Winepress Publishing, 2005.
Smith, Kimberly. *Let Those Who Have Ears to Hear.* Enumclaw, WA: Winepress Publishing, 2001.
Smith, Kimberly and Lee Smith. *Oh, Be Careful Little Ears.* Enumclaw, WA: Winepress Publishing, 1997.
Smith, Nigel. "Perceptions of Homosexuality in Tchaikovsky Criticism." *Context* 4 (Summer 1992–93): 3–9.
Snyder, John L. "Theinred of Dover on Consonance: A Chapter in the History of Harmony." *Music Theory Spectrum* V (Spring 1983): 110–20.
Solie, Ruth A., ed. *Source Readings in Music History Volume 6: The Nineteenth Century.* Rev ed. New York and London: W.W. Norton & Company, 1998.
Song and Service Book for Ship and Field: Army and Navy. New York: A.S. Barnes and Company, Inc., 1941.
Stefani, Wolfgang H. M. "Is Music Morally Neutral?" In *Here We Stand: Evaluating New Trends in the Church.* Edited by Samuel Koranteng-Pipim, 399–417. Berrien Springs, MI: Adventists Affirm, 2005.
Steinbeck, John. *East of Eden.* London: Penguin Books, 1986.
Stevenson, Robert Louis. *The Strange Case of Dr. Jekyll and Mr. Hyde and Other Stories.* New York: Barnes & Noble Classics, 2003.
Sturgis, J. E., ed. *Favorite Hymns: An All Purpose Songbook.* Cincinnati, OH: The Standard Publishing Company, 1933.
Stoquerus, Gaspar. *De Musica Verbali Libri Duo: Two Books on Verbal Music.* Translated by Albert C. Rotola. Lincoln and London: University of Nebraska Press, 1988.
Swaggart, Jimmy and Robert Paul Lamb. *Religious Rock 'n' Roll: a Wolf in Sheep's Clothing.* Baton Rouge, LA: Jimmy Swaggart Ministries, 1987.
Sweatt, Danny M. *Church Music: Sense and Nonsense.* Greenville, SC: Bob Jones University Press, 1981.
Sweney, John R., Gilmour, H. L. and Entwisle, J. H., eds. *Songs of Love and Praise No. 4* Philadelphia and Chicago: John J. Hood, 1897.
Tame, David. *The Secret Power of Music.* Rochester, VT: Destiny Books, 1984.
The Canticle of the Sun of St. Francis of Assisi. New York: Duffield and Company, 1907.
The Child's Christian Year. Philadelphia: Lea and Blanchard, 1842.
The Church Hymnal. Takoma Park, MD: Review and Herald Publishing Association, 1941)
The English Hymnal. London: Oxford University Press, 1933.
The Epworth Hymnal. New York: Hunt & Eaton, 1885.

The Hymnal 1940 Companion. 2nd rev. ed. New York: The Church Pension Fund, 1949.
The Hymnal of the Protestant Episcopal Church in the United States of America. New York: The Church Pension Fund, 1940.
The Liber Usualis. Tournai: Society of St. John the Evangelist, 1952.
The Pius X Hymnal. Rev. ed. Boston, MA: McLaughlin & Reilly Co., 1956.
The Sacred Harp. Rev. ed. Sacred Harp Publishing Company, Inc., 1991.
"The Seal of Love." *The Christian Science Journal* VIII, no. 1 (April 1890): 97.
The Seventh-day Adventist Hymnal. Hagerstown, MD: Review and Herald Publishing Association, 1985.
Thompson, John J. *Raised by Wolves: The Story of Christian Rock & Roll.* Toronto, ONT: ECW Press, 2000.
Thurber, John and Cari Haus. *The Music of Heaven.* Self-published, 2001.
Tinctoris, Johannes. *De Natura et Proprietate Tonorum (Concerning the Nature and Property of Tones).* Translated by Albert Seay. Colorado Springs, CO: Colorado College Music Press, 1976.
Tinctoris, Johannes. *Proportionale Musices (Proportions in Music).* Translated by Albert Seay. Colorado Springs, CO: Colorado College Music Press, 1979.
Tolkien, J. R. R. *Bilbo's Last Song.* New York: Alfred A. Knopf, 1992.
Tolkien, J. R. R. *Tales from the Perilous Realm.* Boston and New York: Mariner Books, 2021.
Tolkien, J. R. R. *The Adventures of Tom Bombadil and other verses from The Red Book.* London: HarperCollins Publishers, 2014.
Tolkien, J. R. R. *The Hobbit.* Boston and New York: Houghton Mifflin Company, 1997.
Tolkien, J. R. R. *The Fellowship of the Ring.* Boston and New York: Houghton Mifflin Company, 2002.
Tolkien, J. R. R. *The Return of the King.* Boston and New York: Houghton Mifflin Company, 2002.
Tolkien, J. R. R. *The Silmarillion.* Boston and New York: Houghton Mifflin Company, 1998.
Tolkien, J. R. R. *The Two Towers.* Boston and New York: Houghton Mifflin Company, 2002.
Tolkien, J. R. R. *Unfinished Tales of Númenor and Middle-earth.* New York: Ballentine Books, 1980.
Tomlinson, Gary, ed. *Source Readings in Music History Volume 3: The Renaissance.* Rev. ed. New York and London: W.W. Norton & Company, 1998.
Torres, Carol A. and Louis R. Torres. *Notes on Music.* St. Maries, ID: LMN Publishing International, Inc., 1990.
Tractatus de Discantu (Concerning Discant). Translated and Edited by Albert Seay. Colorado Springs, CO: Colorado College Music Press, 1978.
Truman, Benjamin. *History of the World's Fair.* New York: Arno Press, 1976.
Trumble, Ernest. "Dissonance Treatment in Early Fauxbourdon." In *Beyond the Moon: Festschrift Luther Dittmer.* Edited by Bryan Gillingham and Paul Merkley. Ottawa: Institute for Mediaeval Music, 1990.

Tsatalbasidis, Karl. *Drums, Rock, and Worship: Modern Music in Today's Church.* Roseville, CA: Amazing Facts, Inc., 2003.
Urang, Gunnar. *Church Music for the Glory of God.* Moline, IL: Christian Service Foundation, 1956.
van Dyke, Henry. *The Poems of Henry van Dyke.* New York: Charles Scribner's Sons, 1914.
Voltaire. *Candide, or Optimism.* Translated by Henry Morley. New York: Barnes & Noble Classics, 2003.
von Goethe, Johann Wolfgang. *Faust: Part 1.* Translated by Peter Salm. Rev. ed. New York: Bantam Books, 1962.
Ward, Michael. *Planet Narnia: The Seven Heavens in the Imagination of C. S. Lewis.* Oxford and New York: Oxford University Press, 2008.
Watts, Isaac. *Divine Songs Attempted in Easy Language for the Use of Children.* London: M. Lawrence, 1715.
Weber, Martin. *Adventist Hot Potatoes.* Boise, ID and Oshawa, ONT: Pacific Press Publishing Association, 1991.
Weiss, Piero and Richard Taruskin. *Music in the Western World: A History in Documents.* New York and London: Schirmer Books, 1984.
Wells, H. G. *The Invisible Man.* New York: Scholastic Inc., 2003.
White, E. E. *Singing With Understanding.* Warburton, Victoria (Australia): Signs Publishing Company, 1968.
White, James F. *Introduction to Christian Worship.* Nashville, TN: Abingdon, 1980.
Whittingham, Elizabeth A. "The Power of Music and Song in Tolkien's Legendarium." In *Music in Tolkien's Work and Beyond.* Edited by Julian Eilmann and Friedhelm Schneidewind, 135–58. Zurich and Jena: Walking Tree Publishers, 2019.
Wiley, Lulu Rumsey. *Bible Music.* New York: The Paebar Company, 1945.
Wohlgemuth, Paul W. *Rethinking Church Music.* Carol Stream, IL: Hope Publishing Co, 1981.
Zacchetti, Corrado. *Franceso d'Assisi e Le 'Laudes Creaturarum.'* Assisi: Tipografia Metastasio, 1904.

Index

Aaron, Pietro, 18
Achilles, 175
Adam: Earthly Adam, 51, 68, 70, 74, 89, 114, 154n18, 155n43, 168, 171, 175, 176, 193; Venusian Adam, 91, 155n43
Adams, Douglas, 209, 222n5
Ad organum faciendum, 115
Africa, 218–21, 225n61
Aghan, 88
the Ainur, 70–76, 80, 81, 84–87, 90, 92, 93n14, 93n20, 94n27, 95n70, 95n73, 101, 108–10, 111n18, 167, 194n7
Albert the Great, 42
Alexander, Cecil Frances, 138
Alford, Henry, 92n5, 140, 141
Ames, Cathy, 184–87, 189, 196n66, 196n71
Anstice, Joseph, 147
Apollo, 27, 33n84, 175
Aquinas, Thomas, 42
Aristides Quintilianus, 31n31, 31n36
Aristotle, 227–29
Artusi, Giovanni Maria, 119–22, 208, 223n18
Arwen, 84
Asclepiades, 12
Aslan, 68, 70, 71, 100, 110n4, 154n18
Aslan's Country, 56n31, 91, 92, 100, 101, 110nn3–4, 194n25

Aufranc, Douglas Albert Raoul, 146
Aulë, 74, 75
Aurelian of Réôme, 10, 13, 18, 20, 28, 113
Ave Maria, 40, 41, 52

Bach, Johann Sebastian, 124, 200, 211, 218, 222n4
Baker, Paul, 217
Banchieri, Adriano, 16
Barach, 88
Barrow-wights, 106, 107
Beach, Curtis, 143
Beatrice, 36, 38–41, 46–49, 51–53, 53n2, 55n24, 57n57
Bede the Venerable, 42
Beethoven, Ludwig van, 124, 147, 200
bentness, 89, 165–93, 194n25, 199, 203
Beren, 109, 110
Berkeley manuscript, 20–21
Bertoglio, Chiara, 72
Bianciardi, Francesco, 117
Bilbo Baggins, 96n89, 103, 158–60, 164n13, 169–71, 176, 194n21
von Bingen, Hildegard, 58n65
Blanchard, John, 220
Blume, Friedrich, 224n45
Boethius, 7–10, 13, 14, 27, 30n3, 30n6, 42, 118, 123, 124, 126, 128n23, 229
Boff, Leonardo, 155n39

241

Boromir, 111n18, 160, 161, 163n8
Brahms, Johannes, 200
da Brescia, Bonaventura, 33n73, 27–28
Bridges, Robert S., 140
Brokenness, 165, 170, 177, 180–90, 193, 196n77
Brontë, Charlotte, 178
Budd, Billy, 175–77, 179, 185, 187
Busoni, Ferruccio, 124, 126

Cacciaguida, 45
Caddell, Cecilia M., 139
Calvin, Jean, 210, 211, 222n14
Cassiodorus, 9, 11, 12
Cecilian Movement, 211
Chaos. *See* void
Charn, 188, 192, 197n81
Chicago World's Fair, 219, 220
Children of Illúvatar, 71, 73, 74, 78, 86, 87, 90, 92, 93n20, 96n101; Drúedain, 87, 88; Dwarves, 74, 75, 82, 103, 157; Elves, 71, 75–77, 82, 95n65, 103, 109, 110, 112n40, 112n43, 157, 161, 163, 166, 194nn6–7; Hobbits, 76, 95n65, 170; Men, 71, 76, 82, 88, 93n20, 102, 109, 112n40, 112n43, 157, 161, 167, 194nn6–7
The Chronicles of Narnia: *The Last Battle*, 64n12, 91, 100, 101; *The Lion, the Witch, and the Wardrobe*, 110n6, 188, 189; *The Magician's Nephew*, 68, 92n5, 154n18, 188, 189; *Prince Caspian*, 110n6; *The Silver Chair*, 56n31, 104; *The Voyage of the Dawn Treader*, 56n36
Church modes, 123
Ciabattoni, Francesco, 39
Ciardi, John, 46, 47, 50, 54n8, 54n11, 55n21, 55n25, 56n32, 56n35, 57n44, 57n46, 57n58
Civil Rights Movement, 208
Claggart, John, 175–77, 179, 185, 187
Cohen, David, 118
Comedia, 35, 37, 39, 53, 59, 61, 150; *Inferno*, 35, 39, 56n28, 59; *Paradiso*, 33n81, 35–53, 60, 61, 63, 67; *Purgatorio*, 35, 39, 56n28
Congo, 166
Conrad, Joseph, 166
Consonance, 3, 4, 92; analogous to light, 78, 81, 82; as character trait, 82–87; in music, 18, 20–23, 26, 28, 31n37, 32nn73–74, 114–20, 122–23, 126–27, 128n13
Constantine, 45
Contrafactum, 217, 218, 225n52
Council of Trent, 210, 211, 213, 223n16
Crocker, Richard, 114
Crüger, Johann, 222n4
Cunningham, Michael, 90

Damian, Peter, 46, 47, 56n37
Dante, 33n81, 35–53, 53n6, 54nn13–14, 55nn24–25, 56n35, 56n39, 57nn48–49, 59, 61–63, 64n2, 65n16, 67, 88, 104, 111n11, 150, 152
David, King, 12, 27, 33n88, 45
Déagol, 158, 163n8
Dearmer, Percy, 148
Debussy, Claude, 124, 125, 127n1, 129n58
De Institutione Musica, 8, 14
Dekad, 19, 128n23
Delle Imperfettioni Della Moderna Musica, 120
the Deplorable Word, 188, 189
Descartes, René, 117
the devil. *See* Satan
Devine, Dick, 180, 182, 195n45
Diamond Jubilee, 142
Dickens, Charles, 222n5
dissonance, 3, 4, 12, 84, 92; analogous to darkness/void, 78, 79, 81–84; as character trait, 72–73, 75, 78, 84–86, 91, 94n40; in music, 75, 116–27, 130n66, 208, 223n18, 229
dominion, 74, 132, 134–36, 142, 143, 161
Donati, Piccarda, 40, 41, 52, 55n19
Donne, John, 168

Draper, William H., 150
Dryden, John, 67, 99
van Dyke, Henry, 147

Eagles of Manwë, 74
Eärendil, 81, 82
East of Eden, 184–86
elements: air, 124, 132, 137, 149–51, 172; earth, 74, 132; fire, 90, 150, 151; water, 76, 77, 85–86, 90, 101, 111n7, 132, 133, 138, 149–51; water (as analogue of music/echo of creation), 76–78, 82
Elendur, 162
Ellerton, John, 141
England, 64n12, 69, 104, 110nn3–6, 175, 189
Enlightenment, 211
Eru, 70–75, 78, 86, 90–92, 93n20, 94n36, 110, 112n40, 167, 192
Eve: Earthly Eve, 70, 89, 155n43, 166, 168, 171, 193; Venusian Eve, 89, 155n43, 171

Farquharson, Walter, 145
Father Time, 100, 101
Fëanor, 81, 86, 87
Felix culpa, 28
Felix peccatum Adae, 28, 88–90
Finrod, 102, 107, 108
Five Pieces for Orchestra, 126
Flieger, Verlyn, 72, 73, 96n91
Forest Bathing, 155n38
Frankenstein, Victor, 172–74, 193
Frankenstein's monster, 172–74, 176, 193, 195n28
Frodo Baggins, 77, 79–85, 87, 95n62, 96n91, 102–6, 112n33, 158–60, 162, 169–72, 176, 177, 194n23
Fuller, Sarah, 115

Gabriel, archangel, 52
Gaffurio, Franchino, 117
Galadriel, 77, 79, 82, 83, 102, 111nn17–18, 163, 163n8

Galton, Francis, 219
Gamelan, 129n58
Gandalf, 79, 80, 86, 95n73, 103, 159, 160, 162, 169, 170
Garden of Eden, 36–40, 52, 61, 68, 74, 91, 114, 166, 193
Gardner, John, 78
de Garlandia, Johannes, 23, 33n74, 116, 129n39, 194n14
Gerhardt, Paul, 140, 153n15
Gimli, 75, 111n18
Glaucus, 39, 54n9
Gloria Patri, 51
goblins. *See* orcs
von Goethe, Johann Wolfgang, 149
Gollum. *See* Sméagol
Gondor, 111n18, 160
Gorgoroth. *See* Mordor
The Great Divorce, 59, 60, 62, 166
the Great Music. *See* music of the Ainur
Green, Fred Pratt, 145
Gregorian Chant, 55n25, 211, 212
Griffin, 166
de Grocheo, Johannes, 11, 14, 17, 20, 21

Hades, 108, 110, 112n40
Handel, George Frideric, 200, 211
Hardy, Thomas, 195n43
Hassler, Hans Leo, 218
Haydn, Joseph, 93n6, 200, 211
Heart of Darkness, 166
Hell, 35, 36, 67, 97n110
Hercules, 175
Herl, Joseph, 224n45
Hermes, 27
Herriot, James, 138
Hezekiah, King, 45
Hill, Rowland, 224n45
Hitler, Adolf, 200
The Hobbit, 103
Hollander, John, 46, 47, 54n8, 57n42
homo erectus, 169
homo incurvatus, 169
homosexuality, 202–4, 205n8

Hosanna, 42, 51, 52
Houseman, Laurence, 149
human senses, 139, 192; hearing, 8, 9, 36–52, 59, 63, 115, 121, 155n38; sight, 13, 36, 37, 39, 42, 44, 46–49, 52, 53, 59, 60, 80, 102, 139, 155n38; smell, 155n38; taste, 63n1, 119, 172; touch, 59–61; understanding, 36, 37, 39, 42, 44, 46, 48, 52, 53, 59
hymn categories; acknowledgement, 132; acknowledgement, aesthetic value, 132, 133, 139–40, 153n16; acknowledgement, existence, 133, 136–39; conservation, 134, 162; conservation, kinship, 134, 149–52; conservation, prompting, 134, 146–48; conservation, stewardship, 134, 160; subjugation, 133, 153n16, 161, 163; subjugation, aesthetic value, 132, 133; subjugation, stewardship, 134, 143–46; subjugation, subduing, 133, 140–43, 160
Hyperion, 175

Illúvatar. *See* Eru
India, 178
invisibility, 79, 82–83
The Invisible Man, 166
Irenaeus, 29, 58n64
Isidore of Seville, 10, 11, 42
Isildur, 158, 161, 162, 163n3
Ives, Charles, 125

Jacoff, Rachel, 36, 39
Jadis, 68, 70, 93n10, 154n18, 188–90, 192, 197n81, 197n83
James the Great, 50
Jane Eyre, 178–79, 195n39
Jensen, Keith W., 91
Jericho, 99
Jesus Christ, 48, 49, 51–53, 89, 99, 114, 133, 135, 183, 196n50, 218, 226n71
John the Apostle, 50
Jonas, Hans, 26
Jones, Paul S., 217, 224n43

Jubal, 19, 33n88
Justinian, 41, 55n21

Ketterley, Andrew, 68, 154n18, 188
Kingsley, Charles, 144
Kipling, Rudyard, 142, 143
Kirke, Digory, 68–70, 154n18, 188, 189, 194n25, 197n83
Kromer, Marcin, 20

Larson, Bob, 220, 221, 226n67
The Last Man, 195n28
Laurelindórenan. *See* Lórien
Lazarus, 183
Legolas, 75, 77, 111n18
Le institutioni harmoniche, 120
Lewis, C.S., 54n13, 59–63, 64n14, 65nn15–16, 67–71, 73, 78, 82, 88, 89, 91, 92, 92n3, 95n5, 99, 100, 102–4, 110, 153n15, 154n18, 155n43, 166, 169, 171, 180, 190, 193n4
Lindar, 77
Linus of Thebes, 33n84
Lippius, Johannes, 10, 12, 13, 17, 18, 20, 21, 23–24, 37
Listenius, Nicolaus, 17, 20
Longfellow, Henry Wordsworth, 46, 54n8, 57n44, 141
Longfellow, Samuel, 141
The Lord of the Rings, 4, 75, 77, 82, 84, 104, 157, 169
Lórien, 82, 102, 103, 111n14, 111nn17–18, 163
Lothlórien. *See* Lórien
Lowry, Somerset Corry, 144
Luca, 120–21
Lucarini, Dan, 215, 216, 220
Luther, Martin, 209, 210, 217, 218, 224nn45–46, 222nn9–10, 222n14
Lúthien, 108–10, 112n36, 112n41

Macrobes, 182, 183, 185
Maia, 27
maior perfectum, 27–30, 38, 53, 62, 88, 89, 91, 92, 119, 126

Mandelbaum, Allen, 46, 54n8, 54n11, 55n21, 55n25, 56n32, 57n54
Mandos, 109, 110, 112n40
Manwë, 73, 80, 85, 86, 91, 102
Martel, Charles, 42
Matins, 43, 69
McBride, Sam, 93n20, 96n95, 94n36
Melian, 85, 109
Melkor, 71–73, 75, 78–81, 86, 87, 90–92, 94n27, 94n36, 95n69, 95n70, 101, 109, 112n40, 166, 167, 192, 194nn6–7, 194n10
Melville, Herman, 175–77
The Metamorphoses of Ovid, 33n83, 54n9, 58n62, 95n67, 112n37
Middle-earth, 82, 95n62, 95n65, 95n73, 101, 110, 157, 161, 162, 166, 167, 169, 172, 194n6
Milton, John, 26, 67–69, 78–80, 97n110, 114, 166, 168
Monteverdi, Claudio, 119–23, 208
Montpellier treatise, 116
Mordor, 158, 160, 161
Morgan, Lewis H., 219
Moses, 99
Mount Doom, 82, 158, 171
Mount Sinai, 99
Mozart, Wolfgang Amadeus, 200
Musica Enchiriadis, 21, 22, 28, 38, 118
musica humana, 10–15, 17, 20, 37, 40, 45, 47, 59, 60, 62, 63, 68, 72, 74, 75, 81, 83–85, 87, 92, 92n3, 94n27, 95n70, 103, 110, 111n18, 113, 115, 116, 121, 124, 127, 131, 134, 141, 144, 147, 148, 152, 163n12, 157, 160, 163, 165, 170, 172, 174–76, 181, 182, 184, 186–90, 192, 195n43, 199–203, 207–10, 213, 218–21, 223n25, 228
musica instrumentalis, 13–18, 21, 27, 30, 68, 72, 77, 81, 85, 94n27, 102, 110, 113, 115–17, 119, 121, 123, 168, 199, 200, 203, 207, 208, 215, 221, 227, 228

musical instruments: Harps. *See* musical instruments, Lyres; Horns, 99–102, 110, 110n6; Lyres, 21, 27, 33n85, 102, 108; Trumpets, 99–101, 110; Voices, 101–10
Musicam Sacram, 214
musica mundana, 8–11, 14, 21, 24, 27, 29, 35, 40, 48, 58n65, 59, 63, 68, 72, 74, 76–78, 81, 85, 92, 100, 103–5, 110, 113–24, 126, 127, 131, 141, 147, 148, 152, 161, 163, 165, 168, 189, 192, 195n43, 199, 200, 203, 207–10, 212–15, 218, 221, 223n2, 228
music of the Ainur, 70–71, 78, 85, 86, 90, 96n95, 99, 108, 109, 112n43
Mussorgsky, Modest, 200, 201, 205n2

Napoleon, 60
Narnia, 67–70, 91, 92, 92n4, 100, 104, 154n18, 172, 180, 189, 192, 194n25, 197n83
Naveh, Reuven, 91
Nemesis, 192–93, 197nn99–100
New England, 185
N.I.C.E., 182–85, 190
Nicomachus, 13
Nile River, 27
Noah, 135
Norton, Charles Eliot, 46, 54n8, 57n47
Númenor, 167, 193, 194n7
numerology, 19, 113, 114, 116

Oatman, Jr., Johnson, 28
the Objectivity Room, 183, 184
Odington, Walter of, 115
Odysseus, 43
the Old Forest, 104, 106
Old Man Willow, 105, 107
Olórin. *See* Gandalf
orcs, 75, 88, 163n3, 159
Oromë, 101
Orpheus and Eurydice, 38, 108–10, 112nn37–38
Ossë, 86, 96n101

Paradise Lost, 67–70, 78, 80, 97n110, 114, 166, 168, 193
Perelandra, 54n13, 63n1, 88
perfectio, 20, 22, 26, 114
Persephone, 108
Peter the Apostle, 49, 50
Pevensie, Edmund, 56n36, 189, 194n25
Pevensie, Lucy, 56n36
Pevensie, Peter, 189
Pevensie, Susan, 110n6
pilgrimage, 135–36, 152
Pius X, 211, 213, 214
planets (as celestial spheres in Dante); the Earth, 36, 40, 43, 44, 97n110; Empyrean, 33n81, 36, 40, 52–53, 64n2; the Fixed Stars, the, 36, 48–51; Jupiter, 36, 45–46, 49; Mars, 36, 45, 49, 56n31; Mercury, 36, 41, 44; the Moon, 36, 40–41, 44, 52; Primum Mobile, 36, 40, 51–52; Saturn, 36, 46–49; the Sun, 36, 42–44, 49; Venus, 36, 41–42, 44
planets (other usages); the Earth, 9, 10, 22, 59, 63n1, 68–69, 89, 91, 113, 114, 135–37, 141, 145, 147, 151, 155n39, 166–68, 172, 180, 182, 189, 193, 194n24, 195n45; Mars, 64n14, 103, 104, 180, 182, 195n45; the Moon, 106, 113, 137, 150, 151; the Sun, 104, 106, 113, 133, 137, 138, 150, 151; Venus, 54n13, 88, 89, 91, 153n15, 155n43, 171, 172, 178, 180, 181, 194n24, 195n45
Plato, 13, 31n26, 122, 228, 229
Plummer, Polly, 68, 70, 154n18, 188, 189, 194n25
Pole, Jill, 56n31, 100, 104, 194n25
Politics, 228
Protestant Reformation, 209, 210, 217, 222n1
Ptolemy, 128n23
Purgatory, 35, 36, 56n29
Pythagoras, 18, 23, 26, 27
Pythagorean comma, 25, 26
Pythagorean quaternary, 19
Pythagorean tuning, 23, 128n23

quadrivium, 9

Rahab, 41
Ransom, Elwin, 54n13, 63n1, 88, 89, 91, 103, 104, 111n21, 153n15, 155n43, 171, 172, 178, 180–82, 194n24, 195n45, 196n56, 196n77
Raphael (the archangel), 68, 114
Raphael (the artist), 15–16
Regina coeli, 49
The Republic, 31n26
Rilian, 104
the Ring of Sauron, 77, 79, 80, 82–85, 87, 96n89, 106, 111nn17–18, 157–63, 163n8, 163n12, 164n13, 166, 169–72, 192, 194n21
Ringwraiths, 169
Rivendell, 77
Rivers, St. John, 177–79, 187, 195n39
Rochester, Edward, 178, 195n39
Russolo, Luigi, 130n66
Rutter, John, 138

Sachs, Hans, 217
Sacrosanctum Concilium, 213–15, 223n29
Samwise Gamgee, 80–85, 87, 102, 105, 160–62, 163n8, 177
Sanctus, 41, 51
Saruman, 160–62, 163n8, 169
Satan, 36, 78, 79, 89, 166, 180, 181, 193
Saul, King, 12
Sauron, 79, 80, 82, 85, 87, 94n36, 95n70, 107–9, 111n18, 112n40, 157, 158, 161–63, 167, 169, 171, 192, 194n7
Sayers, Dorothy, 222n5
Schakel, Peter J., 154n18
Schoenberg, Arnold, 126, 127
Scivias, 58n65
Scrubb, Eustace, 56n31, 56n36, 100, 104
Seal, Emily F., 142

Second Viennese School, 126, 130n63, 229
The Secret Power of Music, 200
Semele, 47, 56n39
Shaw, Martin, 138
Shelley, Mary, 172, 195n28
Shelob, 80–85
Shepherds of the Trees, 74
The Silmarillion, 78, 107, 112n41, 193
Silmarils, 81–83, 86, 91, 101, 109, 166
Sinclair, John D., 38, 47, 50
Skandalkonzert, 127
Sméagol, 84–85, 87, 96n89, 158–60, 169–71, 176, 177
Smith, Kimberly, 221
Solid People, 62, 63
Solomon, King, 42, 139
A Song for St. Cecilia's Day, 67, 99
The Space Trilogy, 88, 91, 166, 169, 171, 180, 182, 193nn3–4; *Out of the Silent Planet*, 64n14, 103, 180; *Perelandra*, 54n13, 63n1, 88, 89, 153n15, 155n43, 171, 180, 182, 183, 196n77; *That Hideous Strength*, 155n43, 172, 182, 190
Spencer, Herbert, 219
Sperent in te, 50
St. Augustine of Hippo, 11, 28
St. Cecilia, 15
Steinbeck, John, 184
Stevenson, Robert Louis, 186, 187
St. Frances of Assisi, 150–52
Stoquerus, Gaspar, 17
straightness, 89, 165, 167, 169, 170, 176, 184, 187, 193, 199, 200
The Strange Case of Dr. Jekyll and Mr. Hyde, 186–87, 189, 193, 196n73, 203
Studdock, Jane, 182, 190–92, 196n59
Studdock, Mark, 182–84, 190–92, 196n59
Swaggart, Jimmy, 226n71
systems of imperfection, 3, 7, 24–27, 29, 30, 33n81, 70, 73, 112n38, 118

systems of perfection, 3, 7, 21–26, 70, 112n38

Tame, David, 25, 200, 203, 204
Tchaikovsky, Pyotr Ilyich, 201–5, 205nn7–8, 205n10
Te Deum laudamus, 50
Terpander of Lesbos, 21
Tess of the d'Urbervilles, 195n43
tetractys, 19, 116, 117, 128n23
tetragrammaton, 19
Theodoric the Great, 7
Thingol, 109
Timaeus, 13, 228
Tinctoris, Johannes, 20, 23
Tolkien, J.R.R., 67, 68, 70–74, 76, 78–80, 82, 84–86, 88–92, 92n3, 93nn13–14, 96n91, 99, 101, 102, 110, 112n43, 157, 166, 169
Tom Bombadil, 95n65, 103, 105–7
Tomlinson, Irving Clinton, 147
tonality, 123–26
Trajan, 45
Tra le sollecitudini, 211, 213
Triad, 20
Tsatalbasidis, Karl, 216, 220
tuning, 24, 25
Tuor, 76, 77, 101, 102
the Two Trees, 81, 82, 85–87, 166

Uinen, 86, 96n101
Ulmo, 76, 85, 86, 90, 96n101, 101, 102
the Undying Lands. *See* Valinor
Ungoliant, 80–82, 86, 101, 194n10
United States, 207, 220, 225n55, 225n59

Valinor, 80, 81, 84, 85, 91, 95n62, 101, 102, 109, 110, 166, 167, 169, 172, 194n10
Varda, 86, 102
Vario, 120–21
Vatican II Council, 213, 214, 218
Verdi, Giuseppe, 200
Virgil, 36, 53

the Virgin Mary, 49, 52, 53
void, 71, 75, 78–80, 83, 95n69, 101, 167
Vulpius, Melchior, 222n4

Wagner, Richard, 200
Ward, Michael, 8
Watts, Isaac, 137
Webern, Anton, 124
Wells, H.G., 166
Weston, Edward, 166, 171, 172, 178–82, 185, 193, 195n45, 196n77
Whiteman, Paul, 220

Whiteman, Sr., Wilberforce, 220
the White Witch. *See* Jadis
Williams, Ralph Vaughan, 150
Wilson, James Steuart, 139
Wodehouse, P.G., 222n5

Yavanna, 73, 74, 81, 85–87

Zarlino, Gioseffo, 8, 23, 117, 120–23, 212
Zeus, 27, 56n39
Zwingli, Huldrych, 222n14

About the Author

David J. Kendall is associate professor of music at La Sierra University in Riverside, California, where he also serves as associate chair of the Department of Music. At La Sierra, he teaches courses in music history, music and worship, humanities, and also supervises student research. He holds a BMus. degree and a performer's certificate from La Sierra University, and an MA and PhD in Historical Musicology from the University of California, Riverside. He has previously held teaching positions at Loma Linda Academy, the University of California, Riverside, and visiting professorships at the University of the Philippines, Diliman, University of Santo Tomás (Manila), Ateneo de Davao University, and University of the Southeastern Philippines.

Kendall has published and presented widely on the liturgical and devotional music of the Philippines during the Spanish and American colonial eras, and also specializes in the Baroque music revivals of the nineteenth century, organology, and the history of music theory. He regularly performs archival research in the Philippines, where he works with various ecclesiastical and governmental bodies in the fields of church history and cultural heritage preservation. He lives in Riverside, California, with his wife Shiela and two daughters Carmina and Mikaëla.

www.ingramcontent.com/pod-product-compliance
Lightning Source LLC
Chambersburg PA
CBHW021351300426
44114CB00012B/1175